3⁰⁰

Rev. C. Kindervater

THE CALL TO HONOUR
1940-1942

Cecil Beaton

CHARLES DE GAULLE

WAR MEMOIRS
VOLUME ONE

THE CALL
TO HONOUR

1940-1942

Translated by
Jonathan Griffin

COLLINS
ST JAMES'S PLACE, LONDON
1955

This book was originally published in
France under the title *Mémoires de
Guerre: L'Appel* 1940-1942 by
Librairie Plon

PRINTED IN GREAT BRITAIN
COLLINS CLEAR-TYPE PRESS: LONDON AND GLASGOW

Contents

*The Documents to which this narrative
refers are published in a separate volume
under the title of* WAR MEMOIRS,
Volume One, THE CALL TO HONOUR
(1940-1942), DOCUMENTS

LIST OF ILLUSTRATIONS

LIST OF MAPS

I. THE SLOPE

ALL MY life I have thought of France in a certain way. This is inspired by sentiment as much as by reason. The emotional side of me tends to imagine France, like the princess in the fairy stories or the Madonna in the frescoes, as dedicated to an exalted and exceptional destiny. Instinctively I have the feeling that Providence has created her either for complete successes or for exemplary misfortunes. If, in spite of this, mediocrity shows in her acts and deeds, it strikes me as an absurd anomaly, to be imputed to the faults of Frenchmen, not to the genius of the land. But the positive side of my mind also assures me that France is not really herself unless she is in the front rank; that only vast enterprises are capable of counter-balancing the ferments of disintegration inherent in her people; that our country, as it is, surrounded by the others, as they are, must aim high and hold itself straight, on pain of mortal danger. In short, to my mind, France cannot be France without greatness.

This faith grew as I grew, in the environment where I was born. My father was a thoughtful, cultivated, traditional man, imbued with the feeling of the dignity of France. He made me aware of her history. My mother had an uncompromising passion for her country, equal to her religious piety. To my three brothers, my sister and myself a certain anxious pride in our country came as second nature. As a young native of Lille living in Paris, nothing struck me more than the symbols of our glories: night falling over Notre Dame, the majesty of evening at Versailles, the Arc de Triomphe in the sun, conquered colours shuddering in the vault of the Invalides.

9

Nothing affected me more than the evidence of our national successes: popular enthusiasm when the Tsar of Russia passed through, a review at Longchamp, the marvels of the Exhibition, the first flights of our aviators. Nothing saddened me more profoundly than our weaknesses and our mistakes, as revealed to my childhood gaze by the way people looked and by things they said: the surrender of Fashoda, the Dreyfus case, social conflicts, religious strife. Nothing moved me so much as the story of our past misfortunes: my father recalling the fruitless sortie from Le Bourget and Stains, in which he had been wounded; my mother conjuring up the despair she had felt as a girl at the sight of her parents in tears: " Bazaine has capitulated ! "

As an adolescent, the fate of France, whether as the subject of history or as the stake in public life, interested me above everything. I was therefore attracted, but also severely critical, towards the play which was performed, day in, day out, in the forum; carried away as I was by the intelligence, fire and eloquence lavished upon it by countless actors, yet saddened at seeing so many gifts wasted in political confusion and national disunity. All the more so since, at the beginning of the century, the premonitory symptoms of war became visible. I must say that in my first youth I pictured this unknown adventure with no horror, and magnified it in anticipation. In short, I did not question that France would have to go through gigantic trials, that the interest of life consisted in one day rendering her some signal service, and that I would have the occasion to do so.

When I joined the Army, it was one of the greatest things in the world. Beneath all the criticisms and insults which were lavished on it, it was looking forward with serenity and even a muffled hopefulness to the approaching days when everything would depend on it. After Saint-Cyr I went through my apprenticeship as officer with the 33rd Infantry Regiment, at Arras. My first colonel—Pétain—showed me the meaning of the gift and art of command. Then, as the hurricane swept me off like a wisp of straw through the shocks of war—my baptism of fire, the calvary of the trenches, attacks, bombardments, wounds and captivity—I was privileged to see France, though deprived of part of her necessary means of defence by an insufficient birth-rate, by hollow ideologies, and by the negligence of the authorities, extract from herself an incredible effort, make up by measureless sacrifices for all she lacked and bring the trial to an end in victory. I was privileged to see her, in the most critical days, pull herself together morally, at first under the ægis of Joffre, at the end under the drive of the " Tiger." I was privileged to see her, later, though exhausted from losses and devastation, with her social structure and moral balance overthrown, resume with tottering steps her march towards her destiny, while the régime, taking once more its former shape and repudiating Clemenceau, rejected greatness and returned to confusion.

During the years which followed, my career passed through various stages: special duty and a campaign in Poland, the professorship of History at Saint-Cyr, the Ecole de Guerre, attachment to a Marshal's personal staff, command of the 19th Battalion of Chasseurs at Trèves, and general staff service on the Rhine and in the Levant. Everywhere I noted the renewal of prestige which her recent successes had earned for France and, at the same time, the doubts about the future which were being awakened by the erratic behaviour of her rulers. In spite of everything, I found in the soldier's trade the powerful interest it has to offer to the mind and to the heart. In the Army, though a mill without grist, I saw the instrument of the great actions which were approaching.

It was clear, in fact, that the outcome of the war had not established peace. Germany was reverting to her ambitions, in proportion as she recovered her strength. While Russia isolated herself in her revolution; while America held aloof from Europe; while England treated Berlin gently in order that Paris might have need of her; while the new States remained weak and disunited: it was on France alone that the burden fell of containing the Reich. She did in fact try, but disjointedly. And so it came about that our policy first applied constraint under the leadership of Poincaré, then attempted reconciliation at the instigation of Briand,

and finally sought refuge in the League of Nations. But Germany was growing big with menaces. Hitler was nearing power.

At this period I was detailed to the Secrétariat Général de la Défense Nationale, a permanent body at the disposal of the Prime Minister for preparing the State and the nation for war. From 1932 to 1937, under fourteen Governments, I found myself involved, in a planning capacity, in the whole range of political, technical and administrative activity concerning the country's defence. I had, in particular, to be familiar with the plans for security and for limitation of armaments presented by André Tardieu and Paul-Boncour respectively at Geneva; to supply the Doumergue Cabinet with the elements for its decisions when it chose to adopt a different course after the arrival of the Führer; to weave the Penelope-web of the bill for the wartime organisation of the nation; and to go into the measures involved by the mobilisation of the civil departments, of industry and of public services. The work I had to do, the discussions at which I was present, the contacts I was obliged to make, showed me the extent of our resources, but also the feebleness of the State.

For the disjointedness of the authorities was rife all over this field. Not—certainly—that the men who figured there lacked intelligence or patriotism. On the contrary, I saw men of incontestable value and, sometimes, of great talent come to the head of the ministries. But the political game consumed them and paralysed them. As a reserved but passionate witness of public affairs, I watched the constant repetition of the same scenario. Hardly had the Premier taken office when he was at grips with innumerable demands, criticisms and bids for favour, which all his energy was absorbed in warding off without ever contriving to master them. Parliament, far from supporting him, offered him nothing but ambushes and desertions. His ministers were his rivals. Opinion, the Press and sectional interests regarded him as the proper target for all complaints. Everyone, indeed—and he first of all—knew that he was there for only a short time. In fact, after a few months, he had to give place to another. As regards national defence, such conditions prevented those responsible from achieving that organic whole of continuous plans, matured decisions and measures carried to their conclusion, which we call a policy.

For these reasons the military, who received from the State no more than spasmodic and contradictory impulses, fell back within their deference to doctrine. The Army became stuck in a set of ideas which had had their hey-day before the end of the previous war. It was all the more inclined that way because its leaders were growing old at their posts, wedded to errors that had once constituted their glory.

Hence, the concept of the fixed and continuous front dominated the strategy envisaged for a future action. Organisation, doctrine, training and armament derived from it directly. It was understood that, in case of war, France would mobilise the mass of her reserves and would build up the largest possible number of divisions, designed not for manœuvring, attacking and exploiting, but for holding sectors. They would be placed in position all along the French and Belgian frontiers—Belgium being, then, explicitly our ally—and would there await the enemy's offensive.

As for the means: tanks, aircraft, mobile and revolving guns, which the last battles of the first world war had already shown to be capable of effecting surprise and the breakthrough, and whose power had since been growing continuously, were to be used only for reinforcing the line and, at need, restoring it by local counter-attacks. The types of weapons were established with this in mind: heavy tanks, armed with light, short pieces and intended for escorting infantry, not for rapid, independent action; interceptor aircraft designed for defending areas of sky, beside which the Air Force could muster few bombers and no dive-bombers; artillery designed to fire from fixed positions with a narrow horizontal field of action, not to push ahead through all sorts of country and fire at all angles. Besides, the front was traced in advance by the works of the Maginot line, prolonged by the Belgian fortifications. Thus the nation in arms would hold a barrier, behind which it would wait—so it was thought—for the blockade to wear the enemy down and the pressure of the free world to drive him to collapse.

Such a conception of war suited the spirit of the régime. Condemned by governmental weakness and political cleavages to stagnation, it was bound to espouse a static system of this kind. But, in addition, this reassuring panacea corresponded too well to the country's state of mind for anyone desirous of being elected, applauded or given space in print not to be tempted to approve it. Public opinion did not care for offensives, yielding to the illusion that by making war against war the bellicose would be prevented from making war, remembering many ruinous attacks, and failing to discern the revolution in military strength produced since then by the internal combustion engine. In short, everything converged to make passivity the very principle of our national defence.

To my mind, such an orientation was as dangerous as could be. I considered that, from the strategic point of view, it handed the initiative over to the enemy, lock, stock and barrel. From the political point of view, I believed that by proclaiming our intention to keep our armies at the frontier, Germany was being egged on to act against the weak, who were from that moment isolated: the Sarre, the Rhineland, Austria, Czechoslovakia, the Baltic States, Poland, and so on; that Russia was being discouraged from forming any bond with us; and that Italy was being assured that, whatever she might do, we would not impose any limit to her malevolence. Lastly, from the moral point of view, it seemed to me deplorable to make the country believe that war, if it came, ought to consist, for her, in fighting as little as possible.

To tell the truth, the philosophy of action, the inspiration and use of armies by the State, the relations between Government and High Command, had preoccupied me for a long time. I had already laid bare my thinking on these subjects by means of several publications: *la Discorde chez l'ennemi*, *le Fil de l'epée*, and a certain number of articles in reviews. I had given lectures in public, at the Sorbonne for instance, on the conduct of war. But in January, 1933, Hitler became master of the Reich. From that moment, things could only move headlong. If no one proposed anything that would meet the situation, I felt myself bound to appeal to public opinion and bring forward my own plan. But as this matter was likely to have consequences, I must expect a day to come when the spotlights of public life would settle on me. It was hard for me to make up my mind to this after twenty-five years spent under military rules.

Under the title *Vers l'armée de métier*,[1] I launched my plan and my ideas. I proposed the creation, as a matter of urgency, of an army of manœuvre and attack, mechanised, armoured, composed of picked men, to be added to the large-scale units supplied by mobilisation. In 1933 an article in the *Revue politique et parlementaire* served me as starting-point. In the spring of 1934 I brought out the book, which set forth my reasons for and my conception of the instrument it was necessary to construct.

Why? Dealing first with the defence of France, I showed that geography (which canalises the invasion of our territory through the north and the north-east), the nature of the German people (which inclines it to vast ambitions, attracts it westwards and marks out as its direction Paris through Belgium), and the character of the French people (which lays it open to surprise at the start of each conflict), imposed on us the need to hold a fraction of our forces always on the alert, ready to deploy in its entirety at any moment. " We cannot," I wrote, " rely on a hasty defensive by uncertain formations, to bear the first shock. The moment has come to add to the mass of our reserves and of our recruits, which is the principal element of the national resistance but is slow to gather and cumbrous to set to work, an instrument of manœuvre capable of acting without delay—that is to say, permanent, coherent and accustomed to arms."

I then argued from technical developments. Since the machine had dominated the military order, like everything else, the quality of those who must work the machines used in war had become an essential element in the effectiveness of the

---

[1] English edition published in 1940 (London and Melbourne; Hutchinson) under the title: *The Army of the Future*. (Translator's note.)

equipment. How true this was, above all, for the new weapons —tanks, aircraft, ships—which had been engendered by mechanical power, were being perfected very rapidly and were reviving mobility! I noted: " It is henceforward a fact that on land, on sea and in the air a carefully chosen personnel, able to get the most out of extremely powerful and varied material, possesses a terrible superiority over more or less confused masses." I quoted Paul Valéry: " We shall see the development of enterprises carried out by chosen men, acting in crews and producing, in a few moments, at a time and place unforeseen, shattering results."

Turning to the conditions imposed by politics upon strategy, I observed that the latter could not limit itself to the strict defence of the territory since the former must extend its field of action beyond the frontiers. " Whether we like it or not, we form part of a certain established order, all of whose elements are interdependent. . . . What becomes, for example, of Central and Eastern Europe, of Belgium or of the Sarre touches us vitally. . . . With how much blood and tears did we pay for the error of the Second Empire in letting Sadowa happen without moving the Army on to the Rhine? . . . We must then be ready to act abroad, at any time, on any occasion. How are we to do so in practice, if in order to undertake anything whatever we have got to mobilise our reserves? . . ." Besides, in the competition which was reviving between Germany and us for military strength, we could not fail to be out-distanced as far as numbers were concerned. On the other hand, " given our gifts of initiative, adaptation and pride, it depended entirely on us to win the upper hand in quality." I concluded this section on the " Why? " as follows: " A weapon for preventive and repressive action—that is what we must provide for ourselves."

How? The internal combustion engine supplied the basis of the answer: " the internal combustion engine which is ready to carry whatever one wants, wherever it is needed, at all speeds and distances; . . . the internal combustion engine which, if it is armoured, possesses such a fire-power and shock power that the rhythm of the battle corresponds to that of its movements." Going on from there, I fixed the aim to be attained: " Six divisions of the line and one light division, motorised throughout, armoured in part, will constitute the sort of army to bring about decisions."

The way in which this army ought to be composed was laid down clearly. Each of the divisions of the line was to include: an armoured brigade of two regiments, one of heavy tanks, the other of medium tanks, and a battalion of light tanks; a brigade of infantry comprising two regiments plus a battalion of chasseurs, all with caterpillared transport; a brigade of artillery, supplied with all-angle guns and formed of two regiments serving respectively short and long-range pieces, and completed by an anti-aircraft group. To second these three brigades, the Division would also have: a reconnaissance regiment; a battalion of engineers: a signals battalion; a camouflage battalion; and sundry services. The light division, designed for scouting purposes and to prevent surprise, would be equipped with faster machines. In addition, the army itself would have its own general reserves: tanks and very heavy guns, engineers, signals, camouflage. Finally, a strong force of reconnaissance aircraft, interceptors and fighters would be integrated with this large corps: a group for each division, a regiment for the whole, without prejudice to the combined operations that would be carried out by the mechanised air army in conjunction with those of the mechanised ground army.

But in order that the army of shock troops might be in a position to get the best possible results out of the complex and costly matériel with which it would be equipped, in order that it might be able to act suddenly, in any theatre, without waiting to be supplemented or learning instead of doing, it would have to be composed of professionals. Total effectives: a hundred thousand men. These troops would therefore be made up of regulars. Serving for six years in the crack corps, they would be moulded in that time by technical skill, emulation and *esprit de corps*. They would later supply cadres to the *contingents* and reserves.

After this came a description of how this strategic battering-ram was to be used to break down a well-established resistance. Positions taken up without warning, in a single night, this being made possible by the motorisation of all elements, by their ability to move in any sort of country and by the use of active and passive camouflage. Attack launched by three thousand tanks, disposed in several echelons on an average front of fifty kilometres, followed and supported closely by the decentralised artillery, and rejoined at the successive objectives by the infantry who would be transported together with their means of fire-power and of ground organisation, the whole being articulated in two or three *corps d'armée* and kept informed and sustained by the Air Force belonging to the divisions and to the Army. Rate of advance of the whole system attaining normally about fifty kilometres in a day's fighting. After which, and if the enemy was still putting up a continuous resistance, a general regrouping, with a view either to enlarging the breach laterally, or to resuming the effort to advance, or to holding the ground gained.

But the wall once pierced, larger possibilities might suddenly lie open. The mechanised army would then deploy fanwise to exploit its gains. On this subject I wrote: " Often, after a success, we shall wish to gather its fruits and to thrust out into the zone of prizes. We shall see the exploitation of gains become a reality, where formerly it was only a dream. . . . Then will lie open the road to great victories, to those victories which, by their deep and rapidly extended effects, lead to a general collapse among the enemy, as the smashing of a pillar sometimes brings down a cathedral. . . . We shall see fast troops range far and wide in the enemy's rear, strike at his vital points, throw his dispositions into confusion. . . . Thus will be restored that strategic extension of tactical results which once used to constitute the supreme end and, as it were, the nobility of the art. . . ." But the hostile people and State might, when their distress and the annihilation of their means of defence reached a certain point, themselves collapse.

All the more so, and the more quickly, since " this aptitude for surprise and for the break-through harmonised perfectly

with the capabilities, from now on vital, of air forces." I pictured
the air army preparing and prolonging by its bombardments
the operations carried out on the ground by the mechanised
army and, vice versa, the latter conferring an immediate
strategic utility upon the destructive actions of the air squadrons
by irrupting into the zones just ravaged.

So profound an evolution of the art made necessary a
similar evolution of the command. After bringing out the fact
that henceforward radio communications provided the means
of binding together the elements of the army of the future, I
ended the work by showing what methods the Command must
employ in order to handle the new instrument. It would no
longer be the job of leaders to direct, by anonymous orders,
from dug-in posts, a distant human material. On the contrary, to be there, see for oneself and set an example would
become once again essential in the midst of that shifting drama,
filled with unforeseen hazards and split-second opportunities,
which the warfare of mechanised forces would be. The personality of the leader would be much more important than
codified formulæ. " If," I asked, " evolution were destined thus
to favour the rise of those who, in the tragic hours when the
storm sweeps away conventions and habits, are the only ones
to remain on their feet and to be, therefore, necessary, would
not that be all to the good? "

In conclusion, I appealed to the State. The Army, no more
than any other body, would in practice transform itself unaided.
Since the specialised corps was bound to bring with it profound changes in military ways, as well as in the technique
and politics of warfare, it was on the Government that the
burden of creating it fell. To be sure, there would be need,
once again, of a Louvois or a Carnot. At the same time such
a reform could only be one part of a whole, one element in
the effort towards a renovation of the country. " But in the
fact that this national recasting must begin with the Army
there would be nothing that would not be in harmony with
the natural order of things. In that case, in the hard toil
which is needed to rejuvenate France, her army will serve

as her stand-by and her inspiration. For the sword is the axis of the world, and greatness is not divisible."

In working out this comprehensive project, I had naturally made use of the lines of thought already set going, all over the world, by the appearance of the fighting internal combustion engine. General Estienne, apostle and first inspector of tanks, envisaged, as early as 1917, bringing a good number of them into action at a great distance in advance of those escorting the infantry. That was why, at the end of 1918, enormous machines weighing sixty tons were beginning to come from the factories. But the armistice had stopped their manufacture and confined the theory within the formula of the concerted action completing an escorting action. The British, who had shown themselves pioneers by engaging the Royal Tank Corps at Cambrai in 1917 in a massive action of deep penetration, continued to keep alive the idea of the autonomous operation by armoured detachments—an idea whose protagonists were General Fuller and Captain Liddell Hart. In France, in 1933, the High Command brought together some scattered elements at Suippes camp and put to the test an embryo light division for preventing surprise and for scouting.

Others had even larger views. General von Seeckt, in his work, *Thoughts of a Soldier*,[1] which appeared in 1929, depicted the possibilities which an army of quality (meaning the Reichswehr with a hundred thousand men on long-term service) had as opposed to masses without cohesion—he was thinking of those of the French. The Italian general, Douhet, calculating the effects which bombardments from the air could produce on the centres of industry and life, estimated that an air army could win a decision unaided. Lastly, the " Maximum Plan," advocated at Geneva by M. Paul-Boncour in 1932, proposed placing under the League of Nations a professional force, which would have disposal of all the tanks and all the aircraft in Europe and would be charged with maintaining collective security. My plan aimed at building into a

---

[1] English version by Gilbert Waterhouse, with introduction by General Sir Ian Hamilton; London: Ernest Benn, 1930. (Translator's note.)

single whole, and for the benefit of France, these fragmentary but converging views.

The book aroused interest at first, but no deep feeling. As long as *Vers l'armée de métier* seemed to be merely a book that set going some ideas of which the hierarchy would make what use it chose, people were willing to see in it an original theory. It entered nobody's head that our military organisation might be modified in consequence. If I had felt that there was no hurry, I would indeed have been content to advocate my thesis in specialist circles, sure that, with evolution on their side, my arguments would make their way. But Hitler was not the man to wait.

Already in October, 1933, he broke with the League of Nations and automatically assumed his freedom of action in the matter of armaments. The years 1934 and 1935 saw the Reich deploy an immense effort in manufacture and in recruitment. The National-Socialist régime made no secret of its determination to smash the Treaty of Versailles by conquering its " Lebensraum." For this policy an offensive military machine was necessary. Hitler was, to be sure, preparing the *levée en masse*. Not long after gaining power he instituted labour service and, later, conscription. But in addition he needed a means of action, to enable him to cut the Gordian knots at Mainz, Vienna, Prague and Warsaw, and to ensure that the Germanic lance, when given a sharp point, should be capable of piercing at one stroke to the heart of France.

The well-informed, indeed, were not unaware that the Führer intended to stamp his mark upon the new German Army; that he listened gladly to the officers formerly grouped around General von Seeckt, such as Keitel, Rundstedt and Guderian, who were partisans of manœuvre, speed and quality, and therefore attracted towards mechanised forces; and finally that, adopting the theories of Goering, he wanted an Air Force whose action could be directly linked with the battle on the ground. I was soon told that he himself had had my book read to him, since his advisers attached importance to it. In November, 1934, it was learnt that the Reich was creating the first three Panzer divisions. A book published at that time by Colonel Nehring of the General Staff of the Wehrmacht specified that their composition would be, practically speaking, identical with that which I was suggesting for our armoured divisions of the future. In March, 1935, Goering announced that the Reich was providing itself with a powerful Air Force, and that this would include, besides many interceptors, numerous bombers and a strong force of dive-bombers. And indeed, although these measures were so many flagrant violations of the treaties, the free world was content to oppose to them a platonic protest from the League of Nations.

I could not bear to see the enemy of to-morrow endowing himself with the means of victory while France was still without them. And yet, in the incredible apathy in which the nation was plunged, no voice in authority was lifted to demand the required action. The stake was so great that it did not seem to me permissible to maintain my reserve, slight as were my importance and my fame. Responsibility for national defence belonged to the Government. I resolved to carry the debate there.

I began by allying myself with André Pironneau, news editor of the *Echo de Paris*, and then editor of *l'Epoque*. He made it his task to make known the plan for a mechanised army and to keep the authorities on the move by the goad of a great newspaper. Tying his campaign up with the news, André Pironneau published forty main articles which rendered the subject familiar. Every time events turned the attention of the public towards national defence, my friendly helper demonstrated in his paper the need for creating the specialised corps. Since it was known that Germany was directing the essential part of her armaments effort towards the engines of attack and of follow-up, Pironneau uttered cries of alarm— but they were obstinately stifled by the general indifference. He proved, twenty times over, that the German armoured mass, supported by the Air Force, could make our defences suddenly cave in and produce among our population a panic from which it would not recover.

While André Pironneau was doing his good work, other journalists and critics were at least raising the question. Such were Rémy Roure and General Baratier in *Le Temps*, Pierre Bourget and Generals de Cugnac and Duval in the *Journal des Débats*, Emile Buré and Charles Giron in *L'Ordre*, André Lecomte in *L'Aube*, Colonel Emile Mayer, Lucien Nachin and Jean Auburtin in various reviews, and so on. Nevertheless the established order of things and ideas was too compact to be affected merely by articles in the Press. The political rulers of the country must be made aware of the problem.

M. Paul Reynaud seemed to me essentially marked out for this undertaking. His intelligence was fully capable of absorbing the arguments; his talent, of putting them effectively; his courage, of fighting them through. In addition, though already an established public figure, M. Paul Reynaud gave the impression of being a man who had his future in front of him. I saw him, convinced him and, from then on, worked with him.

At the tribune of the Chambre des Députés, on 15th March, 1935, he made an arresting speech, showing why and how our military organisation must be completed by a mechanised army of quality. Not long afterwards, when the Government asked Parliament to vote the two years' service, M. Paul Reynaud, while agreeing to this, submitted a bill for " the immediate creation of a specialised corps of six divisions of the line, one light division and general reserves and services, formed of regulars and to be brought completely up to strength by 15th April, 1940, at the latest." During three years M. Paul Reynaud affirmed his position in several speeches which stirred the parliamentary dough profoundly, in a book called *Le problème militaire français*, in vigorous articles and interviews, and finally by conversations on the subject with important politicians and military men. He thus took on the appearance of an innovating and resolute statesman, marked out by nature for the exercise of power in case of serious difficulties.

As I thought it good that the melody should be played on

various instruments, I applied myself to drawing other men in. M. Le Cour Grandmaison, attracted by the aspect of the professional army which answered to our traditions, nobly made himself its apostle. Three left-wing deputies—Philippe Serre, Marcel Déat and Léo Lagrange, whose talent was of the right kind for throwing into relief the revolutionary aspect of the new proposal—agreed to join us. The first did so in fact, and with such brilliance that he gained recognition as a great orator and shortly afterwards entered the Government. The second, the one on whose gifts I counted most, was seduced into an opposite course after his failure in the 1936 election. The third was prevented, by the party of which he was a member, from stating his conviction. But soon men as considerable as M. Paul-Boncour in the Chambre and President Millerand in the Senate gave me to understand that they, too, were in favour of the reform.

Meanwhile, however, the official bodies and their unofficial supporters, rather than recognise obvious necessities and accept the change subject to modification of its formula and application, clung to the system in force. Unfortunately they did so in so categorical a manner that they closed against themselves the way towards learning better. To fight the idea of the mechanised army they set to work to misrepresent it. To fly in the face of technical development they busied themselves denying it. To resist events they affected to be unaware of them. I verified, on this occasion, that the clash of ideas, as soon as it involves the established errors and the men in office, assumes the uncompromising mood of theological disputes.

General Debeney, a glorious army commander in the first world war, who in 1927, in his capacity as Chief of the General Staff, had worked out the laws dealing with military organisation, condemned the project formally. In the *Revue des Deux Mondes* he explained authoritatively that any European conflict would have its decisive phase on our north-east frontier, and that the problem consisted in holding this solidly. He therefore saw nothing to change either in the laws or in practice, and merely insisted that the system resulting from

24

them should be reinforced. General Weygand intervened in his turn, likewise in the *Revue des Deux Mondes*. Admitting, *a priori*, that my idea would separate the Army into two portions: " Two armies—not at any price! " he protested. As for the function I assigned to the specialised corps, he did not deny its interest, but stated that it could be fulfilled by elements already formed: " We have," he explained, " a mechanised, motorised and mounted reserve. There is nothing to create, everything exists." On 4th July, 1939, speaking in public at Lille, General Weygand was to proclaim yet again that we lacked nothing.

Marshal Pétain thought it right to join in. He did so in a preface to General Chauvineau's book, *Une invasion est-elle encore possible?* The Marshal there claimed that tanks and aircraft did not modify the basic factors of warfare, and that the principal element of French security was the continuous front buttressed by fortification. *Le Figaro* published, under the signature of Jean Rivière, a series of inspired and reassuring articles: " Tanks are not invincible," " The weakness of the tank," " When the politicians go wrong," and so on. In the *Mercure de France* a French general who hid his identity under a signature of three stars rejected even the principle of motorisation: " The Germans," he declared, " being naturally aggressive, must naturally have Panzer divisions. But France, being pacific and defensive, is bound to be anti-motorisation."

Other critics had recourse to ridicule. The critic of one of the big literary reviews wrote: " One is hard put to it to assess, with the courtesy one would wish, ideas which touch the fringe of delirium. Let us simply say that Monsieur de Gaulle was anticipated, some years ago, by the Père Ubu, who was likewise a great tactician, with modern ideas. ' When we are back from Poland,' he used to say, ' we will imagine, with the aid of our physical science, a wind machine for transporting the whole army.' "

If the conventionality of the conservative elements came out in fundamental hostility, that of the party of progress was no better disposed. In *Le Populaire* during November and

25

December, 1934, Léon Blum expressed uncompromisingly the aversion and uneasiness inspired in him by the plan. In several articles—" Professional soldiers and professional army," " Towards a professional army? ", " Down with the professional army! "—he too took his stand against the specialised corps. He did so not on grounds of national defence, but in the name of an ideology which he styled democratic and republican and which was traditionally determined to see in everything military a menace to the régime. Léon Blum pronounced the anathema, therefore, against a body of professionals whose composition, spirit and weapons would, if he was to be believed, automatically endanger the Republic.

Thus buttressed to right and left, the official bodies set their faces against all change. M. Paul Reynaud's plan was rejected by the Army Committee of the Chambre. The report on this subject, presented by M. Senac and drawn up with the co-operation of the Army General Staff, concluded that the proposed reform " was useless, undesirable and had logic and history against it." At the tribune of the Assemblée, General Maurin, Minister for War, said in answer to the orators who favoured the corps of manœuvre: " When we have devoted so many efforts to building up a fortified barrier, is it conceivable that we would be mad enough to go ahead of this barrier, into I know not what adventure? " He added: " What I have just told you is the Government's view, and it, at least in my person, is perfectly familiar with the war plan." These words, which settled the fate of the specialised corps, at the same time let those in Europe who had ears to hear know in advance that, whatever happened, France would undertake nothing beyond manning the Maginot line.

As could be foreseen, ministerial reprobation extended to me personally. But this happened in occasional bursts, not by condemnation in due form. Thus it was that at the Elysée, at the end of a meeting of the Conseil Supérieur de la Défense Nationale, whose secretary I was, General Maurin addressed me sharply: " Good-bye, de Gaulle! Where I am there's no place for you! " In his office he would shout at visitors

who mentioned me: "He has got himself a tame writer—
Pironneau—and a gramophone—Paul Reynaud. I shall send
him to Corsica!" While making the thunder rumble, however,
General Maurin had the magnanimity not to launch the
thunderbolt. Shortly afterwards, M. Fabry, who replaced him
at the Rue Saint-Dominique, and General Gamelin, who
succeeded General Weygand as Chief of the General Staff
while remaining head of the Army Staff, adopted the negative
policy of their predecessors towards the scheme and the same
embarrassed and irritated attitude towards me.

At bottom the men in office, although they maintained the
status quo, could not help being secretly sensitive to my arguments. They were, indeed, too well aware of what was going
on to believe entirely in their own objections. When they
declared the ideas I was spreading about what a mechanised
force could do to be exaggerated, they were nevertheless
uneasy about the one which the Reich was forging for itself.
When they pretended to supply the place of the seven shock
divisions by as many large-scale ordinary units of the defensive
type, and when they called these "motorised" because they
would be transported in lorries, they knew, better than anyone, that that was only a play upon words. When they alleged
that by adopting the specialised corps we would be cutting
our army in two, they were affecting not to recognise that the
two years' service, which had been voted since my book had
come out, made it possible, if need be, to introduce into the
corps d'élite a certain proportion of soldiers from the *contingent*;
that there already existed a navy, an air force, a colonial army,
an Africa army, a police force and a *garde mobile*, which were
specialised, without the cohesion of the whole having suffered
damage; and finally, that what makes the unity of the various
national forces is not the identity of their equipment and of
their recruitment but the fact of serving the same country,
under the same laws, and under the same flag.

It made me sad, therefore, to see those eminent men, in
virtue of a sort of upside-down loyalty, constitute themselves
not exactly guides, but reassuring mouth-pieces. Nevertheless,
beneath their apparent conviction, I could feel their wistful-

ness for the horizons now open to them. This was the first episode in a long series of events, in which a part of the French élite, condemning all the ends I would be led to pursue, and yet, deep down in itself, miserable at remaining ineffective, was to grant me, beyond its strictures, the melancholy homage of its remorse.

Destiny followed its course. Hitler, knowing now what to expect from us, opened his series of *coups de force*. Already, in 1935, over the Saar plebiscite, he had created an atmosphere so menacing that the French Government threw in its hand before playing it, and then the people of the Saar, attracted and intimidated by the Germanic fury, voted in a body for the Third Reich. Mussolini, on his side, braving the Geneva sanctions thanks to the Laval Government's support and the Baldwin Cabinet's tolerance, moved on to the conquest of Ethiopia. Suddenly, on 7th March, 1936, the German army crossed the Rhine.

The Versailles treaty forbade the troops of the Reich access to the territories on the left bank, which the Locarno agreement had, in addition, neutralised. In strict law, we could re-occupy them as soon as Germany repudiated her signature. If the specialised corps had existed, even in part, with its fast machines and its personnel ready to march on the instant, the natural force of things would have at once directed it on to the Rhine. As our allies, Poles, Czechs and Belgians, were ready to support us and the British committed in advance, Hitler would certainly have drawn back. He was, in fact, at the beginning of his rearmament effort and still in no condition to face a general conflict. But such a check, inflicted by France at this period, on this ground, could have disastrous consequences for him in his own country. By such a gamble he might, at one go, lose everything.

He won everything. Our organisation, the nature of our resources, the very spirit of our national defence, tempted to inaction an administration which had all too much tendency that way, and prevented us from marching. Because we were only ready to hold our frontier and had imposed on ourselves a self-denying ordinance against crossing it in any case, there was no riposte to be expected from France. The Führer was sure of this. The whole world took note of the fact. The Reich, instead of finding itself compelled to withdraw the troops it had adventured, established them without a blow in the whole of the Rhineland territory, in direct contact with France and Belgium. After that, M. Flandin, Minister for Foreign Affairs, could indeed travel to London with bleeding heart to inform himself of England's intentions; M. Sarraut, the Prime Minister, could indeed declare that the Paris Government " would not admit that Strasbourg should be within range of German guns "; French diplomacy could indeed obtain a theoretical censure of Hitler from the League of Nations: these were only gestures and words in face of the accomplished fact.

To my way of thinking, the emotion aroused by the event could be salutary. The authorities had a chance to use it with a view to filling some deadly gaps. Although people in France were absorbed by the elections and by the social crisis which followed them, everyone was agreed on the need to reinforce the country's defences. If the effort were concentrated upon the creation of the instrument we lacked, what was essential might be saved. Nothing of the kind occurred. The considerable military credits which were opened in 1936 were used to complete the existing system, not to modify it.

I had had some hope, all the same. In the great unrest which then agitated the nation and was canalised politically in an electoral and parliamentary coalition known as the " Popular Front," there was, it seemed to me, the psychological factor which made it possible to break with passivity. It was not inconceivable that, in the presence of National-Socialism triumphing at Berlin, Fascism reigning at Rome and Falangism advancing on Madrid, the French Republic might be willing simultaneously to transform its social structure and to reform its military power. In October Léon Blum, the Prime Minister, invited me to come and see him. It happened that our meeting took place on the very afternoon of the day when the King of the Belgians publicly put an end to the alliance with France and with Great Britain. The King alleged that, if his country were attacked by Germany, this alliance would not protect it. " In practice," he proclaimed, " given what modern mechanised forces are capable of doing, we would in any case be alone."

Léon Blum assured me warmly of the interest he took in my ideas. " And yet," I said to him, " you have opposed them." " One gets a different perspective," he replied, " when one becomes head of the Government." We talked first of what would happen if, as was to be foreseen, Hitler marched on Vienna, Prague and Warsaw. " It's very simple," I pointed out. " According to circumstances we shall have a limited call-up or a full mobilisation. Then, peering between the battlements of our fortifications, we shall watch the enslavement of Europe." " What's that? " cried Léon Blum, " would you have us send an expeditionary force to Austria, to Bohemia, to Poland? " " No! " I said. " But if the Wehrmacht advances along the Danube or the Elbe, why shouldn't we go to the Rhine? While it is debouching on the Vistula, why shouldn't we enter the Ruhr? Besides, the mere fact of our being capable of these ripostes would no doubt prevent the acts of aggression. But our present system forbids us to stir. The armoured corps, on the contrary, would induce us to do so. Isn't it true that a Government may find a certain relief in feeling that its direction is set in advance? " The Prime Minister agreed to that with a good grace, but declared: " It would be deplorable, certainly, if our friends in Central and Eastern Europe were temporarily submerged. All the same, in the last resort, nothing would have been achieved for Hitler, as long as he had not crushed us. How would he manage that? You will agree that our system, ill-adapted though it is to attack, is excellent for defence."

I showed that it was by no means so. Reminding him of the declaration made public that morning by Léopold III, I pointed out that it was the inferiority in which the absence of a *corps d'élite* placed us in relation to the Germans that was costing us the Belgian alliance. The head of the Government did not dispute it, although he thought the attitude of Brussels had other than merely strategic motives. " In any case," he

said, " our defensive front and our fortifications would protect
our territory." " Nothing is less certain," I answered.
" Already in 1918 there was no longer such a thing as an
impregnable front. Well, look at the progress made since then
by tanks and aircraft! To-morrow the concentrated action
of a sufficient number of machines will be capable of smashing,
in a chosen sector, any defensive barrier whatever. Once the
breach is open, the Germans will have a chance of thrusting
far behind our lines a fast-moving armoured mass supported
by their Air Force. If we have the same, all can be repaired.
If not, all will be lost."

The Prime Minister told me that the Government, with the
support of Parliament, had decided on a great programme of
expenditure on national defence over and above the ordinary
budget, and that a considerable part of the credits was to be
devoted to tanks and the Air Force. I drew his attention to
the fact that almost all the aircraft whose construction was
envisaged were to be designed for interception, not for attack.
As for the tanks, nine-tenths of them would be " Renaults "
and " Hotchkisses " of the 1935 type, modern of their kind,
but heavy, slow, armed with short-range guns, made for
co-operation in the infantry battle, but not at all for forming
an autonomous whole with large-scale units. Besides, we had
no such idea. Our organisation would therefore remain what
it was. " We are going," I remarked, " to build as many
machines and spend as much money as would be needed for
the mechanised army, and we shall not have that army."
" The way in which the credits allotted to the War Department
are used," observed the Prime Minister, " is the affair of
M. Daladier and of General Gamelin." " No doubt," I
answered. " Allow me, though, to think that national defence
is the Government's responsibility."

During our conversation the telephone had rung ten
times, deflecting Léon Blum's attention on to petty parliamentary or administrative questions. As I took my leave and
he was again called, he made a great, tired gesture. " Judge,"
he said, " if it is easy for the head of the Government to hold

to the plan you have outlined, when he cannot remain five minutes with the same idea! ”

I soon learned that the Prime Minister, though struck by our interview, was not going to pull down the columns of the temple and that the old plan was to be applied as it was. From that moment our chance of counter-balancing the Reich's new strength before it was too late seemed to me heavily compromised. I was convinced, in fact, that Hitler's character, his doctrine, his age and even the impulse he had given to the German people, made it impossible for him to wait. Things would now move too fast for France to be able to make up the time she had lost—even if her rulers had been willing.

On 1st May, 1937, a complete Panzer division, with hundreds of aircraft flying over it, marched through Berlin. The impression produced on the spectators, and first and foremost on M. François-Poncet, the French Ambassador, and on our military attachés, was of a force that nothing could stop, except a similar force. But their reports produced no modification in the arrangements made by the Paris Government. On 11th March, 1938, Hitler carried out the Anschluss. He launched against Vienna a mechanised division, the mere sight of which rallied the general consent, and with it, that very evening, he entered the Austrian capital in triumph. In France, far from learning the lesson of this rough demonstration, efforts were made to reassure the public by an ironic description of the break-down of a few German tanks in the course of this forced march. There was no greater willingness to be enlightened by the lessons of the Spanish civil war, in which the Italian tanks and German dive-bombers, small as were their numbers, played the principal part in every battle in which they appeared.

In September the Führer, with the complicity of London and then of Paris, executed Czechoslovakia. Three days before Munich, the Chancellor of the Reich, speaking at the Sportspalast in Berlin, had dotted the “ i ”s, in the midst of joyous laughter and hurrahs of enthusiasm. “ Now,” he shouted, “ I can admit publicly what you all know. We have acquired

32

an armed force such as the world has never seen." On 15th March, 1939, he extracted from President Hacha a formal abdication, and entered Prague the same day. After which, on September 1st, he hurled himself upon Poland. In these successive acts of one and the same tragedy, France played the part of the victim that awaits its turn.

As for me, I watched these events without surprise, but not without pain. After having, in 1937, taken part in the work of the Centre des Hautes Etudes Militaires, I had been given command of the 507th Tank Regiment, at Metz. My duties as colonel and the distance from Paris deprived me of the opportunities and contacts required for carrying on my great controversy. At the same time, in the Spring of 1938, M. Paul Reynaud had joined the Daladier Cabinet, first as Minister of Justice, then of Finance. Apart from the fact that he was now bound by ministerial solidarity, the re-establishing of our economic and monetary equilibrium was a task so pressing that it occupied the Minister completely. Above all, the obstinacy of the authorities in cultivating a static military system while Germany's dynamic force was deploying over Europe, the blindness of a régime which went on with its absurd games in face of a Reich that was ready to spring upon us, and the stupidity of the boobies who acclaimed the Munich surrender, were really only the effects of a profound national renunciation. Against that, I could do nothing. Nevertheless in 1938, feeling the tempest rising, I published *La France et son armée*. In it I showed how, from century to century, the soul and the fate of the country were constantly reflected in the mirror of its army: the final warning which, from my modest place, I addressed to my country on the eve of the cataclysm.

When, in September, 1939, the French Government followed the British Cabinet's example and consented to join in the conflict already begun in Poland, I had not the least doubt that it did so with the illusion that, in spite of the state of war, we would not fight all out. It was therefore without astonishment that, as commander of the tanks of the 5th Army, in Alsace, I saw our mobilised forces settle down into stagnation, while Poland was struck down in two weeks by the Panzer divisions and the air squadrons. It is true that the Soviet intervention hastened the crushing of the Poles. But in Stalin's decision to make common cause with Hitler one could discern his conviction that the French would remain stationary, that the Reich therefore had its hands free and that it was better to share its prey than to be its prey. While the enemy forces were almost all being used on the Vistula, we did nothing really, apart from a few token actions, by way of placing ourselves on the Rhine. We did nothing, either, to check Italy by giving her the choice between a French invasion and the pledges for her neutrality. We did nothing, lastly, to realise immediately the junction with Belgium by gaining Liége and the Albert Canal.

Once more the dominant school tried to view this wait-and-see policy as a fruitful strategy. Over the radio the members of the Government, first among them the Premier, and in the Press many notable people, did their best to vaunt the advantages of immobility, thanks to which, so they said, we were maintaining the integrity of our territory without losses. M. Brisson, editor of the *Figaro*, when he asked me my opinion during a visit he paid me at Wangenburg and heard me deploring the passivity of our forces, exclaimed: "Don't you see that we have already *gagné la Marne blanche* (won a platonic Battle of the Marne)?" When I visited Paris in January and dined at M. Paul Reynaud's flat in the Rue de Rivoli, I met Léon Blum. "What's your forecast?" he said to me. "The problem," I answered, "is whether in the Spring the Germans will attack westwards to take Paris or eastwards to reach Moscow." "Do you think so," said Léon Blum, astonished. "The Germans attack to the east? But why should they go and lose themselves in the depths of Russian territory? Attack to the west? But what could they do against the Maginot line?" When President Lebrun visited the 5th Army, I presented my tanks for his inspection. "I am familiar with your ideas," he told me, amiably. "But it does seem too late for the enemy to apply them."

It was too late for us. And yet, on January 26th, I made

a last attempt. I addressed to the eighty chief persons in the Government, the High Command and politics, a memorandum whose aim was to convince them that the enemy would take the offensive with a very powerful mechanised force, on the ground and in the air; that our front might therefore be broken through at any moment; that if we had not ourselves equivalent units of riposte, we were in great danger of being annihilated; that the creation of the required instrument ought to be decided on at once; that, besides pushing on with the necessary manufacture, it was urgent to gather into one mechanised reserve those of the units, already existing or in course of formation, which could, if need be, form part of it.

I concluded: "The French people should not, at any price, fall into the illusion that the present military immobility might be in harmony with the nature of the present war. The opposite is the truth. The internal combustion engine endows modern means of destruction with such force, speed and range that the present conflict will be marked, sooner or later, by movements, surprises, breaks-through and pursuits the scale and rapidity of which will infinitely exceed those of the most lightning events of the past. . . . Let us make no mistake about it! The conflict which has begun might well be the most extended, the most complex, the most violent of all those that have ravaged the earth. The political, economic, social and moral crisis from which it has issued is so profound and so ubiquitous that it is bound to end in a complete upheaval of both the condition of the peoples and the structure of states. And the obscure harmony of things is providing this revolution with a military instrument—the army of machines—exactly proportioned to its colossal dimensions. It is high time for France to draw the conclusion."

My memorandum produced no shock. However, the ideas expressed and the proofs exhibited were at last having some effect. At the end of 1939 there were two light mechanised divisions in existence and a third was being formed. These were, however, only scouting units, which would have been very useful for guiding the manœuvres of an armoured mass, but would be capable of very little as long as there was no such mass. On 2nd December, 1938, the Conseil Supérieur de la Guerre, at the insistence of General Billotte, had decided on the creation of two armoured divisions. One of them was formed by the beginning of 1940. The other was due to be formed in March. These divisions would be armed with some thirty-ton type B tanks, of which the first examples had been in existence for fifteen years and three hundred were being—at last!—made. But each of them, whatever the quality of their machines, would be a very long way from having the power I had proposed. It would comprise 120 tanks; I would have liked 500. It would have only one battalion of infantry transported in lorries; to my mind, seven were required, in caterpillared vehicles. It would possess two artillery groups; seven groups supplied with all-angles pieces were what I judged necessary. It would have no reconnaissance group; to my mind, it needed one. Lastly I could only conceive of mechanical units being employed in the form of an autonomous mass, organised and commanded in the way appropriate to this. All that was envisaged, on the contrary, was to attach the armoured divisions to various *corps d'armée* of the old type—in other words, to fuse them into the general arrangement.

The same faint stirrings of change which, in place of purpose, were appearing on the military plane, were beginning to show in the political field. The sort of euphoria, which the " phony war " had at first maintained among the men in office, was beginning to fade. By mobilising millions of men, devoting industry to the manufacture of arms and undertaking enormous expenditure, the nation was being subjected to upheavals whose effects were already becoming apparent to the alarmed politicians. Besides, there was nothing to indicate that progressive weakening of the enemy which was expected from the blockade. Without any other war policy—for which there were not the means—being suggested out loud, everyone nonetheless turned his uneasiness and bitterness against the one that was being carried out. As usual, the régime, being incapable of adopting the measures that would have saved the situation, but seeking to throw dust in its own eyes and in those of public opinion, started a ministerial crisis. On March 21st the Chambre overthrew the Daladier Cabinet. On the 23rd M. Paul Reynaud formed the Government.

Summoned to Paris by the new Prime Minister, I drew up at his request a short, clear statement which he accepted without change for reading out to Parliament. Then, with intrigues already rustling in the corridors, I went to the Palais-Bourbon to witness from one of the galleries the scene of its presentation.

This was appalling. After the Government's statement of policy had been read out by its head to a sceptical and apathetic House, hardly anyone was to be heard in the debate but the spokesmen of those groups or men who considered themselves injured by the new coalition. The danger in which the country stood, the necessity of a national effort, the co-operation of the free world, were mentioned only to adorn claims and complaints. Léon Blum alone, although he had no place offered him, spoke with greatness. Thanks to him, M. Paul Reynaud won through, though by an extremely narrow margin. The Government received a vote of confidence by a majority of one. "And indeed," M. Herriot, the President of the Chambre, was to tell me later, " I'm not very sure that it had that."

Before regaining my H.Q. at Wangenburg, I remained for a few days with the Prime Minister, who now had his quarters at the Quai d'Orsay. That was enough to show me how far the demoralisation of the régime had gone. In all the parties, in the Press, in the administration, in business, in the trade unions, there were influential groups openly favouring the idea of stopping the war. The well-informed said that this was the opinion of Marshal Pétain, our Ambassador at Madrid, and he was supposed to know, through the Spaniards, that the Germans would gladly lend themselves to an arrangement. " If Reynaud falls," it was everywhere being said, " Laval will take power with Pétain at his side. The Marshal is, in fact, in a position to make the High Command accept an armistice." A leaflet was circulating in thousands of copies:

it bore on its three pages a picture of the Marshal, first as victorious leader in the first world war with the legend: " Yesterday, a great soldier! . . .", then as Ambassador: " To-day, a great diplomat! . . .", and then as a huge, indistinct figure: " To-morrow? . . ."

It must be said that some circles were more inclined to see Stalin as the enemy than Hitler. They were much more concerned with the means of striking at Russia, whether by aiding Finland, or by bombarding Baku, or by landing at Istanbul, than with how to cope with the Reich. Many quite openly professed their admiration for Mussolini. Some, even in the Government, were working to get France to buy the good graces of the Duce by ceding to him Jibuti, the Chad, a share in a condominium over the Tunisian Regency. The communists, on their side, having noisily rallied to the national cause as long as Berlin was opposed to Moscow, started cursing the " capitalist " war as soon as Molotov and Ribbentrop had reached agreement. As for the mass of the people, it was bewildered and, feeling that nothing and nobody at the head of the State was capable of dominating events, wavered in doubt and uncertainty. Clearly a serious reverse would cause the country a wave of astonishment and alarm, which might very well sweep everything away.

In this pernicious atmosphere, M. Paul Reynaud endeavoured to establish his authority. This was all the more difficult because he was in perpetual conflict with M. Daladier, whose successor he was as Prime Minister, but who remained in the Government as Minister of National Defence and War Minister. This strange situation could not be modified, for the Radical Party, without whose forbearance the Government would have fallen, insisted that its leader should remain in it, while waiting to regain the leadership at the first opportunity. At the same time M. Paul Reynaud, in his anxiety to enlarge his tiny majority, was trying to melt the prejudices of the moderates against him. A delicate operation this, for a large fraction of the Right desired peace with Hitler and an *entente* with Mussolini. The Prime Minister thus found himself obliged to summon to his side as Under-Secretary of State

M. Paul Baudouin, who was very active in these circles, and to appoint him secretary of the War Committee which he had just set up.

In reality M. Paul Reynaud had thought of entrusting this work to me. The War Committee, which handled the conduct of the war and brought together, for this purpose, the principal Ministers as well as the Army, Navy and Air Commanders-in-Chief, might play a decisive part. Its secretary's job was to prepare its discussions, be present at its meetings, communicate its decisions and see that they were carried out. Many things might depend on the way this was done. But while M. Paul Reynaud seemed to wish that it should be done by me, M. Daladier would not agree. To the Prime Minister's messenger who came to the Rue Saint-Dominique to make this wish known to him, he replied, straight off: " If de Gaulle comes here, I shall leave this office, go downstairs and telephone M. Paul Reynaud to put him in my place."

M. Daladier was in no way hostile to me personally. He had proved it, some time back, by himself, as Minister, taking the initiative of inscribing me on the list for promotion, when the clerks' cabal was trying to keep me off it. But M. Daladier, who had borne the responsibility for national defence for several years, had wedded himself to the system in force. Feeling that events were going to speak sooner or later, assuming in advance the consequences of their judgment and reckoning that, in any case, it was too late to change the organisation, he was more than ever determined on the positions he had taken up. But for me to act as secretary to the War Committee in spite of the opposition of the Minister of National Defence was manifestly impossible. I left again for the front.

Before this, I had been to see General Gamelin, who invited me to his headquarters in the Château de Vincennes. There he was, in a setting which suggested a convent, attended by a few officers, working and meditating without mixing in day-to-day duties. He left General Georges to command the North-Eastern front,—an arrangement which might work as long as nothing was happening, but would certainly become untenable if battle were joined. As for General Georges, he was installed at La Ferté-sous-Jouarre with part of the Staff, while other officers were functioning at Montry under the direction of General Doumenc as Chief of Staff. In fact, the organism of the supreme command was cut up into three sections. In his ivory tower at Vincennes, General Gamelin gave me the impression of a savant, testing the chemical reactions of his strategy in a laboratory.

He told me, first of all, that he meant to raise the number of armoured divisions from two to four, and informed me of his decision to give me command of the 4th, which would be formed as from May 15th. Whatever my general feelings about our perhaps irremediable lateness in respect of mechanised forces, I felt very proud at finding myself called upon, as a colonel, to command a division. I said so to General Gamelin. He replied simply: " I understand your satisfaction. As for your misgivings, I don't believe they are justified."

The generalissimo then spoke to me of the situation, as he saw it. Unfolding a map which showed the enemy's positions and our own, he told me he expected a German attack in the near future. It would be directed, according to what he foresaw, mainly against Holland and Belgium, and its aim would be the Pas-de-Calais with a view to cutting us off from the British. Various signs led him to think that the enemy would first carry out a covering operation or diversion towards the Scandinavian countries. He himself seemed not only confident in his own arrangements and in the value of his forces, but satisfied and even impatient to see them put to the test. Listening to him I was convinced that, by dint of carrying about with him a certain military system and applying his labour to it, he had made of it a faith. I felt, too, that, referring himself to the example of Joffre, whom he had assisted at close quarters and to some extent inspired in the early days of the first world war, he had persuaded himself that, at his level, the essential thing was to fix one's purpose, once for all, upon a well-defined plan and then not to let oneself be deflected from it by any avatar. This man, in whom intelligence, fineness of perception and self-control attained a very high degree, had certainly no doubt that in the coming battle he was bound in the end to win.

It was with respect, but also a certain uneasiness, that I took leave of this great leader, as he made ready in his cloister to assume all of a sudden an immense responsibility, staking everything for everything on a move I judged to be wrong.

Five weeks later the storm broke. On May 10th the enemy, having first laid hands on Denmark and almost the whole of Norway, began his great offensive. This was destined to be carried out, from one end to the other, by mechanised forces and air power, mass following movement without there ever being any need to engage it fully. In two groups—the Hoth group and the Kleist group—ten armoured and six motorised divisions rushed westwards. Seven of the ten Panzers crossed the Ardennes and reached the Meuse in three days. On May 14th they had got across it at Dinant, Givet, Monthermé and Sedan, while four big motorised units supported and covered them. Dive-bombers co-operated with them ceaselessly and the German bombers, striking at railways and road junctions behind our lines, paralysed our transport. On May 18th these seven Panzers were regrouped around Saint-Quentin, ready to swoop either on Paris or on Dunkirk, having crossed the Maginot line, smashed our positions and annihilated one of our armies. During this time the other three, accompanied by two motorised divisions and operating in the Low Countries and Brabant where the allies had the Dutch army, the Belgian army, the British army and two French armies, threw this total of 800,000 fighting men into a confusion which was to prove irreparable. It can be said that in a week our fate was sealed. Down the fatal slope to which a fatal error had long committed us, the Army, the State, France were now spinning at a giddy speed.

There were, however, 3,000 up-to-date French tanks and 800 motorised machine-guns. The Germans had no more. But ours were, according to plan, distributed up and down the sectors of the front. Also they were not, for the most part, built or armed to form part of a mass for manœuvre. Even the few large mechanised units included in the order of battle were engaged piecemeal. The three light divisions which had been thrown towards Liège and towards Breda for scouting purposes, were quickly forced back and were then spread out to hold a front. The 1st Armoured Division, restored to a *corps d'armée* and launched alone in a counter-attack on May 16th to the west of Namur, was enveloped and destroyed. On the same day the 2nd, having been transported by rail in the direction of Hirson, had its elements, as they were disentrained, swallowed up one by one in the general confusion. On the day before, to the south of Sedan, the 3rd Division, which had just been formed, was immediately split up between the battalions of an infantry division and was engulfed, fragment after fragment, in an abortive counter-attack. Had they been grouped together beforehand, these mechanised units, for all their deficiencies, would have been able to deal the invader some formidable blows. But isolated one from another they were nothing but shreds six days after the German armoured groups had begun to move. As for me, as I discerned the truth through the scraps of news, there was nothing I would not have given to have been wrong.

But battle, even if disastrous, takes a soldier out of himself. This one seized hold of me in my turn. On May 11th I received the order to take command of the 4th Armoured Division,— which indeed did not exist, but whose elements, coming from far distant points, were to be placed at my disposal gradually. From Vésinet, where my H.Q. was fixed to begin with, I was summoned on May 15th to G.H.Q. to be given my instructions.

These were communicated to me by the Chief of Staff. They were wide. "The High Command," General Doumenc told me, "wishes to establish a defensive front on the Aisne and Ailette to bar the way to Paris. The VIth Army, commanded by General Touchon and formed of units mustered in the East (of France), will deploy there. With your division, operating alone in advance in the region of Laon, you are to gain the time necessary for this taking-up of positions. General Georges, commander-in-chief on the North-East front, leaves it to you to decide on the means to be used. You will indeed be responsible solely and directly to him. Commandant Chomel will ensure liaison."

General Georges, when he received me, was calm, cordial, but visibly overwhelmed. He confirmed what he expected of me, and added: "There, de Gaulle! For you who have so long held the ideas which the enemy is putting into practice, here is the chance to act." The administrative services then did their best to get the elements earmarked for me up towards Laon as soon as possible. I observed that the staff, though submerged by the innumerable problems of movement and transport that were raised everywhere by the surprise and disorder suffered during these terrible days, was doing its job as well as possible. But one could feel that hope was departing and that the spring was broken.

I hastened to Laon, set up my headquarters at Bruyères to the south-east of the town, and made a tour of the surroundings. By way of French troops in the district there were only a few scattered elements belonging to the 3rd Cavalry Division, a handful of men holding the citadel of Laon, and the 4th independent Artillery Group, which had instructions to resort to chemical warfare in certain contingencies and had been forgotten there by chance. I annexed this group, formed as it was of fine men armed only with carbines, and disposed them, against surprise, along the Sissonne Canal. Already, that very evening, the enemy patrols made contact.

On the 16th I was joined by the embryo of my staff. I carried out reconnaissances and collected information. The impression I gained was that large German forces which had debouched from the Ardennes through Rocroi and through Mézières were marching, not southwards, but westwards, to reach Saint-Quentin, covering their left with flank guards extending to the south of the Serre. Miserable processions of refugees crowded along all the roads from the north. I saw, also, a good many soldiers who had lost their weapons. They belonged to the troops routed by the Panzers during the preceding days. Caught up, as they fled, by the enemy's mechanised detachments, they had been ordered to throw away their arms and make off to the south so as not to clutter up the roads. "We haven't time," they had been told, "to take you prisoner!"

Then, at the sight of those bewildered people and of those soldiers in rout, at the tale, too, of that contemptuous piece of insolence of the enemy's, I felt myself borne up by a limitless fury. "Ah! It's too stupid! The war is beginning as badly as it could. Therefore it must go on. For this, the world is wide. If I live, I will fight, wherever I must, as long as I must, until the enemy is defeated and the national stain washed clean." All I have managed to do since was resolved upon that day.

To begin with, I would attack next morning with whatever forces might have reached me. Advancing some twenty kilometres north-eastwards, I would try to reach Montcornet on the Serre, the junction of the roads to Saint-Quentin, Laon and Rheims. I would thus cut the first of these, so that the enemy could not use it in his march westwards, and I would bar the other two, which otherwise would lead him straight to the VIth Army's thinly-held front. By dawn on May 17th I had received three battalions of tanks: one of B type (the 46th Battalion), strengthened by a Company of D2s and belonging to the 6th Half-Brigade; the other two of Renault 35s (the 2nd and 24th Battalions), forming the 8th Half-Brigade. I threw them forward as soon as daylight appeared. Sweeping away on their path the enemy units which were already invading that piece of country, they reached Montcornet. Till evening they fought on the outskirts of the place and within it, reducing many nests of snipers and shelling the German convoys that tried to pass. But on the Serre the enemy was in force. Obviously our tanks, with nothing to support them, could not cross it.

In the course of the day there arrived the 4th Battalion of Chasseurs. It was hardly there when I used it to reduce an enemy advance guard near Chivres, which had let our tanks go by and revealed itself later. This was soon done. But from north of the Serre the German artillery was firing on us. Our own was far from being in position. All the afternoon the Stukas, swooping out of the sky and returning ceaselessly,

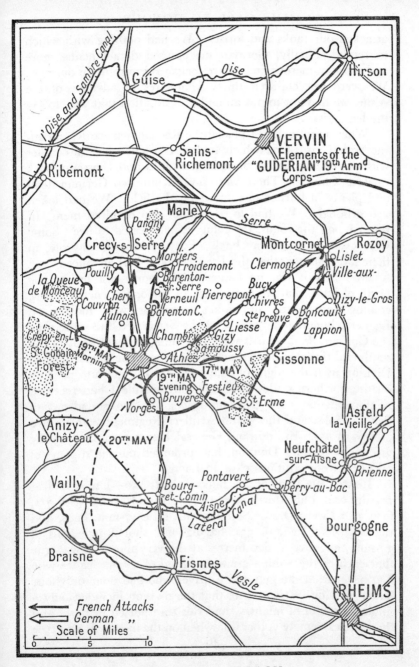

THE ACTION AT LAON

attacked our tanks and lorries. We had nothing with which
to reply. Finally, German mechanised detachments, more
and more numerous and active, began skirmishing in our rear.
We were lost children thirty kilometres in advance of the
Aisne, we had got to put an end to a situation that was, to say
the least, risky.

When night came, I placed the Reconnaissance Regiment,
the 10th Cuirassiers, which had just reached me, in contact
with the enemy, and I brought the tanks and chasseurs back
towards Chivres. There were several hundred German dead
and plenty of burned-out lorries on the field. We had taken
130 prisoners. We had lost less than two hundred men. In
the rear, on the roads, the refugees had ceased to flee. Some
were even on their way back. For the rumour was rife, in
their sad columns, that the French troops had advanced.

And now it was no longer to the north-east but to the
north of Laon that we must act; for important enemy forces,
coming from Marle and going westwards, were moving on
La Fère, hugging the course of the Serre. At the same time
the German flank guards were beginning to spread out to the
south and threatening to reach the Ailette. The 4th Armoured
Division used the night of May 18th-19th to get into position
on the northern outlets of Laon. Meanwhile I had received
reinforcements: the 3rd Cuirassiers, or two squadrons of
Somua tanks, and the 322nd Artillery Regiment with its two
groups of 75s. In addition, General Petiet, commanding the
3rd Light Cavalry Division, had promised me the support of
his guns, from positions close to Laon.

It was true that, of the tanks—about 150—I now had at
my disposal, only thirty were of type B and armed with 75s,
forty or so were D2s or Somuas with little 47-mm. guns, and
the rest were Renault 35s, having only short-range guns of
37 mm., effective at 600 metres at the very most. It was true
that each of the Somua crews consisted of a tank leader who
had never fired the gun and a driver who had done only four
hours' driving. It was true that the division included only a
single battalion of infantry, and this transported in buses and
therefore extremely vulnerable when on the move. It was true

that the artillery had only just been formed out of detachments furnished by many different depots and that many officers were literally meeting their men for the first time on the field of battle. It was true that we had no radio network and that I could command only by despatching motor-cyclists to the subordinate echelons and—above all—by going to see them. It was true that all the units were badly short of the transport, replacements, and victuals they should normally have included. And yet, already, an impression of general enthusiasm was emerging from this improvised body. Come! the springs are not dried up.

On the 19th, at dawn, forward! The tanks of the division, through a succession of objectives, were launched against Crécy, Mortiers and Pouilly. They were to reach the bridges there and cut the enemy's path to La Fère. The artillery accompanied them. To the right, the reconnaissance regiment and the battalion of Chasseurs gave them cover along the Baranton river, and a probe was made towards Marle. The morning went well. We reached the Serre after putting to flight various enemy elements that had been infiltrating into the region. But north of the river the enemy was in position. He held the crossings in force and destroyed those of our tanks that tried to tackle them. His heavy artillery got to work. In fact, we were in contact with the large German units crowding towards Saint-Quentin. To be able to cross the watercourse and push our tanks farther forward we would have needed infantry, which we had not got, and more powerful artillery. During those difficult hours I could not help imagining what the mechanised army of which I had so long dreamed could have done. If it had been there that day, to debouch suddenly in the direction of Guise, the advance of the Panzer divisions would have been halted instantly, serious confusion caused in their rear, and the northern group of armies enabled to join up once more with those of the centre and the east.

But there were only very poor resources to the north of Laon. So it was the Germans who crossed the Serre. They had been doing so since the day before, at Montcornet, where we no longer were. From noon onwards they were crossing also at Marle. With armoured cars in plenty, self-propelled guns, motor-borne mortars, motorised infantry, they attacked our right along the river Baranton and our rear at Chambry. And now came the Stukas! Till nightfall they were to bombard us, with formidable effect on our vehicles unable to leave the roads and our artillery out in the open. Early in the afternoon General Georges sent me the order not to go on. The deployment of the VIth Army had been completed and my division must be used immediately for other tasks. I decided to delay the enemy for yet another day, by regrouping the division for the night around Vorges, ready to attack his flank if he tried to push on from Laon against Rheims or against Soissons, and not retreating across the Aisne till the day after.

The movement was carried out in good order, although the enemy tried to hold us up everywhere. At the exits from the cantonments skirmishing went on all night. On May 20th the 4th Armoured Division made for Fismes and for Braine, literally in the midst of the Germans, who swarmed wherever they went, held many strong points and attacked our columns with plentiful armoured cars. Owing to the tanks, which cleaned up the roads and their approaches as we went along, we reached the Aisne without serious mishap. Even so, at Festieux the 10th Cuirassiers, the reconnaissance regiment, which formed the rearguard with a battalion of tanks, disengaged only with difficulty; and on the plateau of Craonne the division's transport was roughly handled and forced to leave behind some lorries on fire.

While the 4th Division was operating in the Laon district, events farther north were following their course at the rapid rate of the Panzer divisions' march. The German Command, having decided to liquidate the Allied armies in the north before finishing with those of the centre and east, was pushing its mechanised forces towards Dunkirk. These took the offensive again, starting from Saint-Quentin, in two columns: one going straight for the objective *via* Cambrai and Douai, the other slipping up the coast *via* Etaples and Boulogne.

Meanwhile two Panzer divisions seized Amiens and Abbeville and established there, south of the Somme, bridgeheads which were to prove useful later on. On the Allied side, by the evening of May 20th, the Dutch army had disappeared, the Belgian army was retreating westwards, and the British army and 1st French army saw themselves cut off from France.

Certainly the French Command showed the intention of restoring contact between the two fragments of its forces by attacking with the northern group of armies from Arras towards Amiens, and with the left of the centre group of armies from Amiens towards Arras. Those were General Gamelin's orders on the 19th. General Weygand, who replaced him on May 20th and was to visit Belgium next day, took over the idea. Theoretically, the plan was logical. But for it to be carried out, it would have been necessary for the High Command still to have hope and the will to win. The crumbling of the whole system of doctrines and organisation, to which our leaders had attached themselves, deprived them of their motive force. A sort of moral inhibition made them suddenly doubtful of everything, and especially of themselves. From then on, the centrifugal forces were to show themselves rapidly. The King of the Belgians was not slow to contemplate surrender; Lord Gort, re-embarkation; General Weygand, the armistice.

While the Command was dissolving in disaster, the 4th Armoured Division was marching westwards. First there was the question of making it cross the Somme to take the lead in the projected attack northwards. But the idea was abandoned. Then it was proposed to use it, with other forces, to drive back the Germans who had crossed the Somme at Amiens. But the idea of giving it a share in this attempt was given up, although one of its tank battalions was taken from it for the purpose. Finally, during the night of May 26th-27th, the division's commander—promoted general two days earlier—received from General Robert Altmayer, in command of the Xth Army now grouping together the forces that were being hastily brought up to the Lower Somme, the order to make for Abbeville without delay and attack the enemy, who had set up a solidly held bridgehead to the south of the city.

At that moment the division was resting round about Grandvilliers. Starting on May 22nd, and passing through Fismes, Soissons, Villers-Cotterets, Compiègne, Montdidier and Beauvais, it had covered 180 kilometres in five days. It is fair to say that, from its birth in the fields of Montcornet, it had never stopped fighting or marching. The condition of the tanks showed it. Thirty or so were left behind on the way. On the other hand, valuable additions had reached us as we went: a battalion of type B tanks (the 47th Battalion); a battalion of D2s (the 19th Battalion) equipped with 20-ton machines, which I was unfortunately forced to part with before Amiens; the 7th Regiment of motorised Dragoons; an artillery group with 105s; an A.-A. battery; and five batteries of 47-mm. anti-tank guns. Except the battalion of D2s, all these were improvised units. But as soon as they arrived they were caught up in the atmosphere of keenness which hung over the division. Finally, for the operation which had just been allotted to me, the 22nd Colonial Infantry Regiment and the artillery of the 2nd Cavalry Division were placed at my disposal. In all, 140 tanks in working order and six infantry battalions, supported by six artillery groups, were to assault the southern front of the bridgehead.

I decided to attack that very evening. For the enemy air-craft were watching the division all the time, and the only chance of obtaining some effect of surprise was to advance zero hour. The Germans were, in fact, ready for us. For a week they had held, facing southwards, Huppy to the west, Bray-les-Mareuil on the Somme to the east, and between these two villages the woods of Limeux and Bailleul. In the rear they had organised Bienfay, Villers, Huchenneville and Mareuil. Lastly, Mont Caubert, on the same side of the Somme and commanding Abbeville and its bridges, served as a redoubt in their scheme of defence. These three successive lines were the three successive objectives I marked out for the division.

It engaged at 6 p.m.: the 6th Half-Brigade of heavy tanks,

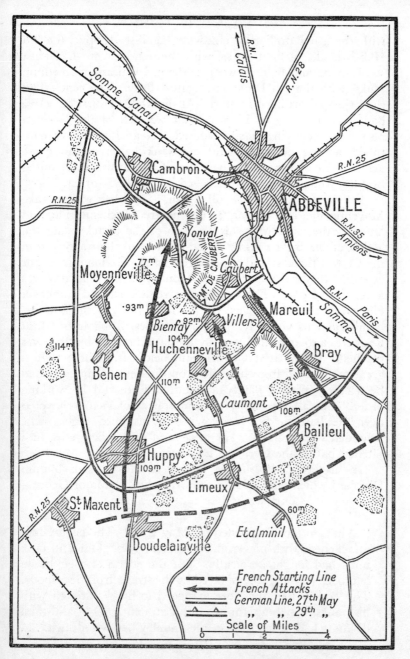

THE ACTION AT ABBEVILLE

with the 4th Battalion of chasseurs, against Huppy; the 8th Half-Brigade, of light tanks, with the 22nd Colonial, against the Limeux and Bailleul woods; the 3rd Cuirassiers, medium tanks, with the 7th Dragoons, against Bray. The centre had the principal artillery support. At nightfall the first objective had been taken. In Huppy what was left of the German battalion occupying it surrendered. Near Limeux we captured, among others, several anti-tank batteries and came across the carcasses of the vehicles of the British mechanised brigade which they had destroyed a few days earlier.

Before dawn we were off again. The left was to take Moyenneville and Bienfay; the centre Huchenneville and Villers; the right Mareuil; the key of the attack being the action of the B-type tanks whose job was to slant across from the west to the east and clip the rear of the German line. For everyone the final objective was Mont Caubert. The day was a very hard one. The enemy was reinforced and stubborn. His heavy artillery, placed on the right bank of the Somme, bombarded us violently. Other batteries, firing from Mont Caubert, also punished us. By the evening the objective was reached. Only Mont Caubert still held out. There were a great many dead from both sides on the field. Our tanks had been sorely tried. Barely a hundred were still in working order. But all the same, an atmosphere of victory hovered over the battlefield. Everyone held his head high. The wounded were smiling. The guns fired gaily. Before us, in a pitched battle, the Germans had retired.

In his book, *Abbeville* (a history of the German Blümm Division, which was holding the bridgehead), Major Gehring was to write, some weeks later:

" What, in fact, happened on May 28th? The enemy had attacked us with powerful armoured forces. Our anti-tank units had fought heroically. But the effects of their blows had been considerably reduced by the strength of the armour. The enemy had therefore managed to break through with his tanks between Huppy and Caumont. Our anti-tank defences had been crushed, the infantry had withdrawn. . . .

". . . When the alarming news poured into divisional
H.Q. and, under the incessant fire of the French artillery,
there was no means of communicating with any of the
battalions in the line, the General commanding the Division went forward himself. . . . He encountered the
routed troops, regrouped them, and led them to prepared
defensive positions some kilometres to the rear of the first
lines. . . .

"But a profound terror of the tanks had got into the
bones of our soldiers. . . . Losses were heavy. . . . There
was, practically speaking, nobody who had not lost beloved
comrades. . . ."

However, reinforcements reached the Germans. During
the night of the 27th-28th, they succeeded in relieving all
their units in the line. Corpses and prisoners gave us proof of
this. During the night of the 28th-29th, a fresh relief. So it
would be fresh troops we would encounter, on the third day
as well as the second. Nothing reached us. And yet we needed
so little to achieve success. Never mind! On May 29th, as
we were, we would attack once more.

On that day, the attack on Mont Caubert; our principal
effort was directed across its western slope. From Moyenneville and Bienfay the last of our B-type tanks were to start,
with the Somuas transferred from the right to the left. The
battalion of Chasseurs reduced by more than a half, the
Reconnaissance Regiment diminished by two-thirds, and a
battalion of Dragoons, were to follow them. Our remaining
Renaults, with the 22nd Colonial, were to be launched from
Villers. To aid us, General Altmayer had ordered the 5th
Light Cavalry Division, which was stretched out along the
Somme downstream from the bridgehead, to push forward its
right against Cambron. But it would in fact be unable to
make progress. He had asked for bombers to help by acting
against the exits from Abbeville. But the aircraft were elsewhere. Five p.m. was our zero hour. The slopes of the hill
were reached, but the crest remained to the enemy. When
night fell, the Germans with powerful artillery support made

a counter-attack on the villages of Moyenneville and Bienfay, but did not succeed in recapturing them.

On May 30th, the 51st Scottish Division under the command of General Fortune, having recently arrived in France, came, all fresh and spruce, to relieve the 4th Armoured Division. This regrouped near Beauvais. With me Colonels Sudre, Simonin and François for the Tanks, de Ham for the Reconnaissance Regiment, Bertrand for the Chasseurs, Le Tacon for the Colonials, de Longuemare for the Dragoons, Chaudesolle and Ancelme for the Artillery, and Chomel for the Staff evaluated the results of the operation. We had not managed to liquidate the Abbeville bridgehead, but it had been reduced by three-quarters. As it now was, the enemy could not debouch from it in force, without first reconquering it. Our losses were heavy; less, however, than those of the other side. We were bringing five hundred prisoners to be added to those of Montcornet, and a large quantity of arms and matériel which had fallen into our hands.

Alas! in the course of the Battle of France, what other ground had been or would be won, except this strip fourteen kilometres deep? Apart from the crews of aircraft shot down in our lines, how many other Germans were to be made prisoner? Instead of one poor division, weak, incomplete, unprovided and isolated, what results would not have been obtained during these last days of May by an armoured *corps d'élite?*—for which many of the elements did, indeed, exist, though deformed and dispersed. If the State had played its part; if, while there was time, it had directed its military system towards enterprise, not passivity; if our leaders had in consequence had at their disposal the instrument for shock and manœuvre which had been often suggested to the politicians and to the High Command; then our arms would have had their chance, and France would have found her soul again.

But on May 30th the battle was virtually lost. Two days before, the Belgian King and army had capitulated. At Dunkirk the British army was beginning to re-embark. What was left of the French troops in the north was trying to do the same—a retreat that was bound to be disastrous. Before long the enemy would start the second, southward phase of his offensive against an adversary reduced by a third and more than ever unprovided with the means of countering the German mechanised forces.

In my cantonment in Picardy I had no illusions. But I was determined not to abandon hope. If the situation could not, after all, be restored in the homeland, it must be re-established elsewhere. The Empire was there, offering its refuge. The fleet was there, to protect it. The people were there, doomed in any case to suffer invasion, but capable of being roused by the Republic to resistance, that terrible occasion for unity. The world was there, able to give us fresh weapons and, later, powerful aid. One question dominated everything: would the Government have the sense, whatever happened, to place the State out of range, to preserve its independence and safeguard the future? Or was it going to surrender everything in the panic of the collapse?

This—as I could easily foresee—would depend largely on the attitude of the High Command. If the High Command refused to lower the flag as long as, according to military regulations, " all the means commanded by duty and honour have not been exhausted," in short, if it adopted, in the last resort, the African solution, it could become the rescue buoy for the shipwrecked State. If, on the contrary, untrue to itself, it were to urge an unstable Government to surrender, what an argument it would supply for the degradation of France!

These reflections haunted my mind as, on June 1st, I went to see General Weygand, who had summoned me. The Commander-in-Chief received me at the Château de Montry. The gift of clarity and the simplicity of manner characteristic of him were, as usual, in evidence. He began by complimenting me on the Abbeville operation, about which he had just given me a most laudatory mention. Then he asked my opinion on what it would be best to do with the modern tanks—1,200 or so—which we still had at our disposal.

I told the general that, in my view, these tanks should be brought together without delay into two groups: the main

one, north of Paris; the other, to the south of Rheims; the
remains of the armoured divisions would provide the nuclei.
To command the first, I suggested General Delestraint,
Inspector of Tanks. To these groups would be attached,
respectively, three and two infantry divisions, provided with
transport, and with a doubled artillery. We would thus have
a *moyen d'infortune* to act against the flank of any of the German
mechanised corps whenever, pushing on in their direction of
advance after breaking through our front, they were more or
less unco-ordinated in breadth and stretched in depth. General
Weygand took note of these proposals. After which, he spoke
to me of the battle.

"I shall be attacked," he said, "on June 6th on the
Somme and on the Aisne. I shall have on my hands twice
as many German divisions as we have ourselves. That means
that the prospects are poor. If things don't go too fast; if I
can recover, in time, the French troops who have escaped
from Dunkirk; if I have arms to give them; if the British
Army comes back to take part in the struggle after being
re-equipped; if the Royal Air Force consents to engage its
whole resources in the fighting on the Continent: then, we
still have a chance." And the Commander-in-Chief added,
shaking his head: "If not . . ."

I knew now. I left General Weygand with heavy heart.

At one go there had fallen on his shoulders a crushing
burden he was not built to bear. When, on May 20th, he had
taken over the supreme command, it was too late, without
any doubt, to win the Battle of France. It seems likely that
the realisation was a surprise to him. As he had never considered the real possibilities of mechanised force, the immense
and sudden effects produced by the enemy's resources had
stupefied him. To face the disaster effectively he would have
had to renew himself; to break, from one day to the next,
with ideas, a rate of action, a set of methods which no longer
applied; to wrench his strategy out of the narrow frame of
the French mainland; to turn the deadly weapon back against
the enemy who had launched it, and to take into his own hand
the trump card of great spaces, great resources and great

speeds, by including distant territories, alliances and oceans. He was not the man to do it. His age, no doubt, was against it as well as his turn of mind—but, above all, his temperament.

Weygand was, in fact, by nature a brilliant second. In this capacity he had served Foch admirably. In 1920 he had made Pilsudski adopt a plan which saved Poland. As Chief of the General Staff he had intelligently and courageously represented to several Ministers, under whose authority he was, the vital interests of the army. But if the qualities demanded for staff service and those required by command are in no way contradictory, they should not be confused. To take action on one's own responsibility, to want no mark upon it but one's own, to face destiny alone, is the harsh, exclusive passion characteristic of a chief, and for this Weygand had neither the inclination nor the preparation. Besides, whether this was due to his own tendencies or to a combination of circumstances, he had not, in all his career, ever exercised command. No regiment, no brigade, no division, no *corps d'armée*, no army had seen him at its head. To choose him for the taking of the greatest risk that had ever occurred in our military history, not because he was known to be up to it, but on the pretext " that he was a banner," was a fruit of the error—habitual in our political life—which is called " taking the line of least resistance."

At any rate, as soon as it was recognised that General Weygand was not the man for the position, he ought to have left it, either by asking to be relieved or by the Government taking the decision as a matter of course. Nothing of the kind happened. From then on, the generalissimo, carried away by a current he was no longer trying to master, was bound to seek the issue within his reach: capitulation. But as he did not intend to assume the responsibility for this, his action would consist in steering the Government towards it. In this he found an ally in the Marshal, who, for different reasons, was demanding the same solution. The régime, having neither faith nor vitality, decided in favour of the worst surrender. The price, for France, was thus to be not only a disastrous military armistice, but the enslavement of the State. So true it is that, face to face with the great perils, the only salvation lies in greatness.

On June 5th I heard that the enemy was resuming the offensive. In the course of the day I went to ask for orders from General Frère, in command of the VIIth Army, in whose zone my division was. As alarming reports were being opened all round him and doubts and reticences could be seen under the outward professional calm, that excellent soldier said to me: " We're sick. Rumour has it that you're to be Minister. It's certainly late in the day for a cure. Ah! at least let's save our honour! "

II. THE FALL

I<small>T WAS</small> during the night of June 5th-6th that M. Paul Reynaud, in re-shuffling his Government, brought me in as Under-Secretary of State for National Defence. I was told the news in the morning by General Delestraint, Inspector of Tanks, who had heard it broadcast. A few moments later, an official telegram brought me confirmation of it. After saying good-bye to my division, I set off for Paris.

When I arrived at the Rue Saint-Dominique, I saw the Premier. He was, as usual, assured, lively, incisive, ready to listen, quick to make up his mind. He explained to me why he had thought it necessary, some days earlier, to take Marshal Pétain into his Cabinet, when neither of us had any doubt that he was the screen for those who desired an armistice. "It's better," said Paul Reynaud, using the customary formula, "to have him inside than out."

"I'm afraid," I answered, "you may be forced to change your opinion. All the more so since events are now going to move very fast, and defeatism may easily submerge everything. The disproportion between our forces and the Germans' is so great that, barring a miracle, we have no longer any chance of winning in metropolitan France, or even of holding there. Besides, the High Command has been overwhelmed by surprise and will not pull itself together. Lastly, you know better than anyone with what an atmosphere of abandon the Government is surrounded. The Marshal and those behind him are going to have things their way from now on. At the same time, if the war of '40 is lost, we can win another. Without giving up the fight on European soil as long as it is possible,

59

we must decide on and prepare for the continuation of the struggle in the Empire. That implies a policy to fit: the transport of resources to North Africa, the choice of leaders qualified to direct the operations, and the maintenance of close relations with the British, whatever grievances we may have against them. I propose to you that I should deal with the measures to be taken for the purpose."

M. Paul Reynaud gave me his consent. " I want you," he added, " to go to London as soon as possible. In the interviews I had on May 26th and 31st with the British Government, I was able to make them realise that we were not excluding the possibility of an armistice. But now what is needed is, on the contrary, to convince the English that we will hold out, whatever happens, even overseas if necessary. You will see Mr. Churchill and you will tell him that the reshuffling of my Cabinet and your presence by my side are the signs of our resolution."

Apart from this general message I was to do, in London, what I could, in my turn, to get the Royal Air Force—particularly the fighter aircraft—to continue to take part in the operations in France. Lastly, I was to ask, as the Prime Minister had already done, for information about the time it would take to rearm the British units that had escaped from the Dunkirk disaster and to send them back on to the Continent. The answer to these two questions involved technical data, which the staffs were competent to supply, but also decisions depending on Mr. Winston Churchill in his capacity as Minister of Defence.

While the liaison bodies were arranging for the meetings I was to have in the British capital, I went on June 8th to make contact with General Weygand at the Château de Montry. I found the Commander-in-Chief calm and master of himself. But a few moments of conversation were enough to make me realise that he was resigned to defeat and resolved upon an armistice. Here, almost word for word, is our dialogue, whose terms have—with good reason!—remained engraved on my mind.

" You see," the Commander-in-Chief said, " I was not

mistaken when I told you, a few days ago, that the Germans would attack on the Somme on June 6th. They are in fact attacking. At this moment they are crossing the river. I can't stop them."

" All right! They're crossing the Somme. And then? "

" Then? The Seine and the Marne."

" Yes. And then? "

" Then? But that's the end! "

" How do you mean? The end? And the world? And the Empire? "

General Weygand gave a despairing laugh.

" The Empire? But that's childish! As for the world, when I've been beaten here, England won't wait a week before negotiating with the Reich."

And looking me in the eyes, the Commander-in-Chief added:

" Ah! if only I were sure the Germans would leave me the forces necessary for maintaining order . . . ! "

Discussion would have been useless. I left, after telling General Weygand that his way of looking at things was the opposite of the Government's intentions. The Government would not give up the struggle, even if the battles went badly. He made no fresh observation and was most courteous when I took my leave.

Before starting back to Paris I chatted for some time with acquaintances of mine among the officers from various staffs who had come that morning to conference with General Weygand. They confirmed my impression that in the higher ranks of the Command the game was considered lost and that everyone, while carrying out his duties mechanically, was suggesting in whispers, and would soon be proposing out loud, that an end be put, somehow or other, to the Battle of France. To steer men's minds and their courage towards the continuation of the war in the Empire, a categorical intervention by the Government was immediately necessary.

I stated this, as soon as I got back, to M. Paul Reynaud, and urged him to take away the command from General Weygand, who had given up trying to win. " It's impossible for the moment," the Prime Minister replied. " But we must think of a successor. What's your view? "

" As regards a successor," I said, " the only one I can see now is Huntziger. Although he is not ideal, he is capable, in my opinion, of rising to the level of a world strategy."

M. Paul Reynaud approved my suggestion in principle, but was not, all the same, willing to put it into practice at once.

Resolved, however, to raise the question again and soon, I set myself to working out the plan for transporting all possible units to North Africa. Already the Army General Staff, in liaison with the Navy and the Air, had begun preparing the evacuation of everything not engaged in the battle to the other side of the Mediterranean. This meant, in particular, the two classes of recruits who were being trained in the depots of the West and South of France and those fractions of the personnel of the mechanised forces which had managed to escape from the disaster in the North, in all, five hundred thousand men of good quality. Later, as the debris of our armies were driven back towards the coasts, many fighting elements could no doubt be embarked. In any case the remains of the bomber air force, the range of whose machines would enable them to cross the sea, the survivors of the fighter groups, the ground staff, the men at the naval bases and finally, and above all, our fleet itself, would have to stand out for Africa. The Navy, whose job it was to carry out this transportation, estimated at five hundred thousand tons the extra merchant shipping required in addition to the French vessels already at its disposal. It was England that would have to be asked for this assistance.

Early on June 9th an aeroplane took me to London. I had with me my aide-de-camp, Geoffroy de Courcel, and M. Roland de Margerie, the Premier's *Chef du cabinet diplomatique*. It was Sunday. The English capital had a look of tranquillity, almost indifference. The streets and parks full of people peacefully out for a walk, the long queues at the entrances to the cinemas, the many cars, the impressive porters outside the clubs and hotels, belonged to another world than the one at war. Certainly the newspapers allowed the real situation to pierce through, in spite of the diluted news and puerile anecdotes with which, as in Paris, semi-official optimism filled them. Certainly the notices people were reading, the digging of shelters, the carrying of masks, suggested the great dangers in the offing. Nonetheless it was obvious that the mass of the population had no idea of the gravity of events in France, so fast had been their pace. It was plain, in any case, that to English minds the Channel was still wide.

Mr. Churchill received me at Downing Street. It was my first contact with him. The impression he gave me confirmed me in my conviction that Great Britain, led by such a fighter, would certainly not flinch. Mr. Churchill seemed to me to be equal to the rudest task, provided it had also grandeur. The assurance of his judgment, his great culture, the knowledge he had of most of the subjects, countries and men involved, and finally his passion for the problems proper to war, found in war their full scope. On top of everything, he was fitted by his character to act, take risks, play the part out-and-out and without scruple. In short, I found him well in the saddle as guide and chief. Such were my first impressions.

What followed only confirmed them and revealed to me, in addition, the eloquence that was Mr. Churchill's own and how well he knew how to use it. Whatever his audience —crowd, assembly, council, even a single interlocutor, whether he was before a microphone, on the floor of the House, at table or behind a desk, the original, poetic, stirring flow of his ideas, arguments and feelings brought him an almost infallible ascendancy in the tragic atmosphere in which the poor world was gasping. Well tried in politics, he played upon that angelic and diabolic gift to stir up the heavy dough of the English as well as to impress the minds of foreigners. The humour, too, with which he seasoned his acts and words, and the way in which he made use now of graciousness, now of anger, contributed to make one feel what a mastery he had of the terrible game in which he was engaged.

The harsh and painful incidents that often rose between us, because of the friction of our two characters, of the opposition of some of the interests of our two countries, and of the unfair advantage taken by England of wounded France, have influenced my attitude towards the Prime Minister, but not my judgment. Winston Churchill appeared to me, from one end of the drama to the other, as the great champion of a great enterprise and the great artist of a great History.

That day I explained to the British Prime Minister what the French Prime Minister had instructed me to tell him as regards our Government's will to continue the struggle even, if need be, in the Empire. Mr. Churchill showed the lively satisfaction which this determination gave him. But would it be carried out? He left me with the impression that he was not convinced. In any case, he no longer believed in the possibility of a re-establishment of the front in metropolitan France, and he made this clear to me by refusing categorically the assistance of his Air Force.

Since the re-embarkation of the British Army at Dunkirk, the Royal Air Force had no longer been co-operating in the battle, save in an episodic fashion. Indeed, with the exception of a fighter group which still followed the fortunes of our Air Force, the British squadrons, being based in Great Britain, were too far away to be of use to a front continually withdrawing southwards. To my pressing request that he should transfer at least a part of the British Army Co-operation Air Force to the aerodromes south of the Loire, Mr. Churchill gave a formal refusal. As for the land forces, he promised to send to Normandy a Canadian division which was arriving from its country, and to keep with us the 51st Scottish Division as well as the debris of the mechanised brigade who were still fighting at our side. But he stated that he could not indicate, even approximately, towards what date the expeditionary corps, which had just escaped destruction in Belgium—but had left there its equipment—would be able to return to the battle.

So, therefore, strategic unity between London and Paris was practically broken. A reverse on the Continent had been enough to make Great Britain desire to absorb herself in her own defence. That meant the success of the Germanic plan, of which Schlieffen, beyond death, was still the inspiration

General de Gaulle on board ship

and which, after the German failures in 1914 and 1918, was at last achieving its object—to separate the French and British forces and, simultaneously, to divide France and England. It was only too easy to imagine what conclusions would be drawn by defeatists at home.

Apart from this interview with Mr. Churchill, I had made contact the same day with Mr. Eden, Minister of War, Mr. Alexander, First Lord of the Admiralty, Sir Archibald Sinclair, Air Minister, and General Sir John Dill, Chief of the Imperial General Staff. I had also conferred with M. Corbin, our Ambassador, M. Monnet, " Chairman " of the Franco-British committee for the co-ordination of purchases of war material, and the heads of our military, naval and air missions. It was clear that in London, if calm reigned over the crowd, the minds of the well-informed were on the contrary filled with foreboding of disaster and doubt as to the firmness of the French Government. In the evening, the aeroplane took me uneasily back to le Bourget, whose aerodrome had just been bombarded.

During the night of June 9th-10th, M. Paul Reynaud had me summoned to his home. Grave information had just reached him. The enemy had reached the Seine below Paris. In addition, everything suggested that, at any moment, the German armoured forces would pass to the decisive attack in Champagne. The capital was therefore immediately threatened from the west, east and north. Lastly, M. François-Poncet announced that he was expecting at any moment to receive from the Italian Government its declaration of war. In face of these bad tidings, I had only one suggestion to make: to take the line of maximum effort and go as soon as possible to Africa, embracing, with all its consequences, a war of coalition.

In the few fractions of day and night which I spent at the Rue Saint-Dominique, I found only too many reasons to reinforce my conviction that there was nothing else to be done. Things were going too fast for it to be possible to regain control of them there. Every scheme at once took on a character of unreality. Recourse was had to precedents from the

1914-18 war which no longer applied at all. The pretence was made of thinking that there was still a front, an active command, a people ready for sacrifices; those were only dreams and memories. In fact, in the midst of a prostrate and stupefied nation, behind an army without faith and without hope, the machine of government was turning in an irremediable confusion.

Nothing made me feel this more clearly than the rapid formal visits I paid to the principal figures of the Republic: first, President Lebrun, to whom I was presented together with the new Ministers, then the Presidents of the Assemblies, and finally the members of the Government. All made a show of calm and dignity. But it was clear that, in the setting where custom placed them, they were now only supers. In the cyclone's heart those Cabinet meetings, instructions on their way down, reports on their way up, public statements and that procession of officers, civil servants, diplomats, members of parliament and journalists, all with something to report on or to ask, gave the impression of a sort of phantasmagoria without aim or effect. On the assumptions and in the surroundings where we were now engaged, there was no way out except capitulation. Unless we resigned ourselves to that—as some were already doing, and those not nonentities—, we must at all costs change our surroundings and assumptions. The so-called " Marne recovery " was possible, but on the Mediterranean.

June 10th was a day of agony. The Government was to leave Paris that evening. The withdrawal of the front was accelerating. Italy was declaring war. The obvious fact of collapse was now borne in on all minds. But at the top of the State the tragedy was being played through as though in a dream. At certain moments, one might even have thought that a sort of terrible humour was seasoning the fall of France, as she rolled from the crest of History down to the deepest hollow of the abyss.

So it was that, that morning, the Italian Ambassador, M. Guariglia, came to the Rue Saint-Dominique on a somewhat strange visit. He was received by Baudouin, who reported what the diplomat said as follows: " You will see that the declaration of war will in the end clarify relations between our two countries! It creates a situation from which, when all is said and done, much good will come. . . ."

Shortly afterwards, when I went to see M. Paul Reynaud, I found Mr. William Bullitt there. I supposed that the United States Ambassador was bringing some encouragement for the future from Washington. But no! He had come to say good-bye. The Ambassador was remaining in Paris with the intention of intervening, if need be, to protect the capital. But, praiseworthy as was the motive which inspired Mr. Bullitt, the fact remained that during the supreme days of crisis there would be no American Ambassador to the French Government. The presence of Mr. A. J. Drexel Biddle, responsible for relations with the refugee Governments, would not, whatever the qualities of this excellent diplomat, remove from our officials the impression that the United States had no longer much use for France.

However, as M. Paul Reynaud was hastily preparing a statement which he was to broadcast and on which he was consulting me, General Weygand arrived at the Rue Saint-Dominique. Hardly had he been announced when he burst into the Prime Minister's office. When the Prime Minister expressed some astonishment, the Commander-in-Chief answered that he had been sent for. "Not by me!" said M. Paul Reynaud. "Nor by me!" I added. "Then it's a misunderstanding!" General Weygand went on. "But the mistake is a useful one, for I have something important to say." He sat down and began to explain the situation as he saw it. His conclusion was obvious. We must, without delay, ask for an armistice. "Things have reached the point," he declared, laying a document on the table, " where everyone's responsibilities must be clearly established. That's why I have put my opinion on paper and am handing you this note."

The Prime Minister, though hard-pressed by the necessity of very soon delivering the broadcast which had been announced, decided to dispute the Generalissimo's opinion. The latter gave no ground. The battle in metropolitan France

was lost. We must capitulate. " But there are other prospects,"
I said at one point. Then Weygand said, mockingly:

" Have you something to suggest? "

" The Government," I replied, " has not suggestions to
make, but orders to give. I am sure it will give them."

In the end M. Paul Reynaud showed the Commander-in-
Chief out, and we separated in a most heavy atmosphere.

The last hours of the Government's presence in the capital
were filled with the arrangements which such an exodus
involved. It was true that many things had been prepared
under a withdrawal plan worked out by the Secrétariat
Général de la Défense Nationale. But there remained all the
unforeseen factors. At the same time the imminent arrival of
the Germans beneath the walls of Paris raised cruel problems.
I myself, as soon as I took up my post, had advocated that the
capital should be defended and had asked the Prime Minister,
as Minister of National Defence and for War, to appoint a
resolute leader as Governor for this purpose. I suggested
General de Lattre, who had just distinguished himself at the
head of a division in the fighting round about Rethel. But
soon afterwards the Commander-in-Chief declared Paris an
" open city," and the Cabinet approved this. Nonetheless it
was necessary to organise, quite suddenly, the evacuation of
a mass of things and a crowd of people. I worked at this till
evening, while everywhere cases were being packed, the last-
minute visitors filled the building from top to bottom with
their rumour, and desperate telephones rang without cease.

Towards midnight M. Paul Reynaud and I got into the
same car. The journey was slow, along a crammed road. At
dawn we were at Orléans and went into the Préfecture, where
contact was made by telephone with G.H.Q., now being set
up at Briare. Shortly afterwards General Weygand rang up,
and asked to speak to the Premier. He took up the telephone
and, to his great surprise, was told that Mr. Winston Churchill
would be arriving that afternoon. The Commander-in-Chief,
through military liaison channels, had begged him to come
urgently to Briare.

" Mr. Churchill must, indeed," added General Weygand,

" be directly informed about the real situation at the front."

" What? " I said to the head of the Government. " Are you allowing the Generalissimo to invite the British Prime Minister like this, on his own authority? Don't you see that General Weygand is pursuing, not a plan of operations at all, but a policy, and that it is not yours? Is the Government going to leave him still in command? "

" You are right! " answered M. Paul Reynaud. " This situation must cease. We spoke of General Huntziger as a possible successor to General Weygand. Let's go at once and see Huntziger! "

But when the cars came up, the Premier told me: " Thinking it over, it's better that you should go alone to see Huntziger. I shall prepare for these interviews with Churchill and the English. We will meet again at Briare."

I found General Huntziger, who was in command of the centre group of armies, at Arcis-sur-Aube, his headquarters. At that very moment this group of armies was being attacked and broken through on the Champagne front by Guderian's armoured corps. Nonetheless, I was struck by Huntziger's coolness. He informed me of the bad situation he was in. I gave him an up-to-date picture of affairs as a whole. In conclusion I said: " The Government sees plainly that the Battle of France is virtually lost, but it means to continue the war by transporting itself to Africa with all the resources that can be got across. That implies a complete change in strategy and in organisation. The present Generalissimo is not the man to be able to carry it out. Would you be the man? "

" Yes! " answered Huntziger simply.

" Well, you will be receiving the Government's instructions."

To reach Briare I went *via* Romilly and Sens, in order to make contact with the commands of various large units. Signs of disorder and panic were in evidence everywhere. Everywhere sections of units were retreating southwards, mixed pell-mell with the refugees. My modest suite was held up for an hour near Méry, so badly blocked was the road. A strange fog—which many took for a gas cloud—increased the terror of that military throng, which was like a shepherd-less flock.

At the Briare G.H.Q. I sought out M. Paul Reynaud and told him of Huntziger's answer. But I could see that for the Premier the immediate replacement of Weygand was no longer an issue and that he had once more adopted the idea of travelling the war road with a generalissimo who wanted to take the peace road. As I entered the gallery I saluted Marshal Pétain, whom I had not seen since 1938.

"You're a General!" he said to me. "I don't congratulate you. What good are ranks in defeat?" "But you yourself, Monsieur le Maréchal, received your first stars during the 1914 retreat. A few days later there was the Marne." Pétain grunted: "No comparison!" In that, he was right. The British Prime Minister was arriving. We went into conference.

During that meeting the ideas and passions which were to dominate the new phase of the war confronted one another openly. All that had served up to then as a basis for action and for attitudes now belonged only to the past. The solidarity of England and France, the strength of the French Army, the authority of the Government, the loyalty of the High Command were ceasing to be factors that could be counted on. Already each of those taking part was behaving no longer as a partner in a game played in common, but as a man who, from now on, takes his own course and plays his own game.

General Weygand made it clear that what he wanted was to liquidate the battle and the war as quickly as possible. Drawing support from the reports of Generals Georges and Besson, he unrolled before the conference the picture of a hopeless military situation. The Commander-in-Chief, who had in addition been Chief of the General Staff from 1930 to 1935, set forth the causes of the defeat of the armies under his orders in the staid, though aggressive, tones of one who attaches the blame without bearing the responsibility. His conclusion was that the ordeal must be brought to an end, for the military organisation might collapse suddenly and give a free run to anarchy and revolution.

The Marshal intervened to reinforce pessimism. Mr. Churchill, wishing to ease the atmosphere, said to him jovially:

" Come, come, Monsieur le Maréchal! Remember the Battle of Amiens in March, 1918, when things were going so badly. I visited you then at your H.Q. You outlined your plan to me. A few days later the front was re-established."

Then the Marshal answered harshly:

" Yes, the front was re-established. You, the English, were done for. But I sent forty divisions to rescue you. To-day it's we who are smashed to pieces. Where are your forty divisions? "

The French Premier, while repeating that France would not withdraw from the struggle and while pressing the British to send the bulk of their Air Force to our aid, made it plain that he would not part with Pétain and Weygand, as if he hoped to see them rally to his policy one day. Mr. Churchill appeared imperturbable, full of vitality, yet to be confining himself to a cordial reserve towards the French at bay, and to be already filled—not, perhaps, without an obscure satisfaction—by the terrible and magnificent prospect of an England left alone in her island, waiting for himself to lead her in her struggle towards salvation. As for me, thinking of what was to come, I had a full sense of how empty and conventional those palavers were, since they were not directed towards the one valid solution: to re-establish ourselves overseas.

After three hours of discussion, which reached no result, we sat down to dinner at the same table. I was next to Churchill. Our conversation fortified my confidence in his strength of purpose. He himself, no doubt, went away with the feeling that de Gaulle, though without means, was no less resolute.

Admiral Darlan, who had not shown up during the conference, appeared after the meal. Pushing in front of him General Vuillemin, the Air Chief of Staff, he came up to M. Paul Reynaud. The object of his visit was decidedly ominous. A combined operation of naval and air bombardment had been prepared against Genoa. According to the plan, it was to begin that night. But Darlan, having changed his mind, wished to countermand it, using as cover the anxieties of General Vuillemin, who was afraid of Italian reprisals against the Berre petrol dumps. None the less, the Admiral was asking for the Government's agreement.

" What do you think ? " M. Paul Reynaud asked me.

" Having got so far," I answered, " the most sensible course is, on the contrary, to show no tenderness. The operation must be carried out as planned."

Darlan won, however, and the counter-order was given. Genoa was, all the same, bombarded later by a small naval detachment, three days after the date planned. This incident made me understand that Darlan, too, was now playing his own game.

During the 12th, while staying at the Château de Beauvais, the property of M. Le Provost de Launay, I worked with General Colson on the plan for transportation to North Africa. To tell the truth, the events I had witnessed the day before and the isolation in which I was now left made me fear the spirit of abandon had gained too much ground and that the plan would never be put into practice. However, I was determined to do all that was in my power to get the Government to adopt it and impose it on the High Command.

Having completed the main part of it, I went over to Chissay where M. Paul Reynaud was living. It was late. The Premier, emerging from the Cabinet meeting which had been held at Cangey and to which I was not invited, arrived towards eleven in the evening, accompanied by Baudouin. While they were dining with their entourage, I took a seat near the table and bluntly raised the question of North Africa. But my interlocutors would talk of only one problem—a related one, indeed, and a very urgent one—, which the Cabinet had just brought up. What should be the Government's next destination? In fact, the Germans, having crossed the Seine, would soon reach the Loire. Two solutions were contemplated: Bordeaux, or Quimper? There followed, over the plates, a discussion that was confused and agitated by fatigue and irritation. No formal decision was taken, and M. Paul Reynaud retired, giving me an appointment for the morning.

I was naturally for Quimper. Not that I had any illusions about the possibility of holding out in Brittany; but if the Government did withdraw there, there would sooner or later be no alternative except to put to sea. For, since the Germans would necessarily have to occupy the peninsula in order to act against the English, there could be no " free zone " in Brittany. Once embarked, the Ministers would in all probability make for Africa, either directly, or after a halt in England. In any case, Quimper was the stage on the way to decisions of energy. Also, as soon as I had joined the Government, when M. Paul Reynaud had spoken to me of the " Breton redoubt " plan, I had supported it. Conversely, it was for motives inspired by their policy and not—whatever they may claim—by military art, that it was opposed by those who, like Pétain, Weygand and Baudouin, were working for capitulation.

Early on the 13th I returned to Chissay. After a long debate and in spite of my arguments, the Prime Minister took the decision to transfer the Government to Bordeaux, alleging that that was the view expressed by the Ministers the night before. This merely made me more persistent in demanding, at least, the signature of an order telling the Commander-in-Chief to envisage and prepare for transportation to Africa. That was really, I knew, M. Paul Reynaud's ultimate intention. But so pressing and exhausting were the contrary intrigues and influences with constant access to him, that I could see this last hope dwindling, hour by hour.

The Premier did, however, sign, towards noon that day, a letter addressed to General Weygand, in which he defined for him what the Government from that time onward expected of him. First: " To hold out as long as possible in the Massif Central and in Brittany." Next: " If we should fail, . . . to instal ourselves and organise the struggle in the Empire, making use of the freedom of the seas." This letter assuredly showed a salutary intention. But it was not, in my view, the categorical order which the circumstances demanded. Besides, after being signed, it was queried again behind the scenes and was not actually sent till the next day.

During the same morning of the 13th, M. Jeanneney, President of the Senate, and M. Herriot, President of the Chamber, had come to Chissay. The former, exhibiting a resolute bearing in the midst of all the agitation, invoked the example of Clemenceau, with whom he had collaborated directly and closely in the Government during the great moments of 1917 and 1918. The latter, affable and accomplished, expressed with eloquence the many and various emotions by which he was swept. Both of them showed themselves favourable to the Prime Minister, opposed to capitulation and entirely ready to cross over to Algiers with the administration. It seemed to me, once again, that M. Paul Reynaud, whatever the defeatist cabals on all sides of him, could remain master of the game, provided he made no concessions.

I was at Beauvais at the beginning of the afternoon when M. de Margerie, M. Paul Reynaud's Chef du Cabinet Diplomatique, rang me up. " A conference is about to start in a moment, at the Préfecture at Tours, between the Premier and Mr. Churchill, who has just arrived with several of his Ministers. I am warning you in haste as I myself was warned. Although you are not invited, I suggest you should come. Baudouin is at work and I don't like the look of it." Such was M. de Margerie's communication.

I drove towards Tours, well aware of all the disquieting possibilities of this unexpected meeting, which the Premier, with whom I had just spent several hours, had not thought fit to mention to me. The courtyard and corridors of the Préfecture were filled with a crowd of members of parliament, civil servants and journalists whom the news had attracted and who formed, as it were, the tumultuous chorus of a tragedy nearing its catastrophe. I entered the office where M. Paul Reynaud was, hemmed in between Baudouin and de Margerie. The conference was adjourned. Margerie told me rapidly that the British Ministers, now in conclave in the garden, were about to give their reply to this question, put to them by the French: " In spite of the agreement of 28th March, 1940, which excludes any separate laying-down of

74

arms, would England consent to France asking the enemy what would be, for her, the terms of an armistice?"

Mr. Churchill sat down, Lord Halifax, Lord Beaverbrook and Sir Alexander Cadogan took their places, also General Spears, who accompanied them. There was a moment of crushing silence. The Prime Minister began to speak, in French. In an even, sad voice, rocking his head, with his cigar in his mouth, he began by expressing his commiseration, that of his Government and that of his people, for the lot of the French nation. " We see plainly," he said, " how things are with France. We understand how you feel cornered. Our friendship for you remains intact. In any case, be sure that England will not retire from the struggle. We shall fight to the end, no matter how, no matter where, even if you leave us alone."

Coming to the prospect of an armistice between French and Germans, which I was expecting to provoke an explosion from him, he expressed, on the contrary, a compassionate understanding. But suddenly, moving on to the question of the fleet, he became very precise and very firm. Obviously the British Government was so afraid of seeing the French fleet handed over to the Germans that it was inclined, while there was still time, to barter its renunciation of the March 28th agreement against guarantees about the fate of our ships. This was, in fact, the conclusion which emerged from that abominable conference. Mr. Churchill, before leaving the room, asked in addition, insistently, that if France ceased to fight she should first hand over to England the four hundred German airmen who were prisoners. This was immediately promised him.

The British were then led by M. Paul Reynaud into the adjoining room, where the Presidents of the Assemblies and several Ministers were waiting. There the tone was very different. MM. Jeanneney, Herriot and Louis Marin in particular spoke only of continuing the war. I went over to M. Paul Reynaud and asked him, somewhat forcibly: " Is it possible that you are thinking of France asking for an armistice? " " Certainly not! " he told me. " But we must give the British a shock, to get more help out of them." I could not, obviously, take this reply as a valid one. After we had separated, in the midst of the confusion in the courtyard of the Préfecture, I went back to Beauvais, overwhelmed, while the Prime Minister telegraphed to President Roosevelt to entreat him to intervene, letting it be understood that, without that, all was lost for us. That evening M. Paul Reynaud stated in a broadcast: "If a miracle is needed to save France, I believe in a miracle."

It seemed to me a foregone conclusion that all would soon be over. Just as a besieged fortress is near surrender as soon as the governor talks of one, so France was heading for an armistice because the head of her Government officially contemplated one. My presence in the Cabinet, secondary though my position might be, was going to become an impossibility. That night, however, at the very moment when I was about to despatch my letter of resignation, Georges Mandel, who had been warned by my *chef de cabinet*, Jean Laurent, sent me a request to go and see him.

André Diethelm took me in to the Minister of the Interior. Mandel spoke to me in a tone of gravity and resolution which impressed me. He was convinced, just as much as I was, that the independence and honour of France could only be safeguarded by continuing the war. But it was because of this national necessity that he recommended me to stay on in the post where I was. "Who knows," he said, "whether we shall not finally get the Government, after all, to go to Algiers?" He described to me what had happened in the Cabinet after the departure of the British: firmness had prevailed there in spite of the scene which Weygand had come to make. He gave me the news that, at that moment, the first German troops were entering Paris. Then, pointing to the future, he added: "In any case we are only at the beginning of a world war. You will have great duties to fulfil, General! But with the advantage of being, in the midst of all of us, an untarnished man. Think only of what has to be done for France, and consider that, in certain circumstances, your present position may make things easier for you." I must say

76

that this argument persuaded me to wait before resigning. On this, perhaps, depended, physically speaking, what I was able to do later on.

June 14th: withdrawal of the Government! I said my good-byes to my hosts, the Le Provost de Launays. *They* would not leave and, surrounded by those of their people who were neither mobilised nor mobilisable, they would await in their home the battles of the retreat and then the arrival of the invader. Towards the end of the afternoon, after a gloomy journey along the road crammed with processions of refugees, I reached Bordeaux and had myself taken to the seat of the military commander, where M. Paul Reynaud was to reside. The deputy and mayor of the town, M. Marquet, was there and gave me the first-fruits of the discouraging thoughts he was getting ready to express to the Premier.

When the Premier had arrived, I said to him: " In the last three days I have realised the speed with which we are rushing towards capitulation. I have given you my modest assistance, but it was for making war. I refuse to submit to an armistice. If you stay here, you will be submerged by the defeat. You must get to Algiers as quickly as possible. Are you—yes or no—resolved on that? " " Yes! " answered M. Paul Reynaud. " In that case," I went on, " I must go to London at once myself to arrange for the British to help us with the transport. I will go to-morrow. Where shall I rejoin you? " And the Premier replied: " You will rejoin me at Algiers."

It was agreed that I should leave that night and on the way stop in Brittany to see what could be embarked there. M. Paul Reynaud asked me, lastly, to summon Darlan to see him next morning. He wanted, he told me, to speak to him about the fleet.

Darlan was on his way to La Guéritoulde. I caught him on the telephone that evening and gave him the appointment. A peevish voice answered me: " Go to Bordeaux, to-morrow? I don't know what the Premier imagines he is doing there. But I've a command, I have, and I've no time to waste." At length he submitted. But the tone adopted by Darlan opened up depressing vistas. A few minutes later I gauged the evolution of certain minds in the course of a short conversation with Jean Ybarnegaray, Minister of State, who till then had shown himself a partisan of war to the end. He came over to me at the Hôtel Splendide, where I was swallowing my dinner in the company of Geoffroy de Courcel. " For me, as an ex-soldier," he said, " nothing counts except obeying my chiefs—Pétain and Weygand! " " Perhaps you will see one day," I answered, " that for a Minister the safety of the State should over-ride all feelings." I went in silence over to Marshal Pétain, who was dining in the same room, to present my respects. He shook me by the hand without a word. I was not to see him again, ever.

What a current was carrying him along, and towards what an ineluctable destiny! The whole career of that exceptional man had been one long effort of repression. Too proud for intrigue, too forceful for mediocrity, too ambitious to be a time-server, he nourished in his solitude a passion for domination, which had long been hardened by his consciousness of his own value, the set-backs he had encountered and the contempt he had for others. Military glory had already lavished on him its bitter caresses. But it had not satisfied him, since it had not loved him alone. And here, suddenly, in the extreme winter of his life, events were offering to his gifts and pride the opportunity—so long awaited!—to expand without limits; on one condition, however,—that he should accept disaster as his elevation's scutcheon and should adorn it with his glory.

It must be said that, in any case, the Marshal considered the game lost. This old soldier, who had put on the harness in the aftermath of 1870, was naturally inclined to view the struggle as no more than another Franco-German war. Beaten in the first one, we had won the second—that of 1914-1918—, with allies, certainly, but allies who played a secondary part. We were now losing the third. It was cruel, but normal. After Sedan and the fall of Paris, the only thing was to end it, negotiate and, if the case arose, crush the Commune, just as, in the same circumstances, Thiers had already done.

In the old Marshal's judgment the world character of the conflict, the possibilities of the overseas territories, and the ideological consequences of Hitler's victory, hardly entered into account. Those were not things he was in the habit of considering.

In spite of everything, I am convinced that in other times Marshal Pétain would not have consented to don the purple in the midst of national surrender. I am sure that, in any case, as long as he remained himself, he would have taken to the road of war again as soon as he could see that he had been wrong, that victory was still possible, that France would have her share in it. But alas! under the outer shell, the years had gnawed at his character. Age was delivering him over to the manœuvres of people who were clever at covering themselves with his majestic lassitude. Old age is a shipwreck. That we might be spared nothing, the old age of Marshal Pétain was to identify itself with the shipwreck of France.

That is what I was thinking of as I drove through the night towards Brittany. At the same time I fortified my resolution to continue the war, wherever that might lead me. Reaching Rennes on the morning of June 15th, I saw General René Altmayer, who was in command of the various elements engaged to the east of Mayenne, General Guitry, commanding the military region, and the Préfet of Ille-et-Vilaine. All three were doing their best in their respective fields. I endeavoured to organise the co-ordination of their efforts and resources for the defence of that part of the country. Then I went on to Brest, overtaking some British convoys on their way there to re-embark. At the Préfecture Maritime I studied, with Admiral Traub and Admiral de Laborde (who was the "Amiral-Ouest"), the shipping available and shipping required for the embarkation of troops at the Brittany ports. In the afternoon I went aboard the destroyer *Milan*, which was to take me to Plymouth together with a mission of chemists headed by General Lemoine, who were being sent by M. Raoul Dautry, the Minister for Armaments, to place the "heavy water" in safety in England. As we left the Brest roadstead, the *Richelieu*, which stood ready to sail for Dakar, gave me the salute. From Plymouth I set off for London, where I arrived on the 16th at dawn.

A few minutes later MM. Corbin and Monnet came into my room at the Hyde Park Hotel, where I was washing. The Ambassador told me, first, that the various appointments I was to have with the British, to discuss the matter of transport, had been arranged for the morning. It was also understood that, unless France asked Germany for an armistice, Mr. Churchill would meet M. Paul Reynaud at Concarneau next day in the morning, to lay down jointly how the embarkations should be carried out. Then my visitors passed on to another subject.

" We know," they said, " that at Bordeaux the mood of surrender is making rapid progress. Indeed, while you were on your way here, the French Government confirmed by telegram the request made orally on the 13th to Mr. Churchill by M. Paul Reynaud with a view to the release of France from the March 28th agreement. We do not yet know what reply the British will give—it is to be sent this morning. But we think they will consent, in return for guarantees regarding the fleet. So we are nearing the last moments. All the more so as there is to be a Cabinet meeting at Bordeaux in the course of the day and, in all probability, this meeting will be decisive."

" It has occurred to us," added MM. Corbin and Monnet, " that some sensational stroke, by throwing a new factor into the situation, might be what is needed to change the state of mind and, in any case, to strengthen M. Paul Reynaud in his intention to go to Algiers. We have therefore worked out with Sir Robert Vansittart, Permanent Under-Secretary at the Foreign Office, a plan which does seem striking. It would consist of a proposal for the union of France and England, to be solemnly addressed by the London Government to the Bordeaux Government. The two countries would decide on the fusion of their administrations, the pooling of their resources and losses, in short a complete linking of their respective destinies. In face of such a proposal, made in such circumstances, it is possible that our Ministers may wish to think again and, at least, postpone surrender. But we still have to get the plan adopted by the British Government. You alone can obtain that from Mr. Churchill. It is arranged that you will lunch with him. That will be the supreme opportunity—if, of course, you approve of the idea."

I examined the text which was put before me. It was clear to me at once that the grandeur of the thing in any case made its rapid realisation impossible. It was obvious that one could not, by an exchange of notes, even in principle fuse England and France together, including their institutions, their interests and their Empires, supposing this were desirable. Even the points in the proposal that were capable of being settled practically—for instance, the sharing of war damage—would demand complex negotiations. But the offer addressed by the British Government to ours did involve a manifestation of solidarity which might take on a real significance. Above all, I thought, like MM. Corbin and Monnet, that the proposal was of a nature to provide M. Paul Reynaud, in the supreme crisis in which he was plunged, with an element of comfort, and, *vis-à-vis* his Ministers, an argument for tenacity. I consented, therefore, to do what I could with Mr. Churchill to get him to adopt it.

The morning was a full one. I began by settling the destination of the *Pasteur*, carrying a cargo of a thousand 75s, some thousands of machine-guns and quantities of ammunition, all from the United States. On the advice of our military mission, the ship, which was still at sea, was diverted by my orders from Bordeaux, whither she was bound, to a port in Great Britain. Given the turn of events, this cargo, then invaluable, had to be prevented from falling into the hands of the enemy. In fact the guns and machine-guns brought by the *Pasteur* helped to re-arm the British, who had lost at Dunkirk nearly all their material.

As for the question of the transports, I found the British sincerely anxious to strengthen our means of getting our troops away and protecting the convoys; the machinery for carrying this out was being set up by the Admiralty in liaison with our naval mission under Admiral Odend'hal. But there was evidently little belief in London that official France would pull itself together. The contacts I made showed that the measures contemplated by our allies in the various fields were based on the assumption of our imminent renunciation of the struggle. Over and above everything, the fate of our Navy literally haunted their minds. During these tragic hours every Frenchman could feel weighing on him the mute or explicit question from every Englishman he met: " What is going to become of your fleet? "

The British Prime Minister also was thinking of that when I came, with MM. Corbin and Monnet, to lunch with him at the Carlton Club. " Whatever happens," I said to him, " the French fleet will not be willingly surrendered. Pétain himself would not consent to that. Besides, the fleet is Darlan's fief. A feudal lord does not surrender his fief. But for it to be possible to be sure that the enemy will never lay hands on our ships, it would be necessary for us to remain at war. Well, I am obliged to tell you that your attitude at Tours came as an unpleasant surprise to me. You appeared there to attach little value to our alliance. Your attitude of resignation plays into the hands of those among us who favour capitulation. ' You can see perfectly well we have no choice,' they say. ' The British themselves are giving us their consent.' No! What you have to do to encourage us in the frightful crisis in which we are is something quite different."

Mr. Churchill seemed disturbed. He conferred for a moment with Major Morton, his private secretary. I supposed that he was making, *in extremis*, the necessary arrangements to modify a decision already taken. Perhaps that was the cause of the fact that at Bordeaux, half an hour later, the British Ambassador came and withdrew from Mr. Paul Reynaud's hands the note which he had brought him, in which the British Government consented in principle to France asking Germany what would be the terms of an armistice if it came to that.

I then raised with Mr. Churchill the proposal for the union of the two peoples. " Lord Halifax has spoken to me about it," he told me. " But it's an enormous mouthful."

"Yes," I answered. "That means that its realisation would involve a great deal of time. But the gesture can be immediate. As things are now, nothing must be neglected by you that can support France and maintain our alliance." After some discussion the Prime Minister fell in with my view. He at once summoned the British Cabinet and went to Downing Street to preside at its meeting. I went with him and, while the Ministers were deliberating, waited with the French Ambassador in an office adjoining the Cabinet Room. I had meanwhile telephoned to M. Paul Reynaud to warn him that I was hoping to send him, before the end of the afternoon and with the British Government's agreement, a most important communication. He answered that he was putting off his Cabinet meeting till five o'clock on this account. "But," he added, "I shan't be able to postpone it longer."

The meeting of the British Cabinet lasted for two hours, during which, from time to time, one or other of the Ministers came out to clear some point with us French. Suddenly they all came in, led by Mr. Churchill. "We are agreed," they exclaimed. And in fact, details apart, the text they produced was the same as the one we had proposed to them. I immediately telephoned to M. Paul Reynaud and dictated the document to him. "It's very important!" said the Premier. "I shall use it at the meeting that is about to start." In a few words I told him all the encouraging things I could. Mr. Churchill then took the telephone: "Hallo, Reynaud! De Gaulle is right! Our proposal may have great consequences. You must hold out!" Then, after listening to the reply, he said: "Well, see you to-morrow! At Concarneau."

I said good-bye to the Prime Minister. He lent me an aeroplane in which to go back at once to Bordeaux. We agreed that the machine should remain at my disposal in case of events which might lead me to return. Mr. Churchill himself had a train to catch in order to board a destroyer for the journey to Concarneau. At 9.30 p.m. I landed at Bordeaux. Colonel Humbert and Auburtin, from my office, were waiting for me at the aerodrome. They told me that the Premier had resigned and that President Lebrun had asked Marshal Pétain to form a Government. That meant certain capitulation. My decision was taken at once. I would leave as soon as morning came.

I went to see M. Paul Reynaud. I found him with no illusion about what the consequences would be of the Marshal taking power and, on the other hand, like one relieved of an intolerable burden. Only those who were eye-witnesses of it can measure what the ordeal of being in power meant during that terrible period. All through days without respite and nights without sleep, the Premier could feel the entire responsibility for the destiny of France weighing upon him personally. For a leader is always alone in face of ill-fortune. He it was who received in their full force the reverses that marked the stages of our fall: the German break-through at Sedan, the Dunkirk disaster, the flight from Paris, the collapse at Bordeaux. Yet he had assumed the leadership only on the very eve of our misfortunes, with no time in which to confront them and after having, for a long time, advocated the military policy which could have averted them. He faced the storm with a steadfastness which did not waver. Never, during those days of drama, did M. Paul Reynaud cease to be master of himself. Never was he seen to lose his temper, give way to anger, or complain. The spectacle of that man's high value, ground down unjustly by a too great weight of events, was a tragic one.

At bottom, the personality of M. Paul Reynaud was the right one for conditions where it would have been possible to conduct the war within a State in running order and on the basis of traditionally established data. But everything was swept away! The Head of the Government saw the system collapsing all around him, the people in flight, the allies withdrawing, and the most illustrious leaders failing. From the day when the Government left the capital, the very business of exercising power became merely a sort of agony, unrolling along the roads amid the dislocation of services, disciplines and consciences. In such conditions M. Paul Reynaud's intelligence, his courage and the authority of his

office were, so to speak, running free. He had no longer any
purchase upon the fury of events.

To seize the reins once more he would have had to wrench
himself out of the whirlwind, cross over to Africa and start
everything afresh from there. M. Paul Reynaud saw this. But
it involved extreme measures: changing the High Command,
getting rid of the Marshal and half the Ministers, breaking
with certain influences, resigning himself to the total occupation of metropolitan France—in short, striking out at all costs
from the ordinary framework and procedure in a situation
without precedent.

M. Paul Reynaud did not think fit to take upon himself
decisions so far outside the orbit of the normal and calculable.
He tried to attain the aim by manœuvring. That explains, in
particular, the fact that he envisaged a possible examination
of the enemy's armistice conditions, provided England gave
her consent. No doubt he judged that even those who were
pushing towards an armistice would recoil when they knew
its terms, and that then there would come into play the
regroupment of all men of value to make war and save the
country. But the tragedy was too harsh to be resolved. Either
make war without sparing anything, or surrender at once:
there was no alternative, only these two extremes. M. Paul
Reynaud, through failing to identify himself wholly with the
first, gave place to Pétain, who completely adopted the second.

It has to be said that at the supreme moment the régime
offered to the head of the last Government of the Third
Republic nothing to fall back upon. Assuredly many of the
men in office looked upon capitulation with horror. But the
authorities, shattered by the disaster for which they felt themselves responsible, did not react at all. At the time when they
were faced by the problem on which, for France, all the
present and all the future depended, Parliament did not sit,
the Government showed itself incapable of adopting as a body
a decisive solution, and the President of the Republic abstained
from raising his voice, even within the Cabinet, to express the
supreme interest of the country. In reality this annihilation
of the State was at the bottom of the national tragedy. By the

light of the thunderbolt the régime was revealed, in its ghastly infirmity, as having no proportion and no relation to the defence, honour and independence of France.

Late in the evening I went to the hotel where Sir Ronald Campbell, the British Ambassador, was residing, and informed him of my intention to leave for London. General Spears, who came and joined in the conversation, declared that he would accompany me. I sent word to M. Paul Reynaud. He made over to me the sum of a hundred thousand francs, on the secret funds. I begged M. de Margerie to send at once to my wife and children, who were at Carantec, the necessary passports for reaching England, which they could just do by the last boat leaving Brest. On June 17th, at nine in the morning, I flew off, with General Spears and Lieutenant de Courcel, in the British aeroplane which had brought me the evening before. There was nothing romantic or difficult about the departure.

We flew over La Rochelle and Rochefort. Ships set on fire by German aircraft were burning in these ports. We passed over Paimpont, where my mother lay very ill. The forest was all smoking from the munition dumps which were being destroyed there. After a stop at Jersey, we reached London in the early afternoon. While I was taking rooms and Courcel was telephoning to the Embassy and the missions and finding them already reticent, I seemed to myself, alone as I was and deprived of everything, like a man on the shore of an ocean, proposing to swim across.

III. FREE FRANCE

G O ON with the war? Yes, certainly! But to what end
and within what limits? Many, even among those who
approved of the undertaking, wanted it to be no more
than aid given by a handful of Frenchmen to the British
Empire, still standing and in the fight. I did not look at the
enterprise in that way for a moment. For me, what had to
be served and saved was the nation and the State.

I thought, in fact, that it would be the end of honour,
unity and independence if it were to be admitted that, in this
world war, only France had capitulated and that she had let
the matter rest there. For in that case, whatever might be the
issue of the conflict,—whether the country, after decisive
defeat, would one day be rid of the invader by foreign arms,
or would remain enslaved—, her self-disgust and the disgust she
would inspire in others would poison her soul and her life for
many generations. As for the immediate future, in the name
of what were some of her sons to be led out, to a fight no longer
her own? What was the good of supplying with auxiliaries the
forces of another Power? No! For the effort to be worth
while, it was essential to bring back into the war not merely
some Frenchmen, but France.

That was bound to involve: the re-appearance of our
armies on the battlefields, the return of our territories to
belligerence, participation by the country itself in the efforts
of its fighting men, and recognition by the foreign Powers of
the fact that France, as such, had gone on with the struggle,
—in short, to bring our sovereignty out from disaster and

from the policy of wait-and-see, over to the side of war and, one day, of victory.

What I knew of men and affairs left me with no illusions about the obstacles to be surmounted. There would be the power of the enemy, which could be broken only by a long process of wearing down and would have the help of the French official machine in opposing the belligerent recovery of France. There would be the moral and material difficulties which a long and all-out struggle would inevitably involve for those who would have to carry it on as pariahs and without means. There would be the mountain of objections, insinuations and calumnies raised against the fighters by the sceptics and the timorous to cover their passivity. There would be the so-called " parallel " but in fact rival and opposing enterprises, to which the French passion for disputation would not fail to give rise, and of which the policy and services of the Allies would make use, in the customary way, in order to control them. There would be, on the part of those whose aim was subversion, the determination to side-track the national resistance in the direction of revolutionary chaos, to result in their dictatorship. There would be, finally, the tendency of the great Powers to take advantage of our weakness in order to push their interests at the expense of France.

As for me, with a hill like that to climb, I was starting from scratch. Not the shadow of a force or of an organisation at my side. In France, no following and no reputation. Abroad, neither credit nor standing. But this very destitution showed me my line of conduct. It was by adopting without compromise the cause of national recovery that I could acquire authority. It was by acting as the inflexible champion of the nation and of the State that it would be possible for me to gather the consent, even the enthusiasm, of the French and to win from foreigners respect and consideration. Those who, all through the drama, were offended by this intransigence were unwilling to see that for me, intent as I was on beating back innumerable conflicting pressures, the slightest wavering would have brought collapse. In short, limited and alone though I was, and precisely because I was so, I had to climb to the heights and never then to come down.

The first thing to do was to hoist the colours. Broadcasting was to hand for that. Already in the afternoon of June 17th I outlined my intentions to Mr. Winston Churchill. Washed up from a vast shipwreck upon the shores of England, what could I have done without his help? He gave it me at once, and to begin with put the B.B.C. at my disposal. We agreed that I should use it after the Pétain Government had asked for the armistice. That very evening the news came that it had done so. Next day, at 6 p.m., I read out at the microphone the well-known text. As the irrevocable words flew out upon their way, I felt within myself a life coming to an end—the life I had lived within the framework of a solid France and an indivisible army. At the age of forty-nine I was entering upon adventure, like a man thrown by fate outside all terms of reference.

It was nonetheless my duty, while taking the first steps in this unprecedented career, to make sure that no authority better qualified than mine was willing to step forward to bring France and the Empire back into the struggle. As long as the armistice was not in force it was possible to imagine, though against all probability, that the Bordeaux Government would at the last moment choose war. Even if there was only the feeblest chance, it must be encouraged. That is why, as soon as I reached London, in the afternoon of the 17th, I telegraphed to Bordeaux to offer my services in carrying on, in the British capital, the negotiations I had begun on the day before about the war material from the United States, the German prisoners and the transport for North Africa.

The reply was a despatch summoning me to return at once. On June 20th I wrote to Weygand, who had taken, in the midst of capitulation, the astonishing title of " Minister of National Defence," to urge him to place himself at the head of the resistance and to assure him of my entire obedience if he did so. But this letter was to be returned to me by him, some weeks later, with a comment of which the least one can say is that it expressed his ill-will. On June 30th the so-called

" French Embassy " notified me of the order to surrender myself at the Saint-Michel prison in Toulouse, there to be tried by the Conseil de Guerre. This condemned me first, to a month's prison. Then—upon an appeal *a minima* demanded by the " Minister," Weygand—it condemned me to death.

Discounting indeed—and rightly!—this attitude on the part of Bordeaux, I had already addressed myself to our authorities overseas. As early as June 19th I had telegraphed to General Noguès, Commander-in-Chief in North Africa and Resident-General in Morocco, to place myself at his orders if he should reject the armistice. That same evening, in a broadcast, I urged " the Africa of Clauzel, of Bugeaud, of Lyautey, of Noguès, to refuse the enemy conditions." On June 24th, by telegram, I renewed my appeal to Noguès and addressed myself also to General Mittelhauser and to M. Puaux, respectively Commander-in-Chief and High Commissioner in the Levant, as well as to General Catroux, Governor-General of Indo-China. I suggested to these high authorities that they should form an organisation for the defence of the Empire, and that I could immediately assure its liaison with London. On June 27th, being apprised of a rather warlike speech made by M. Peyrouton, the Resident-General in Tunisia, I urged him, too, to join the " Defence Committee," at the same time renewing my offers to General Mittelhauser and to M. Puaux. On the same day, in case of need, I booked places for myself and my officers on board a French cargo boat preparing to leave for Morocco.

All I received by way of answer was a message from Admiral de Carpentier, in command of the Navy in the Levant, telling me that M. Puaux and General Mittelhauser had telegraphed to General Noguès to the same effect as I. In addition, one of General Catroux's sons, who was then in London, brought me a telegram from his father, addressed to him, encouraging him to fight and bidding him assure me of his father's sympathetic approval. But at the same time the British, who had sent a Minister, Mr. Duff Cooper, together with General Gort, to North Africa to offer Noguès the assistance of their forces, saw their delegation return to London without even having been received. Finally, General Dillon, head of the British military liaison in North Africa, was asked to leave Algiers.

And yet Noguès's first impulse had been to hoist the flag. As is known, on June 25th, having seen the German terms, he had telegraphed to Bordeaux to let it be known that he was ready to continue the war. Using an expression I myself had used in a broadcast six days before, he referred to " the panic in Bordeaux," as making it impossible for the Government " to appreciate objectively North Africa's possibilities of resistance." He invited General Weygand " to reconsider his orders concerning the carrying-out of the armistice," and protested that, if these orders were maintained, " he could not carry them out without blushing." It is clear that if Noguès had chosen the path of resistance the whole of the Empire would have followed him. But it soon became known that he himself and the other residents, governors and commanders-in-chief were obeying the summonses of Pétain and Weygand and were consenting to the armistice. Only General Catroux, Governor of Indo-China, and General Legentilhomme, in command of our troops on the Somali coast, maintained their opposition. Both of them were replaced, without their subordinates doing much to support them.

But indeed this sort of collapse of most of the " proconsuls " coincided with a total political breakdown at home. The papers that reached me from Bordeaux, and then from Vichy, displayed their acceptance and that of all the parties groups, authorities and institutions. The National Assembly met on July 9th and 10th and gave Pétain full powers, almost without debate. Actually, eighty of the members present voted courageously against this abdication. Also those parliamentarians who had embarked for North Africa aboard the *Massilia* bore witness, by so doing, that for them the Empire had not given up the struggle. Nevertheless it is a fact that not one public man raised his voice to condemn the armistice.

Moreover, even though the collapse of France had plunged the world into stupefaction, even though ordinary people all over the world watched with terror the destruction of that great light, even though this poem by Charles Morgan and that article by François Mauriac brought tears to many eyes, States were not slow to accept accomplished facts. No doubt the Governments of the countries at war with the Axis did recall their representatives from France, whether they did so spontaneously as in the cases of Sir Ronald Campbell or General Vanier, or whether they were asked to do so by the Germans. But there remained, all the same, in London, installed in the building of the French Embassy, a Consul who was in communication with metropolitan France, while M. Dupuis, the Canadian Consul-General, remained accredited to the Marshal, and the Union of South Africa left its representative there. Above all, an imposing diplomatic corps could be seen assembling at Vichy around Monsignor Valerio Valeri, the Papal nuncio, M. Bogomolov, the Soviet Ambassador, and, soon, Admiral Leahy, the United States Ambassador. That was enough to cool the ardour of those personalities whose first impulse might have driven them towards the Cross of Lorraine.

Thus, among the French as within the other nations, the immense convergence of fear, interest and despair caused a universal surrender in regard to France. Though there were many feelings still loyal to her past and many interests eager to take advantage of the shreds yet left to her by the present, no responsible man anywhere acted as if he still believed in her independence, pride and greatness. That she was bound henceforward to be enslaved, disgraced and flouted was taken for granted by all who counted in the world. In face of the frightening void of the general renunciation my mission seemed to me, all of a sudden, clear and terrible. At this moment, the worst in her history, it was for me to assume the burden of France.

But there is no France without a sword. To set up a fighting force was more important than anything. I began work on that at once. There were some military elements in England. First of all there were the units of the Alpine Light Division which, after some brilliant campaigning in Norway under General Béthouart, had been brought back to Brittany in the middle of June and re-embarked there along with the last British troops. There were also some ships belonging to the Navy—nearly a hundred thousand tons in all—which had escaped from Cherbourg, Brest and Lorient with many individuals and auxiliaries on board beside their crews, the whole totalling at least ten thousand sailors. There were, in addition, several thousand soldiers who had been wounded in Belgium and brought to hospital in Great Britain. The French military missions had organised the command and administration of all these elements with a view to keeping them under the orders of Vichy and preparing their general repatriation.

The mere act of making contact with these many, dispersed fractions involved great difficulties for me. To begin with, I had only a very small number of officers, nearly all subalterns, full of immense good-will but powerless to storm the machinery of the hierarchy. What they could do—and did—was to make propaganda among those officers and men whom they managed to meet. The yield was bound to be small. A week after my appeal of June 18th the number of volunteers encamped in Olympia, which the British had leant us, amounted to only a few hundred.

It must be said that the British authorities did little to help our efforts. Certainly they had distributed a leaflet advising members of the French forces that they could choose between repatriation, joining General de Gaulle and serving in His Majesty's forces. Certainly the instructions given by Churchill and the activities of Spears, whom the Prime Minister had made responsible for liaison between Free France and the British services, did sometimes succeed in vanquishing inertia or opposition. Certainly the Press, the wireless, many associations and countless individuals gave our enterprise a warm welcome. But the British High Command, which from one day to another expected the German offensive and perhaps invasion, was too much absorbed by its preparations to busy itself with a task which in its eyes was secondary. Besides, it was inclined by professional decorum and habit to respect the normal order of things—that is to say, Vichy and its missions. Finally it looked with some mistrust upon these allies of yesterday humiliated by misfortune, dissatisfied with themselves and with others and loaded with complaints. What would they do if the enemy gained a bridgehead? Wasn't the most sensible course to ship them away as quickly as possible? And what, after all, was the use of the few battalions without cadres and crews without officers, which General de Gaulle claimed he could rally?

On June 29th I went to Trentham Park, where the Light Mountain Division was encamped. The general commanding the division was himself anxious to return to France, though with the firm intention of getting back into the line one day—which indeed he was destined to do, effectively and with glory, later. But he had arranged for me to be able to see the whole of each unit. This made it possible for me to rally a large part of the two battalions of the 13th Half-Brigade of the Foreign Legion, with their leader, Lieut.-Col. Magrin-Verneret, known as Monclar, and his number two, Captain Koenig, two hundred Chasseurs Alpins, two-thirds of a tank company, some elements of gunners, engineers and signals, and several staff and administrative officers, including Commandant de Conchard and Captains Dewawrin and Tissier. This in spite of the fact that, after I had left the camp, the British Colonels de Chair and Williams, sent by the War Office, had in turn had the troops paraded in order to tell them, literally, this: " You are perfectly free to serve under General de Gaulle. But it is our duty to point out to you, speaking as man to man, that if you do so decide you will be rebels against your Government. . . .."

Next day I wanted to visit the camps at Aintree and at Haydock, where several thousand French sailors were assembled. As soon as I arrived the British Admiral in command at Liverpool told me that he was opposed to my seeing the men because this might be prejudicial to order. I had to return empty-handed. I was luckier at Harrow Park a few days later. In spite of everything, a stream of enlistments was starting among our sailors. A few resolute officers who had joined me at once, such as Capitaines de Corvette D'Argenlieu, Wietzel, Moulec and Jourden, were putting their heart and soul into it. The officers and crews of three small warships had declared themselves at once: the submarine *Rubis* (Commandant Cabanier), then cruising near the Norwegian coast, the submarine *Narval* (Commandant Drogou) which left Sfax immediately after my appeal and reported at Malta, later to be sunk in action in the Mediterranean; and the trawler and patrol craft *Président Honduce* (Commandant Deschatres). The arrival of Vice-Admiral Muselier, who had set many elements in the Navy against him by the incidents of his career and the features of his personality, but whose intelligence and knowledge of the world offered advantages at that adventurous period, made it possible for me to give this embryo of our naval forces a centre and a technical head. At this time also some dozens of airmen, whom I went to see in camp at St. Atham, grouped themselves around Captains de Rancourt, Astier de Villatte and Becourt-Foch, until Commandant Pijeaud was given command of them.

Meanwhile isolated volunteers were reaching England daily. They came mostly from France, brought by the last ships to have left there normally, or escaping in small boats which they had managed to seize, or, again, having with great difficulty got across Spain, evading its police which shut up in the camp at Miranda those it caught. Some airmen saved their machines from the control of Vichy and contrived to get away from North Africa and reach Gibraltar. Some merchant seamen, placed outside French ports by the chances of navigation, or, sometimes, by the escape of a ship—as, for example, the *Capo Olmo* (Commandant Vuillemin),—asked to be enrolled as combatants. Some Frenchmen resident abroad came and demanded to serve. Having called a meeting at the White City of two thousand men who had been wounded at Dunkirk and were convalescing in British hospitals, I got two hundred enlistments. A Colonial battalion, which happened to be in Cyprus, detached from the Armée du Levant, rallied spontaneously under its leader, Commandant Lorette. In the last days of June a flotilla of fishing boats reached

Cornwall, bringing over to General de Gaulle all the able-
bodied men from the island of Sein. Day after day the enrol-
ment of these lads so splendid in their keenness, many of whom
had performed exploits to get to us, strengthened our determination. Messages from all parts of the world piled up on
my table, bringing me, from individuals or from small groups,
moving requests for enlistment. My officers and those of the
Spears mission expended prodigies of ingenuity and obstinacy
to arrange their transport.

Suddenly a lamentable event occurred to stop the stream.
On July 4th the radio and the newspapers announced that on
the previous day the British Mediterranean Fleet had attacked
the French Squadron at anchor at Mers-el-Kebir. At the
same time we were informed that the British had occupied by
surprise the French warships which had taken refuge in
British ports and had taken ashore and interned—not without
some bloodshed—their officers and crews. Finally, on the
10th, the news was made public of the torpedoing, by British
aircraft, of the battleship *Richelieu*, at anchor in Dakar Roads. In
London the official communiqués and the newspapers tended
to represent this series of aggressions as a sort of naval victory.
In the British Government and Admiralty—this was clear—
the fear caused by the danger they were in, the stale reek of
an old naval rivalry, and the resentments accumulated since the
beginning of the Battle of France and brought to the point of
paroxysm with the armistice concluded by Vichy, had exploded
in one of those dark bursts by which the repressed instinct of
this people sometimes smashes all barriers.

It had never, though, been likely that the French Fleet
would of itself open hostilities against the British. Ever since
my arrival in London I had stressed this both to the British
Government and to the Admiralty. Besides, it was certain
that Darlan, quite apart from all the obvious patriotic motives,
would not of his own accord go and surrender to the Germans
his own wealth—the Navy—, as long as it was under his
control. At bottom, if Darlan and his advisers renounced the
chance of playing the magnificent part offered them by events
and becoming the last resort of France at a time when, in

contrast to the Army, the Fleet was intact, it was because they thought they were certain of keeping their ships. Lord Lloyd, the British Minister for Colonies, and Admiral Sir Dudley Pound, the First Sea Lord, when they came to Bordeaux on June 18th, had obtained from Darlan his word of honour that our ships would not be handed over. Pétain and Baudouin, for their part, had given formal undertakings. Lastly—contrary to what the British and American agencies had at first suggested—, the terms of the armistice included no direct provision entitling the Germans to lay hands on the French Fleet.

On the other hand, it must be recognised that, faced by the capitulation of the Bordeaux authorities and the prospect of future flinchings on their part, England might well fear that the enemy would one day manage to gain control of our fleet. In that case Great Britain would have been mortally menaced. In spite of the pain and anger into which I and my companions were plunged by the tragedy of Mers-el-Kebir, by the behaviour of the British and by the way they gloried in it, I considered that the saving of France ranked above everything, even above the fate of her ships, and that our duty was still to go on with the fight.

I expressed myself frankly about this on July 8th, in a broadcast. The British Government, on the advice of its Minister of Information, Mr. Duff Cooper, was clever enough, and elegant enough, to let me use the B.B.C. microphone for the purpose, however disagreeable for the British the terms of my statement may have been.

But it was a terrible blow at our hopes. It showed at once in the recruitment of the volunteers. Many of those, military or civilian, who were preparing to join us, turned on their heels then. In addition, the attitude adopted towards us by the authorities in the French Empire and by the naval and military elements guarding it, changed for the most part from hesitation to opposition. Vichy, of course, did not fail to exploit the event to the utmost. The consequences were destined to be grave as regards the rallying of the African territories.

Still, we resumed our task. On July 13th I went so far as

to announce: "Frenchmen! Realise this! You have still a fighting army." On July 14th in Whitehall, in the midst of a deeply moved crowd, I reviewed our first detachments and then went at their head to place a Tricolour wreath at the foot of the statue of Marshal Foch. On July 21st, at my request, several of our airmen took part in a bombardment of the Ruhr, and I announced that the Free French had resumed the fight. Meanwhile all our troops, in accordance with an idea put forward by d'Argenlieu, adopted as their badge the Cross of Lorraine. On August 24th King George VI came to visit our little army. To see it, one could well believe that " the stump of the blade " would be toughly tempered. But heavens! how short it was!

At the end of July the number of our effectives was barely seven thousand. That was all we would be able to recruit in Great Britain itself: those French troops who had not joined us had now been repatriated. With great difficulty we were recovering the arms and material they had left behind, seized often either by the English or by other allies. As for the ships, we were only able to man some of them, and it was heart-breaking to see the others sailing under a foreign flag. Little by little, in spite of everything, our first units took shape, equipped with an odd assortment of weapons, but formed of resolute men.

These were, in fact, of that strong type to which the fighting men of the French resistance, wherever they might be, were bound to belong. A taste for risk and adventure pushed to the pitch of art for art's sake, a contempt for the cowardly and the indifferent, a tendency to melancholy and so to quarrelling during the periods without danger, giving place to an ardent cohesion in action, a national pride sharpened to its extreme by their country's ill-fortune and by contact with well-equipped allies, and above all, a sovereign confidence in the strength and cunning of their own conspiracy: such were the psychological characteristics of this élite which started from nothing and was to grow, gradually, until it drew after it the whole nation and the whole of the Empire.

While we were trying to forge some forces of our own, the

need to define our relations with the British Government became imperative. The British Government was indeed ready for this, not so much from a taste for juridical definitions as from its desire to see a practical settlement, in His Majesty's territory, of the rights and obligations of those sympathetic but somewhat disconcerting people, the Fighting French.

From the very beginning I had let Mr. Churchill know of my intention to promote, if possible, the formation of a " National Committee " to direct our war effort. To help towards this, the British Government made public two statements on June 23rd. The first denied that the Bordeaux Government possessed independence. The second took note of the proposal to form a French National Committee and expressed, in advance, the intention of recognising it and dealing with it on all matters relative to the carrying-on of the war. On June 25th the British Government issued a communiqué acknowledging the will to resist shown by several high authorities of the French Empire and offering them its assistance. Then, as no response came from any quarter, the London Cabinet found itself once more face to face with General de Gaulle alone and took the decision, on June 28th, to recognise him publicly as " leader of the Free French."

It was therefore in this capacity that I opened the necessary conversations with the Prime Minister and the Foreign Office. The point of departure was a memorandum which I had myself sent to Mr. Churchill and to Lord Halifax on June 26th. The result was the agreement of August 7th, 1940. Several clauses to which I attached importance gave rise to delicate bargaining between the negotiators: Mr. Strang, on behalf of our allies, Professor René Cassin on ours.

Bearing in mind, on the one hand, the hypothesis that the fortunes of war might bring England to a compromise peace and considering, on the other, that the British might perhaps be tempted by this or that overseas possession of ours, I insisted that Great Britain should guarantee the re-establishment of the frontiers of Metropolitan France and of the French Empire. The English in the end consented to promise " the integral restoration of the independence and greatness of France," but without any commitment as regards the integrity of our territories.

Although I was convinced that, given the proportion between the resources, the joint military operations, on land, on sea and in the air, should normally be directed by British commanders, I reserved for myself in all cases the " supreme command " of the French forces and accepted for them only " the general directives of the British High Command." In this way their purely national character was established. I had had it laid down—not without objections on the part of the British—that in no case would the volunteers " bear arms against France." That did not mean that they were never to fight against Frenchmen. The contrary, alas! had to be foreseen, Vichy being what it was and not being—far from it—France. But the clause aimed at guaranteeing that Allied military action, with which our own was merged, should not, even when it came up against the forces of official France, be used against the real France and injure its patrimony or its interests.

Although the expenses relating to the forces of Free France were bound, under the agreement, to fall provisionally upon the British Government, seeing that at the start we had no financial resources, I insisted on having it formulated that these were only advances, to be repaid one day, account being taken of what we furnished in return. The complete repayment did in fact take place, even before the end of the war, so that on balance our war effort remains in no way a charge upon England.

Finally, in spite of the thirst for tonnage by which—all too legitimately!—the British were devoured, we made them with some difficulty agree that a " permanent liaison " should be established between their services and ours to settle " the use to be made of French merchant ships and their crews."

It was at Chequers that Churchill and I signed the document together.

The August 7th agreement had a considerable importance for Free France, not only because it got us out of immediate material difficulties, but also because the British authorities, having now an official basis for their relations with us, no longer hesitated to make things easier for us. Above all, the whole world knew that a new beginning of Franco-British solidarity had been made in spite of everything. The consequences soon made themselves felt in certain territories of the Empire and among the French residents abroad. But in addition, other States, when they saw Great Britain proceeding to a beginning of recognition, took some steps in the same direction. This happened, first of all, with the refugee Governments in England, who possessed, no doubt, little in the way of forces but had retained their international representation and influence.

For in the case of each of the European nations submerged by Hitler's armies, the State had carried its independence and sovereignty across to free shores. It was to be the same for those whose territory was later occupied likewise by Germany or Italy. Not one Government consented to submit to the invader's yoke, not a single one except, alas! that which called itself the Government of France and yet had under its control a vast Empire guarded by large forces and one of the principal navies of the world!

In the course of the disasters of June, Great Britain had seen arrive upon her soil the Sovereigns and Ministers of Norway, Holland and Luxemburg, then the President of the Polish Republic and the Polish Ministers, and, after some delay, the Belgian Cabinet. The Czechoslovaks were busy organising themselves. The King of Albania was making certain contacts. It was from both generous and interested motives that England offered hospitality to these refugee States. However denuded they might be, they had always something left. Several of them brought the gold and foreign exchange of their bank. The Dutch had Indonesia and a by no means negligible fleet, the Belgians had the Congo, the Poles a small army, the Norwegians a good many merchant ships, the Czechs—or more exactly Beneš—intelligence networks in Central and Eastern Europe and active American relations. Moreover, England did not exactly suffer in prestige by appearing as the last rampart of the old world in ruin.

To these exiles Free France, which had nothing, was an interesting experiment. But it above all attracted the most anxious and the most unhappy among them, such as the Poles and the Czechs. In their eyes we who remained faithful to the traditions of France represented, by that very fact, a hope and a pole of attraction. In particular Sikorski and Beneš, suspicious though they were in the midst of the intrigues and susceptibilities which complicated their plight for them, established constant and sustained relations with me. Perhaps never better than at the bottom of that gulf have I felt what the vocation of France meant to the world.

While we endeavoured to obtain for France the beginnings of an international hearing, I was trying to get going the embryo of a political machinery and administration. Almost unknown and wholly without resources as I was, it would have been ridiculous of me to call the elementary organisation which I was forming around me a " Government." Besides, although I was convinced that Vichy would go on from fall to fall till it reached total degradation, and although I had proclaimed the illegitimacy of a régime which existed at the enemy's discretion, I wished to avoid prejudicing the possibility of the State machinery being recast in the mould of war, should the occasion ever present itself. And so I refrained as long as possible from setting up, even as a matter of terminology, anything which might in any circumstances embarrass the regrouping of the State. All I had suggested to the holders of authority in the Empire was that they should unite for its defence. Then, when their failure had been verified, I decided that I myself would form, as soon as possible, a simple " National Committee."

It was necessary, however, that some sufficiently representative people of eminence should be willing to support me. During the first days, certain optimists thought these could easily be found. From hour to hour it was announced that such and such a well-known politician, famous general or revered academician had passed through Lisbon or landed at Liverpool. But the denial soon followed. Even in London, with few exceptions, these well-known Frenchmen who happened to be there, whether on service or by chance, did not join Free France. Many had themselves repatriated. Some stayed where they were, but professed obedience to Vichy. As for those who took sides against the capitulation, some organised their life in exile on their own, either in England or in the United States, others placed themselves at the service of the British or American Governments: the " proved men " who ranged themselves under my banner were few.

" You are in the right! " I was told, for instance, by M. Corbin, the French Ambassador. " I who have devoted the best part of my career to the cause of the Franco-British alliance, have taken sides openly by sending in my resignation the very next day after your appeal. But I'm an old civil servant. For forty years I've lived and worked within a regular framework. Outlawry is too much for me."

" You are wrong," M. Jean Monnet wrote to me, " to set up an organisation which might appear in France as though created under the protection of England. . . . I wholly share your determination to prevent France from abandoning the struggle. . . . But London is not the place from which the effort at insurrection can start."

" I must go back to France," M. René Mayer let it be known, " in order not to separate my fate from that of the people of my religion who are going to be persecuted there."

" You have my approval," M. Bret assured me. " As for me, whether in France or in the Empire, I shall do all I can to help the recovery of France."

" We are going to America," I was informed by MM. André Maurois, Henry Bonnet and de Kerillis. " That is where, indeed, we shall be able to be of most use to you."

" I have been appointed Consul-General at Shanghai," M. Roland de Margerie announced to me, " and I am passing through London not to join you but to reach China. I shall serve the interests of France there, as you are doing here."

On the other hand, M. Pierre Cot, overcome by what had happened, begged me to use him at no matter what task,

" even sweeping the staircase." But he was too conspicuous for that to be desirable.

All in all, whatever the reasons for it, this well-nigh general abstention of Frenchmen of note certainly did not heighten the credit of my enterprise. I had to put off the formation of my Committee till later. The fewer eminent people came, the fewer wished to come.

Some, however, were immediately at my side, and brought to the duties which they assumed *ex tempore* an ardour and an energy thanks to which, in spite of everything, the ship was launched and proved seaworthy. Professor Cassin was my assistant—and what a valuable one!—with regard to all those agreements and other documents upon which, starting from nothing, our internal and external structure was established. Antoine had to run the administration of our first civilian services, a thankless task in that period of improvisation. Lapie, Escarra and then Hackin—the latter doomed soon to perish at sea together with his wife while on a mission—kept in touch with the various departments of the Foreign Office and with the European Governments in exile. They also made contact with the Frenchmen resident abroad to whom I had appealed. Pleven and Denis had charge of our minute finances and worked on the conditions under which the colonies could live when they rallied to us. Schumann acted as the spokesman of Free France on the wireless. Massip studied the Press and kept it informed about us. Bingen settled with our Allies the use of French merchant shipping and seamen.

On the strictly military side, Muselier assisted by d'Argenlieu, Magrin-Verneret by Koenig, and Pijeaud by Rancourt, organised respectively the various naval, land and air units. Morin was in charge of supply. Tissier, Dewawrin and Hettier de Boislambert formed my staff. Geoffroy de Courcel acted as my Chef de Cabinet, aide-de-camp, interpreter and—often—wise adviser. Such were the members of that " entourage " which opposing propaganda denounced as a collection of traitors, mercenaries and adventurers. But they, exalted by the grandeur of the task, stuck to me for better and for worse.

To the British services, whose co-operation was then indispensable to us, our affairs were represented by General Spears. He did so with a tenacity and a dexterity of which it is my duty to say that they were, at these harsh early stages, more than valuable—essential. Yet even he did not find things at all easy on the British side. The conventionality of the official hierarchies made them distrust this man who, as Member of Parliament, officer, business man, diplomat and author, belonged to many categories at once without becoming classifiable in any of them. But to speed up routine he brought into play his intelligence, the fear inspired by his biting sallies of wit and, lastly, the charm he knew how to display on occasion. In addition he had for France, which he knew as well as a foreigner can know her, a sort of uneasy, dominating love.

At a time when so many others considered my enterprise an encumbering adventure, Spears had immediately understood its nature and its scope. It was with ardour that he had taken up his mission to deal with Free France and its leader. But his wish to serve them only made him the more jealous of them. If he approved of their independence towards all the others, he resented it painfully when it rose up before him. That is why, in spite of all that he did to help us at the start, General Spears was destined one day to turn away from our enterprise and to begin fighting against it. In the passion he brought to this, was there not regret at not having been able to lead it and sadness at having left it?

But at its birth Free France did not yet meet with the kind of adversaries which success arouses. It merely struggled among the afflictions which are the lot of the weak. My assistants and I worked in St. Stephen's House on the Embankment, in a flat furnished with a few tables and chairs. Later the British administration placed at our disposal a more convenient building in Carlton Gardens, and there our principal centre was installed. There it was that the daily wave of disappointment broke upon us. But there, too, the flood of encouraging news came to raise us above our normal level.

For testimony was flowing in from France. By the most

ingenious routes, sometimes with the connivance of the censors, simple people were sending us letters and messages. One instance was that photograph taken on July 14th in the Place de l'Etoile as the Germans arrived there, showing a group of women and men, sunk in grief, around the tomb of the Unknown Soldier, and sent on July 19th with these words. "De Gaulle! we have heard you. Now we shall wait for you!" Another was that picture of a grave covered with innumerable flowers put there by passers-by; the grave being that of my mother, who had died at Paimpont on July 16th, offering up her sufferings to God for the salvation of the country and her son's mission.

And so we were able to measure the echoes which our refusal to accept the defeat was arousing deep down among the people. At the same time we had proof that, all over the country, people were listening to the London broadcasts, and that through them a powerful means of war was at our disposal. Indeed, the French who resided abroad returned the same echo of the national feeling. Many placed themselves in contact with me as I had asked them to do and formed groups to help Free France. Malglaive and Guéritte in London, Houdry and Jacques de Sieyès in the United States, Soustelle in Mexico, Baron de Benoist at Cairo, Godard at Teheran, Guérin in the Argentine, Rendu in Brazil, Piraud in Chile, Géraud Jouve at Constantinople, Victor at Delhi, Levay at Calcutta, Barbé at Tokyo, and others, took the first initiatives in this respect. I could soon be certain that in spite of pressure from the Vichy authorities, of the calumnies of their propaganda and of the weakness of a great many, it was to Free France that the people turned what remained to it of pride and hope. The thought of what this supreme appeal from the nation laid upon me has never left me since then for an instant in all I have had to undertake and to endure.

In England itself the Free French were surrounded by esteem and sympathy. The King, first of all, was quick to give them proof of these. Each of the members of his family did the same. The Ministers and authorities, for their part, lost no opportunity of expressing their good wishes. But it would be impossible to imagine the generous kindness which the English people everywhere showed towards us. All sorts of charities were formed to help our volunteers. The people who came to offer their services, their time and their money could not be counted. Every time I had to appear in public, it was in the midst of the most comforting demonstrations. When the London papers announced that Vichy was condemning me to death and confiscating my property, quantities of jewels were left at Carlton Gardens anonymously and dozens of unknown widows sent their wedding-rings in order that the gold might serve the work of General de Gaulle.

It should be said that a tense atmosphere enveloped England at that time. The German offensive was expected from one moment to the next and, faced by this prospect, everyone entrenched himself in an exemplary steadfastness. It was a truly admirable sight, to see each Englishman behaving as if the safety of the country depended on his own conduct. This universal feeling of responsibility seemed the more moving because in reality everything was going to depend on the Air Force.

If ever the enemy managed, indeed, to seize the mastery of the sky, England would be done for! The Fleet, bombarded from the air, would not prevent the German convoys from crossing the North Sea. The Army, whose strength was a bare dozen divisions sorely tried by the Battle of France and without equipment, would be incapable of beating back the troops that had been landed. After which, the large German units would have little trouble in occupying the whole land, in spite of the local resistance organised by the Home Guard. Certainly the King and the Government would have left for Canada in time. But the well-informed whispered the names of politicians, bishops, writers and business men who, in this event, would come to terms with the Germans to assure, under their thumb, the administration of the country.

But those were speculations which did not touch the mass of the people. The British as a whole were getting ready to fight to the bitter end. Each man and each woman joined the network of defence. Everything to do with the building of shelters, the distribution of weapons, tools and implements, work in the factories and fields, services, duties and rationing left nothing to be desired as regards ardour and discipline. The only thing lacking was equipment in this country which, like ours, had long neglected to take precautions. But everything went on as if the English intended to make up by devotion for whatever they lacked. Humour, indeed, was not lacking. One newspaper cartoon showed the formidable German Army already in Great Britain, but held up on the road, with its tanks, its guns, its regiments and its general, in front of a wooden barrier. A notice indicated, in fact, that to pass it one must pay a penny. Not having received from the Germans all the required pennies, the Englishman in charge of the toll-gate, a little old man, courteous but inflexible, was refusing to raise the barrier, in spite of the indignation which ran the whole length of the invaders' monstrous column.

Meanwhile, at the alert on its aerodromes, the Royal Air Force was ready. Among the people many, in their desire to emerge from an almost unbearable tension, went so far as to say out loud that they wished the enemy would risk the attack. Foremost among them Mr. Churchill found the waiting hard to bear. I can still see him at Chequers, one August day, raising his fists towards the sky as he cried: " So they won't come! " " Are you in such a hurry," I said to him, " to see your towns smashed to bits? " " You see," he replied, " the bombing of Oxford, Coventry, Canterbury, will cause such a wave of indignation in the United States that they'll come into the war! "

I expressed some doubt about that, reminding him that two months earlier the distress of France had not made America emerge from her neutrality. " That's because France was collapsing! " stated the Prime Minister. " Sooner or later the Americans will come, but on condition that we here don't flinch. That's why I can't think of anything but the fighter Air Force." He added: " You see I was right to refuse it to you at the end of the Battle of France. If to-day it was destroyed all would be lost for you, as well as for us." " But," said I in my turn, " the intervention of your fighters, if on the contrary that had happened, might perhaps have given new life to the alliance and brought about, in France, the continuation of the war in the Mediterranean. In that case the British would be less threatened and the Americans more tempted to engage themselves in Europe and in Africa."

Mr. Churchill and I agreed modestly in drawing from the events which had smashed the West this commonplace but final conclusion: when all is said and done, Great Britain is an island; France the cape of a continent; America another world.

IV. AFRICA

BY AUGUST Free France had some resources, the beginnings of an organisation, a certain popularity. I had to make use of them at once.

In other respects I may have been assailed by perplexities, but there was no doubt in my mind as to the immediate action to be undertaken. Hitler had managed to win the first round, —in Europe. But the second was about to begin, and it would be on a world scale. One day the opportunity might come of winning a decision where one was possible,—that is to say, on the soil of the old continent. Meanwhile it was in Africa that we French must continue the struggle. The course into which I had tried in vain, a few weeks before, to draw the Government and High Command was the one I naturally intended to follow, as soon as I found that all that had remained in the war—of both of them—was embodied in me.

In the vast spaces of Africa, France could in fact re-create for herself an army and a sovereignty, while waiting for the entry of fresh allies at the side of the old ones to reverse the balance of forces. When that happened Africa, being within reach of the peninsulas of Italy, the Balkans and Spain, would offer an excellent base for the return to Europe, and it would be French. What was more, the national liberation, if accomplished one day thanks to the forces of the Empire, would establish links of solidarity between Metropolitan France and the overseas territories. If, on the contrary, the war were to end without the Empire having made any effort to save the mother country, that would be the end, without a doubt, of the work of France in Africa.

It was also to be foreseen that the Germans would carry the war across the Mediterranean, either to cover Europe, or to acquire some territory there, or to help their Italian associates—and possibly Spanish ones too—to increase theirs. Indeed there was fighting going on there already. The Axis aimed at reaching Suez. If we remained passive in Africa, our adversaries would sooner or later annex some of our possessions, while our allies would be led to lay hands, in the course of operations, on such of our territories as were necessary to their strategy.

To take part in the Battle of Africa with French forces and territories was to bring back, as it were, a fragment of France into the war. It was to defend her possessions directly against the enemy. It was, as far as possible, to deflect England—and perhaps one day America—from the temptation to make sure of them on their own account, for their fighting needs and for their advantage. It was, lastly, to wrench Free France free from exile and install her in full sovereignty on national territory.

But where should we start upon Africa? I could expect nothing positive in the immediate future from the Algeria-Morocco-Tunisia block. It was true that at first many messages of adhesion from municipalities, associations, officers' messes and bodies of ex-servicemen had been addressed to me. But resignation had come quickly, while at the same time penalties and censorship were extending, and the tragedy of Mers-el-Kebir stifled the last schemes of resistance. On the spot, too, it was realised, with a certain " cowardly relief," that the armistice left North Africa outside the occupation. French authority was visibly maintained there in a military and unequivocal form which reassured the French residents and yet did not displease the Moslems. Lastly, certain aspects of what Vichy called " the national revolution "—the appeal to men of substance, the importance given to administration, the parades of ex-servicemen, the display of anti-semitism— answered to many people's inclinations. In short, without ceasing to imagine that North Africa might one day " do something," people were settling down to wait and see. No spontaneous movement in the interior was to be counted on.

As for seizing power there by an action coming from outside, obviously I could not think of it.

Coloured Africa presented quite other possibilities. In the first days of Free France the demonstrations which occurred at Dakar, Saint-Louis, Vagaduga, Abidjan, Konakry, Lomé, Duala, Brazzaville and Tananarive, and the messages which reached me from those places, showed that for these new territories where the spirit of enterprise was dominant the continuation of the war appeared self-evident. No doubt the attitude of resignation finally adopted by Noguès, the unfavourable impression produced by the Oran affair and the activity of Boisson (at first Governor-General of Equatorial Africa and then High Commissioner at Dakar), who dissipated in ambiguity the enthusiasm of those under his rule, had diminished the seething of the Africans. Still, the fire was smouldering in most of our colonies.

It was chiefly in the block of our Equatorial territories that prospects were opening. In the Cameroons, especially, the movement of opposition to the armistice extended to all classes. The population, both French and native, of this active and lively country was indignant at the capitulation. Indeed, no doubt was felt there that the victory of Hitler would bring back the German domination suffered before the first world war. General emotion was caused when tracts were passed round, in which some of the former German colonists, who had retired not long before to the Spanish island of Fernando Po, announced their imminent return to positions and plantations. A committee of action had set itself up under M. Mauclère, the Director of Public Works, and had given me its adherence. It was true that the Governor-General, Brunot, bewildered by the turn of events, was refusing to take sides. But it was possible to suppose that a resolute intervention from outside would bring the solution.

In the Chad conditions seemed better still. The Governor, Félix Éboué, had reacted immediately in favour of resistance. This man of intelligence and heart, this coloured man so ardently French, this humanist philosopher, revolted with his whole being against the submission of France and the triumph

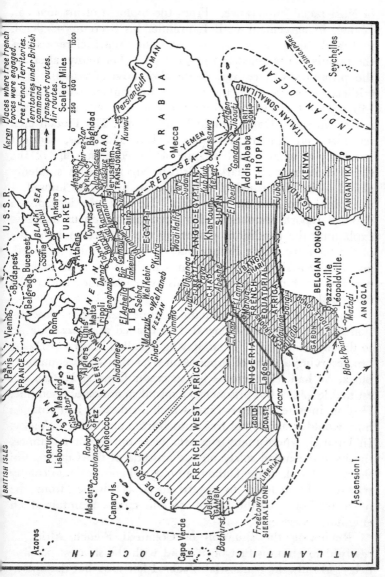

THE BATTLE OF AFRICA AND THE MIDDLE-EAST

of Nazi racial intolerance. From the moment of my first call Éboué, in agreement with Laurentie, his Secretary-General, had made his decision in principle. The French elements and the population inclined to the same side. For many, after all, the promptings of courage were also those of reason. The soldiers, who were at their posts, in contact with Italian Libya, kept the war spirit intact and longed for the reinforcements which de Gaulle might bring them. The French civil servants and traders, like the African chieftains, thought anxiously of what would become of the economic life of the Chad if its normal market, British Nigeria, were suddenly closed to it. Informed of this situation by Éboué himself, I telegraphed to him on July 16th. He sent me, in reply, a detailed report, announcing his intention to join us publicly, explaining the conditions governing the defence and the life of the territory which France had entrusted to him to guard, and finally asking what I was in a position to do to make it possible for him to carry out his responsibilities under the Cross of Lorraine.

In the Congo the situation appeared more obscure. Boisson, the Governor-General, had resided at Brazzaville up to the middle of July. Then, having installed himself at Dakar but reserving a right of supervision over the whole equatorial block, he had left there as his successor General Husson, an estimable soldier but prisoner to a mistaken notion of discipline. Husson, in spite of the grief into which the disaster had plunged him, would certainly not free himself from obedience to Vichy. In Ubangi, where many elements were opting for resistance, the issue depended solely on the attitude of the Congo. On the other hand, in the Gabon, an old and conventional colony traditionally inclined to regard itself as distinct from the other territories of the group, certain circles maintained an enigmatic reserve.

Reviewing the situation of Coloured French Africa, I resolved to attempt first of all, and with the shortest possible delay, to rally the equatorial block. I felt sure that the operation would not require a real engagement of forces, except, probably, in the Gabon. Next, if this first undertaking was a success, I would venture on action in West Africa. But that was an undertaking I could not think of starting on except by a prolonged effort and with considerable resources. ·

The first problem was to go for Fort-Lamy, Duala and Brazzaville. The whole thing would have to be done at one blow and without loosening grip. For Vichy, having control of the ships, aircraft and troops at Dakar, and being able, at need, to call on the forces in Morocco, and even on the Fleet at Toulon, had all the resources required for intervening rapidly. Admiral Platon had indeed been sent by Pétain and Darlan to the Gabon and the Cameroons on a tour of inspection, and had influenced certain military and civilian elements in Vichy's favour. I therefore hurried things on. Lord Lloyd, the British Minister for Colonies, to whom I outlined my plan, understood very well its importance, especially in regard to the security of the British possessions of Nigeria, the Gold Coast, Sierra Leone and Gambia. He gave his governors the instructions I desired and, when the day came, placed an aeroplane at my disposal to transport my team of " missionaries " from London to Lagos.

These were Pleven, Parant and Hettier de Boislambert. They would be required to settle with Éboué, the Governor, the conditions under which the Chad was to join us, and to carry out, with the help of Mauclère and his Committee, the coup d'état in Duala. Just as they were leaving I was able to add to the team a fourth, whose efficiency the future was to show. This was Captain de Hauteclocque. He had just arrived from France through Spain with his head bandaged, having been wounded in Champagne, and pretty tired. He came to report to me, and when I saw what sort of a man I was dealing with I settled his destination at once. It should be the Equator. He had just time to assemble his kit and, under the name of Commandant Leclerc, flew off with the others.

But while hoisting the Cross of Lorraine over the Chad and the Cameroons, it would also be necessary to rally to us the three colonies of the Lower Congo, Ubangi and Gabon, and this would mean, essentially, seizing Brazzaville, the capital of Equatorial Africa, the seat and symbol of authority. This was the task I assigned to Colonel de Larminat. That brilliant and keen officer was then in Cairo. At the end of June, as Chief of Staff to the French Army of the Middle East, he had attempted, without success, to persuade his chief, General Mittelhauser, to continue the struggle, and then had himself organised the departure for Palestine of those elements who did not accept the armistice. But Mittelhauser had succeeded in making them turn back,—helped, indeed, by General Wavell, the British Commander-in-Chief in the Middle East, who was afraid that this exodus might, all in all, bring him more troubles than advantages. Only a few fractions had persevered and reached the British zone. Larminat had been arrested, but had escaped. Making his way to Jibuti, he had there seconded General Legentilhomme in his vain efforts to keep the French Somali coast in the war, and retired after that to Egypt.

There my order to report to London reached him. But on his way he received the further order to proceed to Léopold-ville. In the Belgian Congo he met with discreet but deter-mined support from the Governor-General, Ryckmans, with sympathy from public opinion on his side and, lastly, with active support from the French citizens established in that territory, who were morally grouped together under Dr. Staub. According to my instructions, Larminat was to prepare—from one bank of the Congo to the other—his establishment in Brazzaville, and to co-ordinate action over the whole equatorial block.

When all was ready, Larminat, Pleven, Leclerc and Boislambert, together with Commandant d'Ornano, who had come from the Chad by devious ways, met at Lagos. Sir Bernard Bourdillon, the Governor-General of Nigeria, gave the Free French his active and intelligent support on this occasion, as he was always to do. It was agreed that the Chad should join us to begin with. Next day the Duala business would be carried out. The day after that, that of Brazzaville.

On August 26th, at Fort-Lamy, Éboué, the Governor, and Colonel Marchand, who commanded the troops in the territory, solemnly proclaimed that the Chad was joining General de Gaulle. Pleven had arrived the day before by air, to ratify the event in my name. I announced it myself in a broadcast from London and held up the Chad as an example to the Empire.

On the 27th Leclerc and Boislambert succeeded brilliantly with the *coup de main* in the Cameroons, as planned. And yet they had set out with minute resources. I had at first hoped to obtain for them a military detachment which would make things easier. We had discovered in a camp in England a thousand black sharp-shooters who had been sent from the Ivory Coast during the Battle of France to reinforce certain colonial units and, having arrived too late, were stationed in England, awaiting repatriation. I had agreed with the British that the detachment should go to Accra, where Commandant Parant was to take command of it. It was legitimate to suppose that the return of these coloured troops to Africa would not alarm Vichy. As it turned out, they were landed on the Gold Coast. But they looked so fine that the British officers could not refrain from incorporating them among their own troops. Leclerc and Boislambert, therefore, had at their disposal only a handful of soldiers and a few colonists who were refugees from Duala. Even so, just as they were leaving Victoria, they received from General Giffard, the British Commander-in-Chief, who had suddenly begun to fear the consequences of the operation, an order forbidding them to carry it out. In full agreement with me—I had telegraphed to them that they must act on their own—, they disregarded it and, thanks to the understanding of the British at Victoria, left in native canoes for Duala.

The small band arrived there in the course of the night. A certain number of " Gaullists," who had hastened to the house of Dr. Mauze at the first signal, received it as arranged. Leclerc, having become, as by enchantment, Colonel and Governor, simply occupied the Palais du Gouvernement. Next day, escorted by two companies of the Duala garrison, he arrived by train at Yaunde, where the authorities were. The " transmission " of powers took place there painlessly.

At Brazzaville the business was equally well managed. On August 28th, at the appointed time, Commandant Delange proceeded to the Palais du Gouvernement at the head of his battalion and invited the Governor-General, Husson, to yield. He did so without resistance, though not without protest. The garrison, civil servants, colonists and natives, whose opinion had for the most part been settled in advance under the influence of Médecin-Général Sice, Quartermaster-General Souques, Colonel of Artillery Serres, and Air Lieutenant-Colonel Carretier, accepted the fact with joy. General de Larminat crossed the Congo and immediately took over, in my name, the functions of High Commissioner of French Equatorial Africa with civil and military powers. The same boat which had brought him returned to Léopoldville with General Husson on board.

As for Ubangi, de Saint-Mart, the Governor, who was only waiting for the chance, telegraphed his adhesion as soon as he was notified of what had happened at Brazzaville. However, the Commander of the troops and certain military elements shut themselves up in their barracks and threatened to fire on the town. But Larminat at once came to Bangi by aeroplane and brought these honestly misled men back to their duty. A few officers were, none the less, segregated and sent, at their own request, to West Africa.

And so the greater part of the Equitorial Africa-Cameroons block was attached to Free France without a drop of blood having been shed. Only the Gabon remained detached from the whole. And yet this colony also nearly joined us. At Libreville on August 29th the Governor, Masson, when advised by Larminat of the change of authority, had replied by telegraphing his adhesion. At the same time he publicly proclaimed that the territory was joining us, and notified the commander of the troops.

But at Dakar the Vichy authorities had reacted quickly. Under orders from them, the naval commander at Libreville, who had a sloop, a submarine and several small craft, opposed the Governor and announced the arrival of a squadron. M. Masson then changed his attitude and declared that the decision of the Gabon to join Free France had been the result of a misunderstanding. A naval flying-boat, coming and going between Libreville and Dakar, deported to West Africa those men of note who had " compromised " themselves, and brought to the Gabon officials devoted to Vichy. The situation had been reversed. A hostile enclave, difficult for us to reduce because it gave on to the sea, was thus created within the block of the Equatorial territories. To take advantage of it, Vichy sent to Libreville Air Force General Têtu, with the title of Governor-General of Equatorial Africa and with instructions to re-establish authority all over it. At the same time several Glenn-Martin bombers landed on the aerodrome, and General Têtu put it about that they were only the advance guard of what would soon follow.

Yet on the whole the result was favourable. I drew from it the hope that the second part of the plan for rallying Coloured Africa would likewise succeed.

To tell the truth, this new phase bid fair to be much more arduous. In West Africa the established authority was strongly centralised and, what was more, closely linked with that of North Africa. The military resources there were still considerable. The fortress of Dakar, well armed, equipped with modern works and batteries, supported by several squadrons of aircraft and serving as the base for a naval squadron, including in particular some submarines and the powerful *Richelieu*, whose officers' one dream had been vengeance since the British torpedoes had damaged the ship, constituted a redoubtable defensive and offensive entity. Finally, Governor-General Boisson was a man of energy, whose ambition—greater than his discernment—had made him choose to play on the Vichy side. He proved it as soon as he reached Dakar in the middle of July, by imprisoning Louveau, the administrator-in-chief of the High Volta, who had proclaimed the adherence of that territory to Free France.

With our resources as they were, therefore, I could not think of tackling the place direct. Besides, I considered it essential to avoid a large-scale collision. Not that—alas!— I indulged in illusions about the possibility of achieving the liberation of the country without blood ever being shed between Frenchmen. But at such a moment and on that particular ground, for us to engage in a big battle would, whatever its outcome, have gravely diminished our chances. The course of the Dakar affair cannot be understood if it is not realised that that was the conviction which dominated my mind.

My initial plan therefore ruled out direct attack. The idea was to land at a great distance from the fortress a resolute column, which would proceed towards the objective rallying, as it went, the territories through which it passed and the elements which it encountered. One might hope that in this way the forces of Free France, growing by contagion, would reach Dakar by land. Konakry was the place where I thought of landing the troops. From there one would have the use of a continuous railway and road for the march on the capital of West Africa. But, to prevent the Dakar naval squadron from annihilating the expedition, it was necessary for this to be covered from the sea. I was bound to ask the British Fleet for this cover.

I had confided what I had in mind to Mr. Churchill in the last days of July. He gave me no positive answer straight away, but, some time afterwards, invited me to come and see him. I found him, on August 6th, as usual, in that large room in Downing Street which is used, by tradition, both as the Prime Minister's office and as the place where the Government meets. On the enormous table which fills the room he had had some maps laid out, before which he paced up and down, talking with animation.

"We must," he said to me, "together gain control of Dakar. For you it is capital. For if the business goes well, it means that large French forces are brought back into the war. It is very important for us. For to be able to use Dakar as a base would make a great many things easier in the hard Battle of the Atlantic. And so, having conferred with the Admiralty and the Chiefs of Staff, I am in a position to tell you that we are ready to assist in the expedition. We mean to assign to it a considerable naval force. But we would not be able to leave this force on the coast of Africa for long. The necessity of bringing it back to help in covering England, as well as in our operations in the Mediterranean, demands that we should do things very quickly. That is why we do not agree with your proposal for landing at Konakry and proceeding slowly across the bush,—which would oblige us to keep our ships in the neighbourhood for months. I have something else to propose to you."

Then Mr. Churchill, colouring his eloquence with the most picturesque tints, set to work to paint for me the following picture: "Dakar wakes up one morning, sad and uncertain. But behold, by the light of the rising sun, its inhabitants perceive the sea, to a great distance, covered with ships. An immense fleet! A hundred war or transport vessels! These approach slowly, addressing by radio messages of friendship to the town, to the Navy, to the Garrison. Some of them are flying the tricolour. The others are sailing under the British, Dutch, Polish or Belgian colours. From this Allied force there breaks away an inoffensive small ship bearing the white flag of parley. It enters the port and disembarks the envoys of General de Gaulle. These are brought to the Governor. Their job is to convince him that, if he lets you land, the Allied fleet retires, and that nothing remains but to settle, between him and you, the terms of his co-operation. On the contrary, if he wants a fight, he has every chance of being crushed."

And Mr. Churchill, brimming over with conviction, described and mimed, one by one, the scenes of the future, as they spurted up from his desire and his imagination:

"During this conversation between the Governor and your representatives, Free French and British aircraft are flying peacefully over the town, dropping friendly leaflets. The military and the civilians, among whom your agents are at work, are discussing passionately among themselves the advantages offered by an arrangement with you and the drawbacks presented, on the contrary, by a large-scale battle fought against those who, after all, are the Allies of France. The Governor feels that, if he resists, the ground will give way under his feet. You will see that he will go on with the talks till they reach a satisfactory conclusion. Perhaps meanwhile he will wish, ' for honour's sake,' to fire a few shots. But he will not go farther. And that evening he will dine with you and drink to the final victory."

Stripping Mr. Churchill's idea of the seductive ornaments added to it by his eloquence, I recognised, on reflection, that it was based on certain solid data. Since the British could not divert important naval forces to the Equator for long, a direct operation was the only means to be envisaged for making myself master of Dakar. This, short of taking on the character of a full-dress attack, was bound to involve some mixture of persuasion and intimidation. At the same time I judged it probable that the British Admiralty would be led, one day or another, with or without the Free French, to settle the question of Dakar, where the existence of a great Atlantic base and the presence of the *Richelieu* could not fail to arouse in it both desire and uneasiness.

I concluded that, if we were present, there would be some chances of the operation becoming an adherence, though perhaps a forced one, to Free France. If, on the contrary, we abstained, the English would want, sooner or later, to operate on their own account. In this case the place would resist vigorously, using the fortress guns and the artillery of the *Richelieu*, while the Glenn-Martin bombers, the Curtiss fighters, the submarines,—very dangerous for ships which were not, at that time, provided with any means of detection,—would hold any transport armada at their mercy. And even if Dakar, crushed by shellfire, were finally forced to surrender with its ruins and its wrecks to the British, there would be reason to fear that the operation would end to the detriment of French sovereignty.

After a short delay, I returned to Mr. Churchill to tell him that I accepted his suggestion. I worked out the plan of action with Admiral John Cunningham, who was to command the British squadron, and whom I was to find, during this painful affair, sometimes troublesome to work with, but an excellent sailor and a man of feeling. At the same time I organised the resources,—very meagre they were!—which we

French would be able to engage in the enterprise. They consisted of three sloops: the *Savorgnan de Brazza*, the *Commandant Duboc* and the *Commandant Dominé*, and two armed trawlers: the *Vaillant* and the *Viking*. There were, also,—on board two Dutch liners, the *Pennland* and *Westerland*, since we had none, at the time, that was French,—a battalion of the Foreign Legion, a company of recruits, a company of Marines, the personnel of a tank company, that of an artillery battery, and finally some embryo services: in all, a couple of thousand men. There were, in addition, the pilots of two air squadrons. Lastly, there were four French cargo boats, the *Anadyr*, *Casamance*, *Fort-Lamy* and *Nevada*, carrying the heavy material: tanks, guns, Lysander, Hurricane and Blenheim aircraft in cases, vehicles of various kinds, and some victuals.

As for the British, their squadron was not destined to include all the ships of which Mr. Churchill had spoken at first. It was finally composed of two old-fashioned battleships —the *Barham* and the *Resolution*, four cruisers, the aircraft carrier *Ark Royal*, some destroyers and a tanker. In addition, three transports would bring, in case of need, two battalions of Marines under the command of Brigadier Irwin, with apparatus for landing. On the other hand, a Polish brigade, which at first was to have taken part in the affair, had been dropped. It looked as if the General Staffs, less convinced than the Prime Minister of the importance, or else of the chances, of the enterprise, had whittled down the resources envisaged at the start.

A few days before we set sail, a bitter discussion was raised by the British about what, in case of success, I intended to do with a very important stock of gold which was at Bamako. This was bullion deposited there by the Bank of France on its own account and for the Belgian and Polish national banks. The reserves and deposits of the Bank of France had, in fact, at the moment of the German invasion, been in part evacuated to Senegal, while another portion had been placed in safety in the vaults of the Federal Reserve Bank, and the balance was on its way to Martinique. Through blockade, across frontiers, between guard posts, the Bamako gold was being watched attentively by the intelligence services of the various belligerents.

The Belgians and the Poles desired, very legitimately, that their share should be given to them, and I gave M. Spaak and M. Zaleski the appropriate assurances. But the British, who of course laid no claim to the ownership of any of it, intended, none the less, to use this gold as a means of paying directly for their purchases in America, alleging that they were doing so in the interests of the coalition. At this period, in fact, the United States was selling nothing to anybody that was not paid for in cash. In spite of the insistence of Spears, and even of his threat that I might see the British give up the expedition which had been agreed on, I rejected this claim. In the end it was conceded, as I had suggested from the first, that the French gold at Bamako should be used to cover only that part of the purchases in America which England would be obliged to make on behalf of Fighting France.

Before we embarked, the news of the adherence of the Chad, the Cameroons, the Congo and Ubangi had come, just in time to enliven our hopes. Even should we not succeed in laying hold of Dakar, at least we counted on organising in the centre of Africa, thanks to the reinforcements we were bringing, a base for action and sovereignty for belligerent France.

The expedition left Liverpool on August 31st. I myself, with part of the French units and a small staff, was on board the *Westerland*, which flew the French flag beside the Dutch, and whose commander (Captain Plagaay), officers and crew were to prove, like those of the *Pennland*, models of friendly devotion. Spears accompanied me, delegated by Churchill as liaison officer, diplomat and informant. In England I left our forces in course of formation under the orders of Muselier, an embryo administration under the direction of Antoine, and, in the person of Dewawrin, an element of liaison and direct information. In addition, General Catroux was expected shortly from Indo-China; and in a letter which was to be handed to him as soon as he arrived I explained to him my projects as a whole and what I had in mind for him. I reckoned that, in spite of my absence, and provided it did not last long, the reserves of wisdom accumulated by my companions would prevent internal quarrels and intrigues from outside from shaking the still very fragile edifice too profoundly! None the less, on the deck of the *Westerland*, after leaving the port in the middle of an air-raid warning with my small troop and my tiny ships, I felt crushed, as it were, by the dimensions of duty. Out in the open, in black night, on the swell of the ocean, a poor foreign ship, with no guns, with all lights extinguished, was carrying the fortunes of France.

Our first destination was Freetown. According to the plan, we were to regroup there and collect the latest information. We did not arrive there till September 17th, having sailed at the slow speed of our cargo boats and made a wide détour into the Atlantic to avoid German aircraft and submarines. During the voyage, radiograms received from London had given us a piece of news about the Vichy forces which might well lead to everything being reconsidered. On September 11th three large modern cruisers, the *Georges-Leygues*, *Gloire* and *Montcalm*, and three light cruisers, the *Audacieux*, *Fantasque* and *Malin*, having started from Toulon, had passed the Straits of Gibraltar without being stopped by the British Fleet. But hardly had we anchored at Freetown, when a new and grave piece of information completed our perplexity. The squadron, reinforced at Dakar by the cruiser *Primauguet*, had just weighed anchor and was heading southwards at full speed. A British destroyer, detached to watch it, was keeping in touch with it at a distance.

I could have no doubt that this powerful naval force was bound for Equatorial Africa, where the port of Libreville was open to it, and where it would find it easy to re-take Pointe-Noire and Duala. If such a thunder-clap did not suffice to reverse the situation in the Congo and Cameroons, these magnificent ships could easily cover the transport and landing of forces of repression from Dakar, Konakry or Abidjan. The hypothesis was confirmed, indeed, almost immediately, when the cargo vessel *Poitiers*, coming from Dakar and bound for

Libreville, having been hailed by the British, was scuttled by her captain. It was clear that Vichy was starting a large-scale operation to re-establish itself in the territories which had rallied to Free France, and that the despatch of seven cruisers towards the Equator was conceivable only with the full consent, if not at the orders, of the Germans. Admiral Cunningham fell in with my view that the Vichy squadron must be stopped at once.

We agreed that the intruders should receive the injunction to return, obviously not to Dakar, but to Casablanca. Failing this, the British squadron would open hostilities. We felt sure, indeed, that the threat would suffice to make these errant ships change course. For if the speed of the British ships—which was notably inferior—did not permit them to intercept those of Vichy, their power—which was double—would assure them the advantage over the others, as soon as these were obliged to moor in some Equatorial roadstead undefended by any battery. The aggressor would then have either to give in or to accept battle in unfavourable conditions. The chances that the leader of the expedition would let himself be reduced to such a choice were slight.

In fact, the British cruisers which made contact with Admiral Bourraguet, the commander of the untimely squadron, had no difficulty in making it change course when its leader learned, to his complete surprise, of the presence of a Franco-British fleet in the region. But the Vichy ships, defying all pursuit, made straight for Dakar. Only the cruisers *Gloire* and *Primauguet*, which were slowed down by engine trouble, and with which Commander Thierry d'Argenlieu, now on board the destroyer *Ingerfield*, got into direct touch on my behalf, submitted to the terms and went to Casablanca, after declining my offer of repairs at Freetown.

In this way Free French Africa escaped a very great danger. This fact alone justified over and over again the expedition we had fitted out. At the same time, the behaviour of the squadron that had come from Toulon, setting course for the Equator as if we were not there, then renouncing its mission the moment it perceived that we were, suggested that Vichy was not sure of our real destination. But after congratulating ourselves on having made our adversaries' plan come to nothing, we had to admit that our own was gravely compromised. In fact, the Dakar authorities were henceforward on their guard and had received a most valuable reinforcement of ships. We learned almost at once, through our intelligence agents, that to serve the shore batteries naval gunners had been substituted for the men of the colonial artillery, who were considered less reliable. In short, our chances of occupying Dakar appeared, from now on, very small.

In London Mr. Churchill and the Admiralty reckoned that, in these circumstances, it was better to do nothing. They had telegraphed this to us as early as September 16th, proposing that the fleet should simply escort our vessels as far as Duala and then move on elsewhere. I must say that to give up in this way seemed to me the worst possible solution. In fact, if we left everything at Dakar as it was, all Vichy would have to do, to resume its attempt on Equatorial Africa, would be to wait for the British ships to return northwards, as they soon would. With the sea open to them, Bourraguet's cruisers would swoop once more towards the Equator. In this way the combatants under the Cross of Lorraine, including General de Gaulle, would sooner or later be mewed up in these distant territories and, even if they did not succumb to it, would be absorbed by a sterile struggle carried on against other Frenchmen in the bush and forest. No prospect for them, in these conditions, of fighting Germans or Italians. I had no doubt that those were the intentions of the enemy, of which the Vichy puppets inevitably made themselves the instruments, conscious or not. It seemed to me that, at the stage things had now reached, we ought in spite of everything to try to enter Dakar.

Besides, I must admit that the adherences already obtained in Africa had filled me with a secret hope, confirmed by the good news which, since we had left London, had come from elsewhere. On September 2nd the French Settlement of Oceania, under the provisional government of MM. Ahne, Lagarde and Martin, had joined Free France. On September

9th Governor Bonvin proclaimed that the French Settlements in India were placing themselves at our side. On September 14th, at Saint-Pierre and Miquelon, the Ex-Servicemen's General Assembly sent me its formal adhesion, after which the British Government urged the Canadian Government to support their movement. On September 20th Governor Sautot, having himself brought New Caledonia over on July 18th, had gone by my orders to Nouméa. There the " De Gaulle Committee," presided over by Michel Verges, had made itself master of the situation with the enthusiastic support of the population, and this allowed Sautot to take over the government. Lastly, I had seen Bourraguet's squadron turn about at the first summons. Who could be sure that we would not find at Dakar that mood of consent to which the most formal instructions adjust themselves? In any case, we must try.

Admiral Cunningham reacted in the same way. We telegraphed to London arguing, most pressingly, that we should be allowed to attempt the operation. Mr. Churchill, as he told me later, was surprised and enchanted by this insistence. He willingly consented and the action was decided on.

Before starting, however, I was subjected to an energetic intervention by Cunningham, who claimed to take me and my modest forces under his orders, and offered me, in compensation, hospitality on his flagship, the *Barham*. I declined, of course, both the demand and the invitation. That evening there were some stormy passages on board the *Westerland*, where the interview took place. In the course of the night, the Admiral wrote me a note full of cordiality, giving up his claims. We weighed anchor on September 21st. At dawn on the 23rd, in the midst of a very thick fog, we were before Dakar.

The fog was bound to compromise our enterprise seriously. In particular, the moral effect which, according to Churchill, the sight of our fleet was to produce upon the garrison and population would not come into play at all, since not a thing was to be seen. But postponement was obviously impossible.

The plan as prepared was therefore put into execution. At six o'clock I addressed the Navy, the troops and the inhabitants by radio, announcing our presence and our friendly intentions. Immediately afterwards two small " Lucioles," French touring aircraft, unarmed, took off from the deck of *Ark Royal*: they were to land at the aerodrome of Ouakam and there set down three officers—Gaillet, Scamaroni and Soufflet—with a fraternisation mission. In fact, I quickly learned that the " Lucioles " had landed without difficulty, and that the signal " Success ! " was displayed on the airfield.

Suddenly ack-ack fire was heard at various points. Some of the guns of the *Richelieu* and of the fortress were firing at the Free French and British machines which were beginning to fly over the town, dropping friendly leaflets. And yet, sinister though this cannonade might be, it seemed to me to have something hesitant about it. I therefore gave the order to the two pinnaces with the spokesmen on board to enter the port, while the Free French sloops, together with the *Westerland* and *Pennland*, approached in the mist as far as the entrance to the roads.

There was at first no reaction. Commander d'Argenlieu, Major Gotscho, Captains Becourt-Foch and Perrin and Sub-Lieutenant Porgès ordered their boats to be moored, landed on the quay, and asked for the port commander. When he presented himself, d'Argenlieu told him that he was the bearer of a letter from General de Gaulle for the Governor-General, which letter he was instructed to deliver to him personally. But the port commander, with unconcealed embarrassment, informed the spokesmen that he had orders to have them arrested. At the same time he showed his intention of calling the guard. Seeing which, my envoys returned to the pinnaces. As these drew away, some machine-guns opened fire on them. D'Argenlieu and Perrin were brought on board the *Westerland*, seriously wounded.

Thereupon, the Dakar batteries began aiming at the British and French ships an intermittent fire which for several hours remained without reply. The *Richelieu*, having been moved within the harbour by tugs so that its guns might be put to better use, began firing in its turn. Towards eleven, the cruiser *Cumberland*, having been badly hit, Admiral Cunningham addressed this message by radio to the fortress: " I am not firing on you. Why are you firing on me? " The reply was: " Retire to twenty miles' distance! " Upon which, the British in their turn sent some broadsides. Meanwhile time was passing without a sign, on one side or the other, of real fighting ardour. No Vichy aeroplane had taken off up to midday.

From these indications as a whole I did not draw the impression that the place was determined on a desperate resistance. Perhaps the Navy, Garrison and Governor were waiting for something to happen which could serve them as pretext for conciliation? Towards noon, Admiral Cunningham sent me a signal to let me know that this was his feeling too. Certainly, there could be no thought of getting the squadron into the harbour. But would it not be possible to land the Free French somewhere near the fortress, which they would then attempt to approach by land? This alternative had been considered in advance. The small port of Rufisque, outside the range of the works, seemed suitable for the operation, provided always that this did not meet with determined resistance. In fact, while our sloops could reach Rufisque, our transports could not, because of their draught. The troops would therefore have to be disembarked by lighter, which would deprive them of their heavy weapons and make complete peace essential. However, having received from Cunningham the assurance that he was covering us from the sea, I set all in motion towards Rufisque.

Towards 3 p.m., still in the fog, we arrived at the spot. The *Commandant Duboc*, with a section of marines on board, entered the port and sent some sailors ashore in a boat to prepare the berthing. On shore a crowd of natives was already running up to welcome the patrol, when the Vichy troops in position in the neighbourhood opened fire on our sloop, killing and wounding several men. A few moments earlier, two Glenn-Martin bombers had flown over our little force at a low altitude, as if to show it that they held it at their mercy

—which was indeed the case. Lastly, Admiral Cunningham signalled that the cruisers *Georges Leygues* and *Montcalm* had left Dakar roads and were in the mist at a mile's distance from us, and that the British ships, occupied elsewhere, could not protect us from them. Decidedly, the affair was a failure! Not only was the landing not possible, but, what was more, a few shots fired by the Vichy cruisers would be enough to send the whole Free French expedition to the bottom. I decided to make for the open again, which was done without further incident.

We passed the night on tenterhooks. Next morning the British Fleet, having received from Mr. Churchill a telegram inviting it to push on actively with the affair, addressed an ultimatum to the Dakar authorities. They replied that they would not surrender the place. From then on, the day was spent by the British in exchanging a rather lively cannonade with the shore batteries and ships in the roads, firing blind in the mist, which was thicker than ever. By the end of the afternoon, it seemed evident that no decisive result could be obtained.

As evening fell, the *Barham* came up quite close to the *Westerland*, and Admiral Cunningham asked me to come and see him, to discuss the situation. On board the British battleship the atmosphere was gloomy and strained. They were sorry, certainly, not to have succeeded. But the dominant feeling was that of surprise. The British, being practical people, could not understand how and why the authorities, naval forces and troops at Dakar expended such energy upon fighting against their compatriots and against their Allies, at a time when France lay beneath the invader's boot. As for me, I had from that moment given up being astonished at it. What had just happened showed me, once for all, that the Vichy rulers would never fail to misuse, against the interests of France, the courage and discipline of those who were in subjection to them.

Admiral Cunningham summed up the situation. " Given," he declared, " the attitude of the place and of the squadron supporting it, I do not think bombardment can result in a solution." General Irwin, who commanded the landing units, added " that he was ready to send his troops ashore to assault the fortifications, but that it must be clearly understood that this would mean a great risk for each boat and each soldier." Both of them asked me what would become of the Free France " movement " if an end were put to the expedition.

" Up to now," I said, " we have not made an all-out attack on Dakar. The attempt to enter the harbour peaceably has failed. Bombardment will decide nothing. Lastly, a landing against opposition and an assault on the fortifications would lead to a pitched battle which, for my part, I desire to avoid and of which, as you yourselves indicate, the issue would be very doubtful. We must, therefore, for the moment, give up the idea of taking Dakar. I propose to Admiral Cunningham that he should announce that he is stopping the bombardment at the request of General de Gaulle. But the blockade must be maintained in order not to allow the ships now at Dakar their liberty of action. Next, we shall have to prepare a fresh attempt by marching against the place by land, after disembarking at undefended or lightly defended points, for instance at Saint-Louis. In any case, and whatever happens, Free France will continue."

The British admiral and general fell in with my view as regards the immediate future. In the falling night I left the *Barham* on board a launch which danced on the waves, while the officers and crew, drawn up along the hand-rails, sadly gave me a ceremonial send-off.

But during the night two facts were to make Admiral Cunningham go back on what we had agreed. First, a fresh telegram from Mr. Churchill expressly called upon him to pursue the enterprise. In it the Prime Minister showed astonishment and irritation at the idea of the affair coming to nothing,—the more so because, already, political circles in London and, above all, in Washington, were beginning to grow agitated, impressed by the Vichy and Berlin radios. At the same time, the fog was lifting, and this at once seemed to give the bombardment another chance. The fighting therefore began again at dawn,—this time without my having been consulted,—with an exchange of gunfire between the fortress and the British. But towards evening the battleship *Resolution*, torpedoed by a submarine and in danger of sinking, had to be taken in tow. Several other British ships had been badly hit. Four aircraft from the *Ark Royal* had been shot down. On the other side, the *Richelieu* and various other ships had taken some hard punishment. The destroyer *Audacieux*, the submarines *Persée* and *Ajax* had been sunk; a British destroyer had managed to pick up the latter's crew. But the stalwarts of the fortress still went on firing. Admiral Cunningham decided to cut the losses. I could not but agree. We headed for Freetown.

The days which followed were cruel for me. I went through what a man must feel when an earthquake shakes his house brutally and he receives on his head the rain of tiles falling from the roof.

In London a tempest of anger, in Washington a hurricane of sarcasms were let loose against me. For the American Press and many English newspapers it was immediately a matter of course that the failure of the attempt was due to de Gaulle. "It was he," the echoes repeated, "who thought of this absurd adventure, misled the British by imaginative reports on the situation at Dakar, and insisted, quixotically, that the place be attacked when the reinforcements sent by Darlan made any success impossible. . . . Besides, the cruisers from Toulon had come only as the result of the incessant indiscretions of the Free French, which had put Vichy on the alert. . . . Once for all, it was clear that no reliance could be placed on people incapable of keeping a secret." Soon Mr. Churchill, too, was roughly handled for having, so it was said, so easily let himself be carried away. Spears, with a long face, kept bringing me telegraphed reports from his correspondents suggesting it as probable that de Gaulle in despair, abandoned by his partisans, dropped by the British into the bargain, would renounce all activity, while the British Government would take up afresh with Catroux or Muselier, on a much more modest scale, the recruitment of French auxiliaries.

As for the Vichy propaganda, it triumphed without

restraint. The Dakar communqués gave the impression that the thing had been a great naval victory. Innumerable messages of congratulation, addressed to Governor-General Boisson and to the heroic fighters of Dakar, were published and commented upon by the newspapers of both zones and by the so-called " French " radios. And I, in my narrow cabin, in a harbour crushed by the heat, was completing my education in what the reactions of fear could be, both among adversaries taking revenge for having felt it and among allies suddenly alarmed by a set-back.

However, it very soon became clear to me that, in spite of their reverse, the Free French remained unshakeable. Among the men of our expedition—and I visited them as soon as we had anchored,—not one wished to leave me. On the contrary, all of them had been hardened by the hostile attitude of Vichy. So it happened that, when an aeroplane from Dakar came and flew over our ships at anchor, a furious fusillade greeted it from every vessel,—which would certainly not have been the case a week before. Soon warm telegrams came from Larminat and Leclerc, to tell me that, for them and those about them, resolute loyalty was less than ever in doubt. From London no defection was reported to me, in spite of the tumult of bitter reproaches now breaking against our people. This confidence on the part of all those who were linked to me, gave me powerful comfort. It meant that the foundations of Free France were indeed solid. Come! We must go on! Spears, his serenity somewhat restored, quoted to me Victor Hugo: " Le lendemain, Aymeri prit la ville."

It must be said that in London, if ill-will was active, the Government on the contrary had managed to avoid it. Mr. Churchill, although he himself was being strongly harassed, did not disown me any more than I disowned him. On September 28th, in the House of Commons, he gave an account of what had happened, with all the objectivity that could be expected, and declared that " all that had happened had only strengthened His Majesty's Government in the confidence they extended to General de Gaulle." It is true that at that moment the Prime Mininster knew, although he was unwilling to say, how the squadron from Toulon had managed to pass the Straits of Gibraltar. He told me himself when, two months later, I returned to England.

A telegram sent from Tangier by Captain Luizet, a French intelligence officer who had secretly joined Free France, had given London and Gibraltar news of the movement of the Vichy ships. But this message had arrived at a time when the bombing of Whitehall by German aircraft kept the personnel in the cellars for hours on end and so led to a prolonged dislocation of the work of the staff. The deciphering of the message took place too late for the First Sea Lord to be able to warn the fleet at Gibraltar in time. Much worse! When the Vichy naval attaché at Madrid had himself, in all innocence(?), warned the British attaché and the admiral in command at Gibraltar had thus been given the alarm from two different sources, nothing had been done to stop the dangerous ships.

The Prime Minister's public attitude towards the " Gaullistes " helped greatly to allay the agitation in Parliament and in the newspapers. But in spite of everything, the Dakar affair was destined to leave in the hearts of the British a wound which remained raw, and in the minds of the Americans the idea that, if one day they themselves had to land on territory held by Vichy, the action should be carried out without Free French and without British.

For the time being, in any case, our British Allies were determined not to renew the attempt. Admiral Cunningham told me expressly that we must give up the idea of resuming the affair in any way whatever. All he himself could do now was to escort me as far as the Cameroons. We headed for Duala. On October 8th, when the French vessels were about to enter the estuary of the Wouri, the British saluted them and made for the open.

The enthusiasm, however, which broke over the town as soon as the *Commandant Duboc*, on board which I had made the passage, entered the port of Duala, was extreme. Leclerc was there, waiting for me. After the review of the troops, I went to the Palais du Gouvernement, while the troops that had come from England were disembarking. The civil servants, French colonists and native leaders, with whom I made contact, were swimming in a full tide of patriotic optimism. They forgot, however, no part of their special problems, of which the chief one was that of keeping up the export of the territory's produce and of bringing in what was needed to live on and was not to be found there. But, above anxieties and differences of opinion, the moral unity of the Free French, whether they had joined up in London or rallied to the cause in Africa, was instantly apparent.

This identity of nature between all those who took their stand beneath the Cross of Lorraine was to be, from then on, a sort of permanent factor of the enterprise. No matter where, and no matter what happened, one could now know in advance, to all practical purposes for certain, what the " Gaullistes " would think and how they would behave. For example, the enthusiastic emotion I had just encountered: I was to find it again always, in all circumstances, as soon as the crowd was present. I must say that for me its result was to be a perpetual bondage. The fact of embodying for my comrades the fate of our cause, for the French multitude the symbol of its hope, and for foreigners the image of a France indomitable in the midst of her trials, was to dictate my bearing and to impose upon my personality an attitude I could never again change. For me this meant, without respite, a stubborn self-supervision as well as an extremely heavy yoke.

For the moment what counted was to keep the whole of French Equatoria going and mobilise it to take part in the battle of Africa. My intention was to establish, on the borders of the Chad and Libya, a Sahara theatre of operations, ready for the day when the evolution of events would permit a French column to seize the Fezzan and debouch from there upon the Mediterranean. But because of the desert and the unparalleled difficulties of communication and supply, it would not be possible to devote to this more than limited and specialised effectives. I therefore wished at the same time to send to the Middle East an expeditionary force which would join up with the British there. The distant objective for everyone was French North Africa. However, it was first necessary to liquidate the hostile enclave in the Gabon. At Duala, on October 12th, I gave the necessary orders.

While this painful operation was preparing, I left the Cameroons to visit the other territories. I went first to the Chad, after a short stop at Yaunde. The career of the leader of Free France and of those accompanying him nearly came to an end in the course of this journey. For the Potez 540 which was taking us to Fort-Lamy had engine trouble, and it was a marvel that it managed to land, without too much damage, in the middle of a swamp.

In the Chad I found an atmosphere of tense excitement. Everyone had the feeling that the beam of history had just lighted upon this land of merit and suffering. Nothing, certainly, could be achieved there except by supreme effort, so heavy were the servitudes imposed by the distances, by isolation, by the climate, by lack of means. But, to make up for this, that heroic mood in which great actions germinate was already abroad there.

Éboué received me at Fort-Lamy. I could feel he was giving me his loyalty and confidence, once for all. At the same time I noted that he was sufficiently large-minded to embrace the vast plans with which I wanted to associate him. He formulated views full of common sense, yet never raised objections to risk or effort involved. And yet, for the Governor, nothing less was involved than undertaking an immense job of creating communications, to make the Chad capable of receiving from Brazzaville, Duala and Lagos, and then of transporting right to the frontiers of Italian Libya, all the material and all the supplies which the Free French forces would require for carrying on active warfare. The territory would have, by its own means, to blaze or to maintain 4,000 miles of tracks. In addition, it would be necessary to develop the country's economy, in order to feed the fighting men and workers and to export produce to cover the costs. The task was all the more difficult because a good many of the colonists and civil servants were going to be mobilised.

With Colonel Marchand, commander of the troops in the Chad, I flew as far as Faya and the desert posts. There I found troops who were resolute but terribly short of supplies. There were, by way of mobile elements, only some camel units and a few motorised sections. And so, when I told the officers that I was counting on them to seize the Fezzan one day and reach the Mediterranean, I could see stupor plain upon their faces. Some German and Italian raids, which they would have plenty of trouble in repulsing if they came, seemed to them much more probable than the far-reaching French offensive whose prospect I outlined. Not one of them, indeed, showed any hesitation about continuing the war, and already the Cross of Lorraine had been hoisted everywhere.

Meanwhile, farther to the west, in the territories of the Niger and the Sahara oases, the comrades of these officers, of the same stuff as they were, and posted, like them, on the borders of Libya, but not having above them, anywhere in the hierarchy, a single leader who dared break the spell, were holding themselves ready to fire on anyone who should claim to lead them to fight against the enemies of France! Among all the moral torments inflicted on me by the culpable errors of Vichy, none made me suffer more than the spectacle of this stupid sterility.

To set against this, I was to find, on my return to Fort-Lamy, a signal encouragement. It was brought to me by General Catroux. When he had arrived in London, after my departure for Africa, certain experts on ulterior motives imagined that the British would try to make themselves an alternative trump card out of this full general accustomed to big posts, while certain sticklers for etiquette wondered if he himself would consent to serve under a mere brigadier. He had seen Churchill more than once, and there was much chatter about these interviews, in the course of which it did seem that the Prime Minister had in fact suggested to him that he should take my place—doubtless not with the idea that he should try his hand at it, but with the classic objective of dividing in order to rule. A few days before Dakar, Churchill had all of a sudden telegraphed to me that he was sending Catroux to Cairo to work upon the Levant, where there was

hope of some favourable opportunity arising. I had reacted
sharply, not against the idea, which certainly did not seem to
me a bad one, but because the initiative required my approval
first. Churchill had then given a satisfactory explanation, on
the ground of urgency.

And now here was Catroux, arrived from Cairo. At the
meal, I raised my glass in honour of this great leader, for
whom I had always had feelings of deferential friendship. He
answered, in a very noble and very simple way, that he placed
himself under my direction. Éboué and all those present recognised, not without emotion, that for Catroux de Gaulle was,
from now on, outside the ladder of rank and invested with a
duty that knew no hierarchy. No one made any mistake about
the weight of the example thus given. When, after determining
with him his mission, I parted from General Catroux near the
aircraft which was taking him back to Cairo, I felt he was
going away greater than he had come.

At Brazzaville, where I arrived on October 24th, things
were looked at, on the whole, with the same conviction as at
Duala and at Fort-Lamy. But they were looked at level-
headedly. That was natural for the " capital." The administration, the general staff, the services, business circles and the
missions measured the difficulties which the Equatorial
territories—the poorest in the whole Empire—would have to
surmount in order to live for years cut off from the Mother
Country and to support the war effort. Some of their products
—oil, rubber, timber, cotton, coffee, hides—would indeed be
easy to sell to the British and the Americans. But as there
were no factories, nor indeed any minerals apart from a little
gold, the total exports would not make it possible to balance
all that would have to be bought abroad.

To second Larminat in this field, I appointed Pleven
Secretary-General. When he had got the machine running,
he would go to London and Washington to settle the questions
of exchange and payments. His capabilities, supported by
Larminat's authority, turned out to be most efficient. Admini-
strators, planters, traders and carriers, seeing that there was a
great deal to do and that it was worth while, started upon that

period of intense activity which was to transform the life of the Equatorial territories profoundly, even in the midst of war. The journey I made at the end of October to Ubangi, where I was welcomed by Governor de Saint-Mart, and then the one which took me to Pointe-Noire, administered by Daguin, made it possible for me to give, on the spot, the impulse for which all were waiting.

Finally, on October 27th, I went to Léopoldville, where the authorities, Army and people, as well as the French residents in the Belgian Congo, gave me a most moving reception. Governor-General Ryckmans, who, like me, was cut off from his native land, but wanted his country to take part in the war, was in sympathy with Free France. And indeed Free France was a protection to the Belgian Congo against the spirit of capitulation which had come near to investing it from the north. Ryckmans was destined, all the way through, to maintain close relations with his French neighbour on the other bank of the Congo. It may be noted that it was the same with their British colleagues, Bourdillon in Nigeria and Huddleston in the Sudan. Instead of the rivalries and intrigues which had formerly set the neighbours at loggerheads, there was established between Lagos, Duala, Brazzaville, Léopoldville and Khartoum a personal solidarity among governors, which was a weighty factor in favour of the war effort and of maintenance of order in Africa.

Meanwhile all had been made ready for ending the Gabon affair. Before my arrival at Duala, Larminat had already taken the first steps. Under the orders of Commandant Parant a few troops, raised in the Congo, had advanced as far as Lambaréné, on the Ogowe. But they had been stopped by resistance from the Vichy forces. At the same time a small column, sent from the Cameroons and commanded by Captain Dio, was besieging the post at Mitzic. At Lambaréné and Mitzic, " Gaullists " and Vichyists were in contact and were exchanging a few shots, and plenty of arguments. Sometimes a Glenn-Martin from Libreville would come and drop a few bombs and a great many leaflets on our men. A "Bloch 200 " from Brazzaville would do the same, next day, to the other side. These dragging, aching hostilities offered no solution.

As soon as I arrived I had decided to have Libreville captured directly, and had determined the plan of action. There could unfortunately be no doubt that serious resistance would be put up to our forces. General Têtu, whose headquarters were at Libreville, had at his disposal four battalions, some artillery, four up-to-date bombers, the sloop *Bougainville* and the submarine *Poncelet*. He had mobilised a certain number of colonists. Besides, the instructions he had received obliged him to fight. To prevent him from receiving reinforcements, I had had to ask Mr. Churchill if he would agree to warn Vichy that, if this happened, the British Fleet would oppose it. Following my telegram, Admiral Cunningham had come to see me at Duala. We had settled that his ships should not take part directly in the Libreville operation, but that they should station themselves out at sea to prevent the Dakar people from again sending their cruisers, if this should by any chance be their intention. For our part, we looked forward to the affair with heavy hearts, and I announced, in the midst of a general assent, that there would be no mentions in despatches for anyone on this painful occasion.

On October 27th the post at Mitzic was taken. On November 5th the garrison at Lambaréné laid down its arms. Immediately afterwards the vessels carrying the column bound for Libreville left Duala. Leclerc was in over-all command; Koenig was at the head of the land troops: a Legion battalion, and a mixed colonial battalion of Senegalese and colonists from the Cameroons. The landing took place at La Mondah Point during the night of November 8th, and some rather violent fighting broke out on the 9th in the approaches to the town. On the same day, under the direction of Commandant de Marmier, several of the Lysander aircraft, which we had brought in cases from England and which had been hastily assembled at Duala, flew over the field and dropped some bombs. It was then that d'Argenlieu, on board the *Savorgnan de Brazza*, followed by the *Commandant Dominé*, entered the roadstead, where the *Bougainville* lay. In spite of messages of friendship, repeated many times by our men, the *Bougainville* opened fire. The *Brazza's* reply set her on fire. During this time the Legion was breaking the resistance of the Vichy elements on the aerodrome. D'Argenlieu having conveyed to General Têtu a message urging him to stop fighting, the surrender was concluded. Koenig occupied Libreville. Parant, whom I had appointed Governor of the Gabon, took up his post. There were, alas! some twenty killed.

On the previous day the submarine *Poncelet*, having left Port-Gentil and met with one of Cunningham's cruisers out at sea, had fired a torpedo at it. Attacked with depth-charges, the submarine surfaced, and while the crew was being picked up by the British her commander, Capitaine de Corvette de Saussine, scuttled his ship and went down bravely with her.

There remained the task of occupying Port-Gentil. This was done on November 12th, after long discussions but without resistance from the fortress. The only victim of this final operation was Governor Masson, who, after having brought the Gabon over to us in August, had later retreated. The poor man, in despair at this error and its consequences, had taken up his quarters on board the *Brazza* after the capture of Libreville, and had landed at Libreville in order to ask the administrator and garrison not to open, on their side, a fratricidal struggle. This action had helped to prevent calamity. But M. Masson, worn out by the nervous torments he had just been through, hanged himself in his cabin in the course of the return journey.

I went to Libreville on November 15th, and to Port-Gentil on the 16th. The dominant feeling among the population was satisfaction at being out of an untenable situation. At the hospital I visited the wounded of both sides, who were being cared for side by side. Then I had the cadres of the Vichy units presented to me. A few elements joined Free France. The majority, who had been made by their chief to give their word that they would "remain faithful to the Marshal," preferred intern-ment. They waited for the re-entry of North Africa into the war before going back to service, and from that moment, like many others, did their duty valiantly. General Têtu was entrusted to the hospitality of the Fathers of the Holy Spirit and, later, transferred to the Hospital at Brazzaville. From there, in 1943, he, too, left for Algiers.

The Dakar, Vichy and Paris radio indulged in furious insults, after having, a few weeks earlier, exaggerated its cries of triumph. I was accused of having bombarded, burned and pillaged Libreville, and even of having shot the notables, beginning with the Bishop, Monseigneur Tardy. It seemed to me that, by inventing such lies, the Vichy people wished to cover some infamous action. At the time of the Dakar affair they had arrested the three Free French airmen who had been landed unarmed on the Ouakam airfield, and later Boislambert, Bissagnet and Kaouza, whom I had sent secretly into the town, together with Dr. Brunel, to spread the good word there. Of these " missionaries " Brunel alone had managed, after the fighting, to get out again into British Gambia. The accusations hurled by Dakar made me think that perhaps the people there were proposing to take vengeance on the prisoners. The more so since when, with the necessary discretion, I had a proposal conveyed to Boisson for exchanging these against Têtu and his officers, the Dakar broadcasts had immediately made my move public, with many outrageous and provocative statements. I then warned the Vichy High Commissioner that I had enough of his friends in my hands to answer for the life of those Free French whom he held in prison. The tone of the opposing radio was lowered instantly.

For the rest, various signs revealed the disorder into which the Vichy rulers were being thrown by what had happened. The sort of base optimism, into which the armistice had plunged them, had rapidly dispersed. Contrary to what they had announced in order to justify their capitulation, the enemy had not finished off England. At the same time, the rallying of several colonies to de Gaulle, then the Dakar affair, and finally that of the Gabon, made it evident that, even if Free France did know how to use the radio, it was something quite other than " a handful of mercenaries grouped round a microphone." All at once people in France were beginning to catch sight of a refuge that was truly French, while the

Germans were compelled to include in their calculations the growing difficulties which would be caused for them by resistance. Deep in Africa, I could perceive the jolts which this state of affairs was already giving to the behaviour of the Vichy people.

On the morrow of Dakar, violence had been their first reaction. Aircraft from Morocco had dropped bombs on Gibraltar. But immediately afterwards an attempt was made at appeasement. Telegrams from Mr. Churchill and Mr. Eden informed me of conversations which had been opened, on October 1st at Madrid, by M. de la Baume, the Ambassador, with his British colleague, Sir Samuel Hoare. The object was to persuade the British to let cargoes coming from Africa pass over to France, on the strength of a guarantee that the Germans would not get hold of them. But in addition M. de la Baume declared, on behalf of Baudouin, that " if the enemy seized these supplies, the Government would be transferred to North Africa, and France would resume the war by the side of the United Kingdom."

While noting the disarray revealed by such declarations, I had put the British on their guard. It was hard to see how people who had themselves placed the State under the enemy's law and condemned those who wanted to fight, could suddenly become the champions of resistance because the invader helped himself to a few supplies over and above those which he was taking every day. In fact, in spite of the efforts made by the London Government to encourage Vichy in the good intentions of which it was making a display, in spite of the personal messages addressed to the Marshal by the King of England and by the President of the United States, in spite of the contacts made by the British with Weygand, now installed at Algiers, and with Noguès, still in Morocco, all illusion was soon to disappear under German pressure. On October 24th there took place the meeting between Pétain and Hitler at Montoire. Vichy's collaboration with the enemy was officially proclaimed. Finally, in the first days of November, Vichy put an end to the Madrid negotiations.

From now on, obvious reasons ordained that I should deny

to the Vichy rulers, once for all, the right of legitimacy, should constitute myself the trustee of the interests of France, and should exercise in the liberated territories the attributes of a government. The Republic was the source of this provisional power, as also the objective I assigned to it, and I proclaimed my obedience and responsibility towards the sovereign people, engaging myself solemnly to render account to it as soon as it should have regained its liberty. I determined this national and international position on October 27th at Brazzaville, in French territory, by means of a manifesto, two ordinances and an " organic declaration " which, taken together, were to constitute the charter of my activity. I believe I never departed from it until the day, five years later, when I remitted to the representatives of the nation the powers I had assumed. At the same time I set up the Defence Council of the Empire, designed to aid me with its advice, and made members of it, at the start, Catroux, Muselier, Cassin, Larminat, Sicé, Sautot, d'Argenlieu and Leclerc. Finally, I laid down, once for all, in a note addressed to the British Government on November 5th, the attitude which Free France was adopting, and which she invited her Allies to take, towards both the Vichy Government and its pro-consuls such as Weygand and Noguès, of whom some obstinate optimists were trying to believe that they would one day move over into action against the enemy.

On the whole, if our African enterprise had not attained all the results at which it had aimed, at least the basis of our war effort was solidly established, from the Sahara to the Congo, and from the Atlantic to the basin of the Nile. In the first days of November I set up the Command which was to direct activities there. Éboué, appointed Governor-General of French Equatorial Africa, had his headquarters at Brazzaville, with Marchand as commander of the troops. Lapie, summoned from London, became Governor of the Chad, and Administrator Cournarie Governor of the Cameroons, where he replaced Leclerc. The latter, in spite of the objections dictated to him by his desire to go on with what he had begun at Duala, was sent to the Chad to command the Sahara operations, in which he was destined to make the harsh and disturbing acquaintance of glory. Finally, Larminat, as High Commissioner with civil and military powers, was to guide the whole.

Before leaving for London, I laid down with him the plan of action for the next months. Our aim was, on the one hand, to set in motion the first motorised and air raids against Murzuk and Kufra. We aimed, at the same time, at sending to Eritrea a mixed brigade and also a bomber group, which would take part in the fighting against the Italians. This latter expedition would be the beginning of French intervention in the Middle East campaign. But it was also necessary to recruit, officer and arm the elements which would go, as and when ready, to reinforce these advance guards, both in the Sahara and on the Nile. It is impossible to imagine what efforts were to be required, in the immensities of Central Africa, under the Equatorial climate, for the mobilisation, training, equipping and transport of the forces which we meant to create and send into battle at colossal distances. It is impossible to measure, either, what prodigies of activity all concerned were to bring to this.

On November 17th I left Free French Africa for England, via Lagos, Freetown, Bathurst and Gibraltar. As, under the autumnal rain, the aircraft skimmed the ocean, I pictured the incredible détours by which, in this strange war, the Fighting French must henceforth pass to get at the Germans and the Italians. I sized up the obstacles which barred their way, and the greatest of which—alas!—were raised against them by other Frenchmen. But at the same time I encouraged myself with the thought of the ardour which the national cause was exciting among those who were free to serve it. I thought of all there was to exalt them in an adventure whose dimensions were those of the earth. Harsh though the realities might be, perhaps I would be able to master them, since it was possible for me, in the phrase of Chateaubriand, " to lead the French there by dreams."

V. LONDON

In London, as that winter began, fog had settled about men's minds. I found the British strained and depressed. Certainly they thought with pride of how they had just won the air battle, and how the risks of invasion had greatly diminished. But, as they cleared their ruins, other terrors were swooping down upon them and upon their poor Allies.

The submarine war was raging. With growing anxiety the British people saw German submarines, aircraft and raiders effecting the destruction of the ships on which depended the course of the war and even the level of rations. For the Ministers and services the one question was " shipping." Tonnage became an obsession, a tyrant dominating everything. The life and glory of England were staked, every day, upon the sea.

In the East, active operations were beginning. But the Mediterranean, owing to Vichy's defection, was becoming inaccessible to the slow British convoys. The troops and material which London was sending to Egypt had to go round the Cape, following a sea-route as long as half-way round the world. What was sent there from India, Australia and New Zealand likewise arrived only after interminable journeys. At the same time the mass of raw materials, armaments and food-stuffs—sixty million tons in 1941,—which Great Britain imported for her industry, her Armies and her population, could no longer come to her except from a long way away, from America, Africa or Asia. It required a colossal tonnage, sailing in zig-zags over immense distances, ending up in the narrow neck of the Mersey or the Clyde, and demanding considerable escort forces.

British uneasiness was all the heavier because on no side did happy prospects lie open. Contrary to what many English people had hoped, the bombing of their towns and the victory of the Royal Air Force did not decide America to come in. Certainly public opinion in the United States was hostile to Hitler and Mussolini. At the same time, President Roosevelt, as soon as he was re-elected on November 5th, strengthened his efforts to draw America towards intervention both by his diplomatic activity and by his public statements. But the official attitude of Washington was still neutrality, which indeed was imposed by law. Therefore, during this dark winter, the British had to pay for their purchases in the United States in gold and foreign exchange. Even such indirect help as the President's casuistic cleverness contrived to give them was the object of lofty reprobation in Congress and in the Press. In short the British, at the rate of payments imposed by their needs, saw the moment approaching when, for want of cash, they would no longer be able to receive what they required for fighting.

As regards Soviet Russia, no crack was to be seen in the bargain which bound her to the Reich. On the contrary, after two journeys by Molotov to Berlin, a Germano-Russian trade agreement, concluded in January, was to give powerful aid in the feeding of Germany. Meanwhile, in October, 1940, Japan had signed the Tripartite Pact, and so proclaimed her menacing solidarity with Berlin and Rome. At the same time the unity of Europe under German hegemony seemed to be becoming a reality. Hungary, Roumania and Slovakia adhered to the Axis in November. Franco met Hitler at San Sebastian and Mussolini at Bordighera. Lastly Vichy, unable to maintain even the fiction of independence granted to it by the armistice, was entering into effective collaboration with the invader.

With the horizon dark outside, very heavy burdens were pressing on the British people within. Mobilisation was sending off twenty million men and women to the armies, to

148

the factories, to the land, to the public services and to passive
defence. For everybody consumption was rigorously limited,
and the courts dealt with the black market, as and when it
arose, with extreme severity. At the same time the enemy's
air activity, though no longer aiming at decisive results, continued nevertheless, harassing the ports, industry and railways,
all of a sudden crushing Coventry, the City of London, Portsmouth, Southampton, Liverpool, Glasgow, Swansea, Hull,
and so on, keeping the inhabitants on the alert night after
night, wearing out the first-aid and defence teams, compelling
a multitude of poor people to leave their beds and go down
to the cellars, to the shelters and even, in London, to the
underground stations. At this close of 1940 the British,
besieged in their island, felt they were at the darkest part of
the tunnel.

The many trials that the British were undergoing did not
make our relations with them easier. Concentrated as they
were on their own preoccupations, our special problems seemed
to them ill-timed. Indeed, the fact that we complicated things
for them made them all the more inclined to absorb us. It
would, in fact, have been more convenient for them, from the
administrative as well as from the political point of view, to
treat the Free French as elements incorporated in the British
forces and services, rather than as allies full of ambitions and
claims. Besides, during this period when the war was
settling down and at the same time destitution threatened, there
was not much inclination, in governing circles in London, to
innovate, or even to settle anything. In the midst of pressing
but insoluble problems, general staffs and ministries fell
naturally into the system of pending questions and disputed
functions, while the Government, under fire from critics in
Parliament and in the Press, had difficulty in taking agreed
decisions. " You know," Churchill said to me one day, " what
a coalition is. Well! the British Cabinet is one."

Nevertheless, Free France had need of everything, and
urgently. After the improvisations of the summer and autumn
and before the fresh enterprises which I had decided to set
going in the spring, we had to obtain from the British what

was indispensable, while maintaining towards them a resolute independence. From this state of things, frequent friction was bound to arise.

All the more so since the shifting and composite character of our organisation justified, to some extent, the circumspection of the British, while at the same time it made their attempts to interfere easier. It was inevitable that Free France, recruited in haste, man by man, should not at once find its internal balance. In London each of its categories—Army, Navy, Air, Finance, Foreign Affairs, Colonial Administration, Information, liaison with France—formed itself and functioned with a strong desire to do well. But experience and cohesion were cruelly lacking. Besides, the adventurous spirit of certain individuals, or simply their inability to conform to the rules and obligations of a public service, imparted some rude jolts to the machine. So it was that, during my absence in Africa, André Labarthe had left our administration and Admiral Muselier had fallen foul of the other services. Some bitter personal conflicts and office tragi-comedies had arisen at Carlton Gardens, scandalising our volunteers and worrying our Allies.

As soon as I got back at the end of November, I set to work to put people and things in their place. But hardly had I begun this reorganisation when I found myself up against a startling error on the part of the British Government, itself led astray by " Intelligence."

The siege fever with which England was then afflicted made information and security organisations increase and multiply there. " Intelligence," which to the British is a passion quite as much as a service, had obviously not failed to thrust out antennæ in the direction of Free France. On this it employed both some who were well-meaning and others who were not. In short, at the instigation of certain undesirable agents, the British Cabinet was suddenly to inflict on Free France a wound which just missed being disastrous.

In the evening of January 1st, when I was in Shropshire with my family, Mr. Eden sent me a request to come and see him urgently at the Foreign Office, where he had recently replaced Lord Halifax, now appointed Ambassador to the United States. I went straight there the next morning. As he welcomed me, Eden showed signs of being deeply disturbed. " Something lamentable," he said, " has occurred. We have just had proof that Admiral Muselier is secretly in touch with Vichy, that he attempted to transmit the plan of the Dakar expedition to Darlan at the moment when it was being prepared, and that he is planning to hand over the *Surcouf* to him. The Prime Minister, as soon as he heard, gave the order to arrest the Admiral. It has been approved by the Cabinet. Muselier is therefore in prison. We have no illusions about the impression this dreadful affair will make on your people and on ours. But it was impossible for us not to act without delay."

Mr. Eden then showed me the documents on which the accusation was based. They consisted of typed notes on the headed paper and with the stamp of the French Consulate in London,—still occupied by a Vichy official,—and apparently signed by General Rozoy, formerly head of the Air Mission and recently repatriated. These notes gave an account of information allegedly supplied by Admiral Muselier to Rozoy. The latter was supposed to have passed them on to a South American legation in London, from which they were to reach Vichy. But on their way, according to Mr. Eden, certain clever " Intelligence " agents had intercepted the documents. " After a thorough inquiry," he added, " the British authorities were, alas! forced to believe in their authenticity."

Though dumbfounded at first, I immediately had the feeling that " it was laid on a bit too thick " and that the thing could only be a huge mistake arising from some machination. I said so clearly to Mr. Eden and told him that I was going to see for myself what there might be in it, and that, meanwhile, I was treating this extraordinary affair with every possible reserve.

Not, however, at first, going so far as to imagine that the affair could have been staged under cover of a British service, I attributed it to Vichy. Might not some of Vichy's henchmen have manufactured and left in England this delayed-action bomb? After forty-eight hours of inquiry and reflection, I went to see the British Minister and said to him: "The documents are ultra-suspect, both in their context and in their supposed source. In any case, they are not proofs. Nothing justifies the shocking arrest of a French vice-admiral. Besides, he has not been heard. I myself am not allowed to see him. All this is unjustifiable. For the moment, at the very least, Admiral Muselier must come out of prison and be treated honourably until this dark business has been cleared up."

Mr. Eden, though disconcerted, did not consent to give me satisfaction, alleging the seriousness of the inquiry made by the British services. In a letter, then in a memorandum, I confirmed my protest. I visited Admiral Sir Dudley Pound, First Sea Lord, and invoking the admirals' international, invited him to intervene in this dishonouring quarrel picked with one of his peers. As the result of the steps I had taken, the attitude of the British authorities showed some hesitation. And so I obtained permission, as I had demanded, to go and see Muselier at Scotland Yard, not in a cell but in an office, without guard and without witnesses, in order to demonstrate to everyone, and to tell him, that I rejected the imputation of which he was victim. Finally, certain indications having led me to think that two individuals, who had been incorporated in our own "security service" during my time in Africa, in French uniform but at the insistence of the British, had had something to do with the affair, I sent for them and became convinced, at the sight of their terror, that this was decidedly an "Intelligence business."

To General Spears, summoned by me on January 8th, I formally confirmed my certainty. I told him that I gave the British Government twenty-four hours in which to set the Admiral free and make reparation to him, failing which all relations between Free France and Great Britain would be broken off, whatever might be the consequences. That same day Spears came, crest fallen, to tell me that the error was admitted, that the "documents" were simply fakes, that the men to blame had confessed and that Muselier was coming out of prison. Next day, the Attorney-General visited me, told me that legal proceedings were being instituted against the authors of the machination, in particular several British officers, and asked me to appoint someone to follow the inquiry and the trial in the name of Free France ; which I did. That afternoon at Downing Street Mr. Churchill and Mr. Eden, obviously much put out, expressed to me the British Government's excuses and its promise to repair, in regard to Muselier, the insult which had been done him. I must say this promise was kept. Indeed, the reciprocal change of attitude on the part of the British and of the Admiral was so complete that it soon turned out to be excessive, as will be seen later.

I will not conceal that this lamentable incident, by setting in relief the element of precariousness always present in our situation relative to our Allies, did not fail to influence my philosophy on the question of what should definitely be our relations with the British State. However, the immediate consequences of the trouble were not all bad. For the British, no doubt desirous of making up for their error, showed themselves more disposed to discuss with us the matters awaiting settlement.

So it was that, on January 15th, I signed with Mr. Eden a " jurisdiction " agreement concerning the Free French in British territory and especially our own courts, which would operate " in accordance with the national military legislation." At the same time we were able to open negotiations with the British Treasury with a view to a financial, economic and monetary agreement. Cassin, Pleven and Denis were charged, on our side, with these negotiations, which achieved their aim on March 19th.

The problems which we had to resolve in this connection were such that it was essential for us to break out from the practice of hand-to-mouth expedients. How were we to make viable, as a whole, the territories that had rallied to us in Africa and Oceania,—we who had not yet a bank, or a currency, or transport or communications, or commercial representation recognised abroad? How keep up the forces of

Free France, dispersed as they were all over the world? How balance the value of the material and services supplied to us by our allies and that of those we supplied to them? Under the terms of the agreement it was understood that every payment, whatever its purpose, should be effected in London between the British Government and General de Gaulle, and not arranged haphazard with the local French authorities. The rate of exchange adopted was 176 francs to the pound,— that is to say, the same as that which was in force before the armistice concluded by Vichy.

Pursuing the same policy, we were led, a little later, to set up the " Caisse centrale de la France Libre." This Bank was to effect all payments out—clearances, salaries, purchases, and so on—and to receive all payments in—contributions from our territories, advances from the British Treasury, gifts from French people abroad, etc. It became, at the same time, the only bank of issue for Free France, anywhere in the world. Thus, while their rallying to de Gaulle bound all our elements together morally, their administration also was now strongly centralised. Because there were, in our midst, no budgetary and economic fiefs, any more than there were political and military ones, and because at the same time England forbade all local intervention by financial means, unity was established over the whole, improvised and dispersed though it was to the last degree.

And yet, while consolidating our overseas base, it was of Metropolitan France that we were chiefly thinking. What to do there? How? With what? We had at our disposal no means of action in France and could not even see where to start on the problem, but this did not prevent us from being obsessed by the largest schemes in the hope that the country would support them massively. And so we had in mind nothing less than an organisation which would enable us, at one and the same time, to give light to the Allied operations by means of our intelligence about the enemy, to rouse within the country resistance in all fields, to equip forces there which, at the right time, would take part in the battle for liberation at the enemy's rear, and, finally, to prepare the national regrouping which, after victory, would set the country going again. In addition we wanted this manifold contribution by Frenchmen to the common war effort to be made so as to benefit France, and not be divided up into services rendered directly to the Allies.

But clandestine action was a field entirely new to us all. No preparations had ever been made in France with a view to the situation into which the country had been hurled. We knew that the French intelligence service was still active to some extent at Vichy. We were not unaware that the Army Staff was trying to keep certain stocks of material out of the hands of the armistice commissions. We suspected that various military elements were trying to make arrangements on the assumption that hostilities might be resumed. But these fragmentary efforts were being carried on apart from us, on behalf of a régime whose *raison d'être* consisted precisely in not using them, and without the authorities ever seeking or accepting the least contact with Free France. In short, there was nothing in Metropolitan France to which our action could attach itself. The service which was to operate on this special field of battle would have to be drawn out of the void.

There was not, certainly, any shortage of applicants round about me. By a sort of obscure foresight of nature's, it happened that in 1940 part of the adult generation was set, in advance, towards clandestine action. Between the two wars the young had shown a marked taste for stories of the Deuxième Bureau, secret service, detection, and even sabotage and conspiracy. Books, newspapers, the theatre and the cinema had devoted themselves largely to the adventures of more or less imaginary heroes who were prodigal of shadowy exploits in the service of their country. This psychology was destined to make recruitment for special missions easier. But it involved, also, the risk of introducing into them romanticism, irresponsibility, and sometimes fraud, and these would be the most dangerous reefs. In no field were there to be more applications for jobs, or more need for those in responsible positions to show themselves sober as well as bold.

Luckily there were some good ones. Commandant

Dewavrin, known as Passy, was their chief. Passy had had no preparation for this unprecedented mission. But in my eyes this was preferable. As soon as he was appointed, indeed, a sort of cold passion for his job took hold of him, which was destined to sustain him along a dark road where he was to be mixed up with both the best there was and the worst. All through that daily drama, the action within France, Passy, seconded by Manuel and later by Vallon, Wybot, Pierre Bloch, and others, kept the ship afloat in face of a succession of alarms, intrigues and disappointments. He himself proved capable of resisting his disgust and guarding against conceit, the familiar demons of this kind of activity. That is why, whatever changes the " Bureau Central de Renseignements et d'Action " [B.C.R.A.] had to undergo in the light of experience, I kept Passy where he was, through thick and thin.

The most urgent thing was to install an embryo organisation within the national territory. The British, for their part, would have liked to see us simply send over agents with instructions to gather, in isolation, information about the enemy with reference to defined objectives. Such was the method used for espionage. But we meant to do better. Since the action in France would be carried on in the midst of a population which would, we thought, be teeming with well-wishers, we meant to set up networks. By binding together hand-picked elements and communicating with us through centralised means, these would give the best return. The first experiments were made by d'Estienne d'Orves and Duclos, who landed on the Channel coast, by Fourcault, who went in through Spain, and by Robert and Monnier, who came from Tunisia to Malta and were sent on into North Africa. Shortly afterwards Rémy, in his turn, began that career as a secret agent in which he was to show a kind of genius.

Then began the struggle on this hitherto unknown battlefield. Month after month, or rather moon after moon, for many operations were dependent on the luminary of night, the B.C.R.A. set its work in motion: recruitment of fighters for the clandestine war; orders to be given to the missions; reports to be gone through; transport by trawler, submarine, aircraft; routes through Portugal and Spain; parachute landings; making contact with those ready to help in France; comings and goings for inspection and liaison; radio communications, couriers and agreed signals; work with the Allied services which formulated the requests from their Staffs, supplied the material, and made things easier or complicated them as the case might be. Later on, this action was to grow wider and to include the armed groups within the country and the resistance movements with their multiple activities. But we were not yet at that stage, during this dark winter!

Meanwhile we had to work out a *modus vivendi* with the English, which would make it possible for the B.C.R.A. to operate and at the same time to remain national. That was indeed a tricky business. Certainly the British understood the advantages to be gained from the help given by the French from the intelligence point of view—the only one which interested them at first. But direct contacts were what the British bodies concerned were chiefly seeking. A regular competition therefore started immediately, with us appealing to the moral and legal obligation of Frenchmen not to join a foreign service, and the British using the means at their disposal to try and gain for themselves agents, and then networks, of their own.

As soon as a Frenchman arrived in England, unless he was somebody well known, he was confined by " Intelligence " in the " Patriotic School " buildings and invited to join the British Secret Services. It was only after a whole series of remonstrances and requests that he was allowed to join us. If, however, he had yielded, he was kept away from us and we would never see him. Even in France, the English used equivocation to recruit their auxiliaries. " De Gaulle and Great Britain are the same thing! " was the line. As for the material means, for which we were almost entirely dependent on our Allies, we sometimes obtained them only after obstinate bargaining. To what friction this behaviour led is obvious. It is true that, if the British often went near the limit, they never went beyond it. At the right moment they put the brake on and yielded, at least partially, to our firmness. Then would follow a period of useful collaboration,—until, suddenly, fresh storms rumbled.

But what we were trying to do could only be of some value, in this respect as in the others, if French opinion was with us. On June 18th, when I broadcast for the first time in my life and imagined, with a certain dizziness, the women and men who were listening-in, I realised what a part was going to be played in our enterprise by broadcast propaganda.

The British, among other merits, had that of immediately discerning, and of using in masterly fashion, the effect which a free radio was capable of producing upon imprisoned peoples. They had at once begun to organise their French propaganda. But in that, as in everything else, although they sincerely desired to reinforce the national response aroused by de Gaulle and Free France, they also claimed the right to profit by it while keeping the control in their own hands. As for us, we intended to speak only on our own account. For my part, it goes without saying that I never admitted any supervision, nor even any foreign advice, over what I had to say to France.

These different points of view shook down together into a practical compromise, according to which Free France had the use of the wavelengths for five minutes twice every day. At the same time, and independently of us, the well-known team " Les Français parlent aux Français " worked under the direction of M. Jaques Duchesne, a Frenchman employed by the B.B.C. Several Free French, such as Jean Marin and Jean Oberlé, took part in it with my approval. It was, indeed, understood that the team would keep in close liaison with us, which was in fact for a long time the case. I must say that the talent and effectiveness of this group decided us to give it all the help we could. We did as much, indeed, for the review " France Libre," which owed its existence to the initiative of MM. Labarthe and Raymond Aron. We treated in the same way the " Agence Française Indépendante " and the newspaper *France*, run respectively by Maillaud (known as Bourdan) and by M. Comert, with the direct support of the British

Ministry of Information but without being in any way attached to us.

Things went on like this, with a few incidents, as long as the interests and policies of England and Free France remained parallel. Later there arose crises in which the propagandists of " Les Français parlent aux Français," the " Agence Française Indépendante " and the newspaper *France* did not take up our quarrel. It is true that through the wireless station at Brazzaville we always had the means of making public what appeared to us useful. Our modest African radio had, in fact, functioned actively from the beginning, and I myself used it often. But we wanted to enlarge it and increase its coverage. The necessary apparatus was ordered in America. To get it we had not only to wait a long time and pay a great many dollars, but also to outwit a great deal of intrigue and forced bidding in the United States. It was not until the spring of 1943 that the small installation that was part of the heroic beginnings was relieved, on the Congo, by the powerful Fighting France station.

The importance we attached to our brief broadcasts from London will be understood. Every day the man who was to speak in our name entered the studio imbued by the sense of his responsibility. As is well known, it was Maurice Schumann who did so most often. With what talent, is also well known. About once a week I spoke myself, with the moving impression that I was accomplishing, for the millions who were listening to me in dread through frightful jamming, a sort of priestly duty. I based my broadcasts on very simple elements: the course of the war, which was demonstrating the error of the capitulation; the national pride which, on contact with the enemy, was stirring men's souls profoundly; and lastly, the hope of victory and of a new greatness for " our lady France."

And yet, favourable though the effect produced might be, we were forced to recognise that, in both zones, opinion inclined to passivity. Certainly people listened in to " the London radio " with satisfaction, often even with fervour. The Montoire interview had been criticised severely. The students' demonstration in Paris, when they went on November 11th to the Arc de Triomphe in procession behind two rods—" deux gaules "—and were broken up by the Wehrmacht with rifle and machine-gun fire, sounded a moving and encouraging note. The temporary dismissal of Laval looked like an official impulse towards recovery. On January 1st, as I had asked, a large part of the population, above all in the occupied zone, had stayed at home, emptying the streets and squares, for an hour: " the hour of hope." But no sign led one to suppose that French people in appreciable numbers were resolved on action. The enemy, wherever he was, ran no risk in our country. As for Vichy, few were those who contested its authority. The Marshal himself remained very popular. A film, which had reached us, of his visits to the principal towns of the Centre and of the South gave obvious proofs of this. At bottom, the great majority wanted to believe that Pétain was playing a deep game and that, when the day came, he would take up arms again. The general opinion was that he and I were secretly in agreement. In the last resort, propaganda had, as always, only slight value in itself. Everything depended on events.

For the moment, what mattered was the battle of Africa. Free France was beginning to figure in it. As early as July 14th I had got into direct touch with General Wavell, British Commander-in-Chief in the Middle East, to ask him to group the French elements in his zone into properly-formed units and to send them as reinforcements to General Legentilhomme at Jibuti. Then, when it became clear that the French Somali Coast was submitting to the armistice, I had obtained Wavell's agreement that the Marine Infantry Battalion, which had joined us in Cyprus in June and had been completed by some of the French in Egypt, should take part in the first offensive carried out by the English in Cyrenaica in the direction of Tobruk and Derna. In France and outside, many patriots had thrilled when they heard that, already on December 11th, Commandant Folliot's brave battalion had distinguished itself in the battle of Sidi-Barrani. But the great effort, now, was to bring a division—alas! a light one—to the Red Sea from

Equatorial Africa, and to arrange for it to take part, as such, in the operations.

It was in Eritrea and Ethiopia that the British command wished to bring force to bear, in the spring, so as to liquidate the army of the Duke of Aosta before starting anything else on the shores of the Mediterranean. Whatever the distances, I intended that a first French echelon should take part in the action. On December 11th and 18th I had given Larminat and Catroux the necessary instructions. They involved the Foreign Legion half-brigade, a Senegalese battalion from the Chad, a company of marines, a tank company, an artillery battery and some rearward services, the whole placed under the orders of Colonel Monclar. Already a squadron of Spahis, brought from Syria in June, 1940, by Commandant Jourdier, and a few airmen, some of whom had come from Rayak with Captain Dodelier, the others from Tunisia with Lieutenants Cornez and de Maismont, were fighting side by side with the British. I had had arrangements made for transporting the Legion brigade to Port Sudan, with Wavell's agreement; the tanks and artillery were to follow, likewise by sea. As for the Chad battalion, it had left Khartoum quite simply by field tracks, using small local lorries. It was, indeed, destined to arrive without trouble, in spite of the ominous predictions of experienced Africans, and, as early as February 20th, to be engaged near Kub-Kub under Commandant Garbay and to win a signal success. Later, four other Senegalese battalions joined these leading elements and formed, with them, an appreciable battle unit. At the same time a French bombardment group, equipped with Blenheim machines which we had brought from England, was to be sent to Khartoum. Lastly, the gallant sloops *Savorgnon de Brazza* and *Commandant Duboc* were on their way to the Red Sea.

How much more important the French part in the battle of Abyssinia would have been, if the French Somali Coast, with its garrison of ten thousand well-armed men and its port of Jibuti, railhead of the Addis Ababa railway, had become belligerent again! Therefore, while pressing on with the despatch of troops towards Ethiopia, I wanted to try to bring this French colony over. Now at Jibuti, after some thoughts of refusing the armistice, they had submitted to Vichy's orders. But would perhaps the fact that, in that very region, a battle was being joined with the enemy, and that Frenchmen were arriving to take part in it, bring about a change of attitude? If so, Jibuti was the place where the troops of Free France should be landed, in order to combine them with the garrison there. From that moment a really important French force would be able to take the offensive, starting from there and joining its efforts with that of the British. If, on the contrary, the Somali Coast did not consent to rally, the Free French expedition would fight alone side by side with the British.

In London our Allies agreed to this programme. I instructed General Legentilhomme to try to bring his old troops at Jibuti into the fight, and in any case to command those that were being or would be sent to the Red Sea from Equatorial Africa. He left at once for Khartoum. To General Catroux and General Wavell I defined the conditions within which Legentilhomme and the forces under his orders were to act. At the same time I begged Mr. Churchill to make the best of the French initiative, of which at first he appeared to be fighting shy.

While we were trying to reinforce the action of the British forces in the Middle East, we were opening on the frontiers of the Chad and Libya a strictly French front. This, to tell the truth, with very feeble resources and over immense expanses. But we could depend only on ourselves there, and I regarded it as essential that it should be so.

Since his arrival in the Chad, Lerclerc, under the orders of High Commissioner Larminat, who gave him all he could, had been preparing with extreme activity the first operations ordered in the desert. In January, with Lieutenant-Colonel d'Ornano, who was killed in this affair, he thrust out a brilliant reconnaissance, in which a British patrol from the Nile had joined, as far as the Italian post at Murzuk. At the end of January, at the head of a carefully-formed column supported by our aircraft, Leclerc hurled himself at the Kufra oases, a thousand kilometres away from his bases. During several weeks of manœuvring and of fighting, he attacked the Italians in their posts, repelled their mobile troops and, on March 1st, made the enemy surrender.

At the same moment the rapid advance of the British in Libya seemed able to offer us still larger prospects. This is why, on February 17th, I ordered General de Larminat to prepare for the conquest of the Fezzan. The later course of events in Libya was destined to prevent us from carrying this out at the time. But Leclerc and his Saharans were, from now on, keyed up towards this main objective. I had been led, meanwhile, to define the position of France in relation to that of the British concerning the future of Kufra and the Fezzan. We would remain at Kufra, although the oases had formerly been attached to the Anglo-Egyptian Sudan. One day, when the Fezzan had been conquered by us, and provided that England recognised our right to stay there, we would be able to evacuate Kufra.

And yet, whatever the British and, with them the Free French, might do, the strategic initiative still belonged to the enemy. The direction taken by the war depended on him. In default of being able to invade England, would he come flooding over North Africa through Suez and Gibraltar? Or would he wish to settle accounts with the Soviets? In any case there were signs that he was about to start one or other of these enterprises. Whatever might happen, the arrangement we had drawn up made it possible, we thought, for Free France to engage profitably what forces she had. But in addition, and in spite of the terrible weakness amid which we struggled, I was determined, in face of each of the problems which the new offensive by Germany and her allies would set the world, to speak in the name of France and to do so suitably.

In November, 1940, Italy had attacked Greece. On March 1st, 1941, the Reich forced Bulgaria to join the Axis. In the first days of April, German troops were to enter Greece and Yugoslavia. By thus laying hands on the Balkans the enemy might equally well be aiming at debouching against the Middle East and at denying the British any bridgehead in the rear of the Wehrmacht should it penetrate into Russia. Right at the start of the Italian offensive in Greece I had telegraphed to General Metaxas, Hellenic Prime Minister, that it might be known publicly on which side were the prayers and the loyalty of France. The reply from Metaxas showed that he had understood. Nevertheless I was unable to get the British to agree to the transport to Greece of a small detachment which I was anxious to send there as a token. It must be said that Wavell, absorbed by the operations in Libya and Eritrea, was not himself, at that time, sending any of his own forces to Greece.

At the beginning of February we had learned of the arrival in Syria of the German mission of von Hintig and Roser. The agitation which this mission was bound to stir up in the Arab countries might serve either to prepare for the irruption of the Axis forces, or to create a diversion there which would be useful in case of an attack by those forces in the direction of Kiev and Odessa.

At the same time, in the Far East, the Japanese menace was becoming definite. Certainly it was impossible to make out if we had to deal with a fixed determination by the Japanese to enter the war in the near future, or simply with pressure intended to tie down in South-East Asia the largest possible proportion of British forces and American precautions while Germany and Italy deployed their strength either towards Moscow or across the Mediterranean. But in any case the Japanese wanted to make sure of the control of Indo-China at once. In addition, if they should come in, New Caledonia, our archipelago in the Pacific, the French Settlements in India and even Madagascar, would be threatened.

In Indo-China, Japanese intervention had begun as soon as it was clear that France was losing the battle in Europe. In June, 1940, General Catroux, the Governor-General, had considered himself forced to give satisfaction to the first Japanese demands. Before making up his mind to this, he had had the British and Americans sounded and had concluded that no help from outside could be expected. Thereupon Vichy had replaced Catroux by Decoux. As for me, not being in a

position either to arouse in Indo-China a movement capable
of taking matters in hand, or to smash on the spot the Japanese
intervention which such a movement would not have failed to
provoke, or to decide the Allies to oppose Japanese encroachments there, I found myself forced to sit and wait till further
notice. It is easy to guess with what feelings I had telegraphed,
from Duala on October 8th, to Inspector-General of Colonies
Cazaux, director of finance at Saigon, in reply to a moving
message in which he informed me of the sympathy of a large
part of the population towards the Free French, but also of
the impossibility of Indo-China acting as she desired. To me,
steering a very small boat on the ocean of war, Indo-China
seemed like a great ship out of control, to which I could give
no aid until I had slowly got together the means of rescue.
As I saw her move away into the mist, I swore to myself that
I would one day bring her in.

At the beginning of 1941, the Japanese were pressing Siam
to take possession of both banks of the Mekong, and even of
Cambodia and Laos. At the same time they were increasing
their own demands, claiming for themselves, to begin with, a
sort of economic control over Indo-China, and then military
occupation of the essential points. I was informed of the
developments of this grave affair, not only by the British and
the Dutch in London, but also by the representatives Free
France had at the principal centres of the world: Schompré,
then Baron and Langlade, at Singapore; Garreau-Dombasle
at Washington; Égal at Shanghai; Vignes at Tokyo; Brenac
at Sydney; André Guibaut, then Béchamp, at Chungking;
Victor at New Delhi. It seemed to me that the various policies
were, in point of fact, as unsure as they were complex, but
that in any case no one would do anything to help Indo-
China to resist the Japanese. Free France obviously had not
the means. Vichy, which had them but had handed them
over to the Germans, was denied by these the chance of using
them. The British, although they felt that the storm would
one day reach Singapore, wanted only to gain time, and their
representative at Bangkok showed himself above all desirous
of keeping friendly relations with Siam, whatever might be

the fate of the Mekong territories. As for the Americans, who were not ready either materially or morally to face conflict, they did not intend to intervene.

In these conditions what we could do, and what was done, consisted first of all in notifying everyone that Free France would hold as null and void any abandonment in Indo-China to which Vichy might agree. It consisted also—without our friends going over to the policy and doctrine of Vichy—in not embarrassing by any internal movements the resistance which the local authorities might wish eventually to put up against the Japanese and Siamese. It consisted, again, in concerting our action in the Pacific with that of other threatened Powers and trying—but in vain—to obtain a joint mediation by England, the United States and Holland in favour of Indo-China. It consisted, lastly, in organising the defence of New Caledonia and Tahiti, in common with Australia and New Zealand.

In this last connection I saw the Australian Prime Minister, Mr. Menzies, when he passed through London in March, and settled the essential points with this man of great good sense. After which Governor Sautot negotiated and concluded, in my name, a detailed agreement with the Australians, all precautions being taken that there should be no encroachment on French sovereignty.

We soon heard that the Thailanders were attacking on the Mekong and that, after suffering some serious set-backs on land and sea, they were nonetheless gaining possession of the coveted territories, thanks to merciless pressure by the Japanese at Saigon and at Vichy under the name of " mediation." Later Japan herself was to impose her control on Indo-China. There was no opposition, not even any protest, on the part of any other Power interested in the Pacific. From that moment it was clear that the entry of the Japanese into the world war would be only a question of time.

As the reasons for common action became more concrete, relations between French and British multiplied. And indeed, as the days went by, we had got to know each other. It is my duty to say that, as those of the British who were running their country had my whole-hearted esteem, so, it appeared to me, did they personally bestow theirs on me. First of all, the King, who was exemplary and always informed, the Queen and each of the members of their family sought out many occasions on which to show it. Among the Ministers, it was clearly with Mr. Churchill that I was chiefly in contact, public and private. But I saw also, at this period, whether on business or at friendly gatherings, principally Mr. Eden, Sir John Anderson, Mr. Amery, Sir Edward Grigg, Mr. Alexander, Sir Archibald Sinclair, Lord Lloyd, Lord Cranborne, Lord Hankey, Sir Stafford Cripps, Mr. Attlee, Mr. Duff Cooper, Mr. Dalton, Mr. Bevin, Mr. Morrison, Mr. Bevan, and Mr. Brendan-Bracken. Among the leading high officials, civil and military, it was most often Sir Robert Vansittart, Sir Alexander Cadogan, Mr. Strang, Mr. Morton, Generals Sir John Dill and Ismay, Admiral Sir Dudley Pound and Air-Marshal Portal whom I had to meet. But whether they were members of the Government, military leaders, high officials or personalities from Parliament, the Press or the business world, and so on, all displayed a striking and imposing loyalty and assurance with regard to British interests.

Not, certainly, that these men were in any way devoid of critical sense, or even of idiosyncrasies. How often, indeed, have I savoured the humour with which, over-worked though they were, they judged men and events in the midst of the drama which was sweeping us all about as the sea sweeps the pebbles! But there was in each of them a devotion to the public service, and between all of them a community of aims, which bound them together. The whole gave the impression of a cohesion among those in authority which I very often envied and admired.

But of which I had also to suffer the grip. For to resist the British machine, when it set itself in motion to impose something, was a severe test. Without having experienced it oneself, it is impossible to imagine what a concentration of effort, what a variety of procedures, what insistence, by turns gracious, pressing and threatening, the English were capable of deploying in order to obtain satisfaction.

First of all there would be allusions, poured out on this hand and on that but striking in their agreement, to put us on the alert and subject us to a methodical preparation. Suddenly, in the course of a meeting called with due decorum, the right person would produce the British request, or demand. If we did not consent to go down the proposed paths,—and I must say that this was frequent,—there began the trial of "pressure." Everyone around us got to work on it, in all ways, at all levels. There were official conversations, or informal ones, in which those in the most diverse positions invoked friendship, interest or fear, according to the occasion. There was the action of the Press, skilfully restrained as regards the subject of the dispute itself, but creating an atmosphere of criticism and gloom about us. There was the attitude of the people with whom we were in personal touch, who all, instinctively in agreement, endeavoured to persuade us. Everywhere, in mass and all at once, there would be remonstrances, complaints, promises and signs of anger.

Our British partners were aided in this by the natural propensity of the French to yield to foreigners and become divided. Among those of us who, in their career, had had to do with foreign affairs, whether from afar or close to, concession was most often a habit, if not a principle. To many, from having lived under a régime devoid of consistency, it was practically an understood thing that France never said "No!" Therefore, at those moments when I was holding out against the British demands, I could see signs, even in my own circle, of astonishment, uneasiness, anxiety. I could hear people whispering behind my back and could read in people's eyes the question: "Where does he thing he's going?" As if it were inconceivable that one should go anywhere but towards acceptance. As for those French émigrés who had not rallied to us, they took sides against us almost automatically. Most of them followed the bent of their school of politics, for which France was always in the wrong as soon as she asserted herself. And all disapproved of de Gaulle, whose firmness, which they called dictatorial, appeared to them suspect in relation to the

General de Gaulle and Mr. Churchill

General de Gaulle and H.M. King George VI, August 1940

spirit of surrender which they had the arrogance to confound with that of the Republic!

After these manifold influences had been given full play, suddenly silence spread. A sort of void was created around us by the British. No more interviews, or correspondence; no more visits or lunches. Questions remained pending. Telephones no longer rang. Those of the British with whom chance brought us nonetheless in contact were sombre and impenetrable. We were ignored, as if for us the page of the alliance, and even that of life, had henceforth been turned. In the heart of concentrated and resolute England, an icy coldness enveloped us.

Then would come the decisive attack. A solemn Franco-British meeting would take place unexpectedly. At it, all means would be brought to bear; all the arguments produced; all the complaints given utterance; all the tunes chanted. Although among the responsible British there were different degrees of dramatic skill, each one of them played his part like an artist of distinction. For hours on end heart-rending and alarming scenes followed one another. It would break up on a solemn warning of what would happen if we did not yield.

A little while more and there would come the epilogue. Various British sources would give out signals for an easing of tension. Intermediaries would come and say that there was doubtless a misunderstanding. Suitable people would ask how I was. Some benevolent paragraph or other would appear in the newspapers. Thereupon there would arrive a British proposal for accommodation over the disputed question, with a good deal of resemblance to what we ourselves had proposed. The terms becoming acceptable, the matter would be quickly settled, at least in appearance. The rounding-off would be done at a friendly party, not without our partners attempting, at a venture, in the midst of the optimism arising from restored understanding, to obtain some advantage by surprise. Then relations would become as close as before; the basis of things remaining, however, undetermined. Because, for Great Britain there was no such thing as a case tried and done with.

At the beginning of March, 1941, I felt beyond doubt that

the war was on the point of confronting us, in the Middle East and in Africa, with great trials in face of the enemy, obstinate opposition from Vichy and grave dissensions with our Allies. I would have to take the necessary decisions on the spot. I decided to go there.

Before leaving, I spent the week-end with the Prime Minister at Chequers, and he told me two things, besides saying good-bye. On March 9th, at dawn, Mr. Churchill came and woke me up to tell me, literally dancing with joy, that the American Congress had passed the " Lend-Lease Bill," which had been under discussion for several weeks. There was, indeed, matter of comfort here for us, not only from the fact that the belligerents were from now on assured of receiving from the United States the material necessary for fighting, but also because America, by becoming, in Roosevelt's phrase, " the arsenal of the democracies," was taking a gigantic step towards war. Then, wishing no doubt to profit by my good humour, Mr. Churchill formulated his second communication. " I know," he said, " that you have some complaints against Spears as head of our liaison with you. However, I am most anxious for you to keep him on and to take him with you to the Middle East. It is a personal service you will be doing me." I could not refuse, and on that we parted.

As I flew towards the Equator on March 14th, I felt, this time, that Free France possessed a serviceable framework. Our Empire Defence Council, dispersed though its members were, formed a valuable and coherent whole, recognised indeed, since December 24th, 1940, by the British Government. In London our central administration had gained in strength; men of quality like Cassin, Pleven, Palewski, Antoine, Tissier, Dejean, Alphand, Dennery, Boris, Antier, and others, formed the bones of it. At the same time, from the military point of view, several valuable officers, such as Colonels Petit, Angenot, Dassonville and Brosset, who had come from South America where they had been *en mission*, Bureau, transferred from the Cameroons, Capitaine de Frigate Auboyneau, who had hurried to us from Alexandria, and

Colonel de l'Air Valin, who was joining us from Brazil, were giving our staffs a firmer consistency. In the Middle East Catroux, in Africa Larminat had things well in hand. Under the drive coming from Garreau-Dombasle for the United States, Ledoux for South America, Soustelle for Central America and d'Argenlieu and Martin-Prevel for Canada, our delegations were planting themselves all over the New World. Our committees abroad were developing all the time, in spite of the activity exercised on the spot by the representatives of Vichy, the ill-will of most of the French notables and the quarrels usual among our compatriots. The Order of Liberation, which I had instituted at Brazzaville on 16th November, 1940, and established in London on 29th January, 1941, was arousing emulation in the best sense among the Free French. At last we could feel, across the sea, France looking towards us.

These gains by Free France in resources and solidarity were apparent to me already, along my route, in the attitude of the British Governors with whom I broke the journey, at Gibraltar, Bathurst, Freetown and Lagos. I had found them cordial before; I now found them full of consideration. Next, as I passed through the French Equatorial block, I nowhere felt anxiety or uncertainty. Everyone, assured now in his faith and in his hope, had his eyes fixed on the outside world and was ambitious to see our strength emerge from its distant cradle, grow by fresh rallyings, strike at the enemy, draw near to France.

VI MIDDLE EAST

Towards the involved Orient I flew with simple ideas. I knew that, in a welter of intricate factors, a vital game was being played there. We therefore had to be in it. I knew that, for the Allies, the key was the Suez Canal, whose loss would lay Asia Minor and Egypt open to the Axis, but whose retention would, on the contrary, make it possible one day to act from the east westwards upon Tunisia, Italy and the South of France. That meant that everything required us to be present at the battles of which the Canal was the stake. I knew that between Tripoli and Baghdad, passing through Cairo, Jerusalem and Damascus, and between Alexandria and Nairobi, passing through Jeddah, Khartoum and Jibuti, political, racial and religious passions and ambitions were being sharpened and drawn tenser under the excitement of the war, that France's positions there were sapped and coveted, and that there was, on any hypothesis, no chance of her keeping any of them if, for the first time in history, she remained passive when everything was in the melting-pot. My duty, then, was to act, there as elsewhere, in place of those who were not doing so.

As for the resources which belonged to France in this part of the world, there were, to begin with, those of which I had already disposed: combat troops and reserves in course of formation, but also the Chad territory, which put us in a position to act in Libya from the south and, in addition, gave the Allied Air Forces the advantage of bringing their aircraft by air direct from the Atlantic to the Nile instead of transporting them by sea all the way round the Cape. There were, at the same time, the assets which Vichy was busy losing: the presence of France in the Levant States, where she had an army, and where the petrol debouched; our colony at Jibuti; and our naval squadron at Alexandria. While, from tactical reasons or necessity, I could consider leaving one or other of these elements outside the war for a time, and could also measure how far the temporising of the subordinates was often excusable and their obedience explicable, I was none-theless resolved to bring them all to heel as soon as possible. At the moment of leaving London I had, indeed, collected the opinions of the members of the Defence Council on what it would be best to do if, faced by some direct threat from the Germans, England and Turkey decided to make sure of the Syrian and Lebanese territories. In short, I was arriving in the Middle East determined to let no considerations stand in the way of extending the action of France and of safeguarding all that could be safeguarded of her position.

I landed first at Khartoum, the base for the battle of Eritrea and the Sudan. This was being directed—extremely well—by General Platt, an alert and dynamic leader, who had in fact just taken the Italians' principal line of defence on the Keren heights. Colonel Monclar's brigade and Commandant Astier de Villatte's air group had taken a brilliant part in this. As for the troops at Jibuti, although General Legentilhomme had made some contacts with them, they had not decided to come over, and Governor Noailhetas was repressing by every means, including the death penalty, the stirrings which showed themselves in favour of rallying.

To bring Jibuti back into the war it would be wrong, therefore, to count on a spontaneous adhesion. At the same time I did not think it right to go in by force of arms. There remained blockade, which was certainly capable of bringing to its right mind a colony whose subsistence came to it by sea from Aden, Arabia and Madagascar. But we never managed to induce the English to do all that was necessary.

Certainly their military command was favourable in principle to an adhesion which would result in reinforcements. But other British influences were less keen. " If," they probably thought, "the competition which has set Great Britain, France and Italy at loggerheads near the sources of the Nile for the last sixty years ends in a strictly British triumph; if, when the Italians have been finally crushed, it is apparent that the French have remained passive and impotent, what an unparalleled situation England will have thenceforth in the whole area—Abyssinia, Eritrea, Somaliland and the Sudan! For the sake of a few battalions which Jibuti might engage in a battle already virtually won, is it right to forgo such a result?" This state of mind, more or less widespread among the British, explains, in my opinion, why the Vichy authorities succeeded, for two years, in feeding the colony and thereby maintaining it in a pernicious obedience.

Their default only rendered more meritorious the services of the French troops who did fight in Eritrea. I went to spend the days of March 29th and 30th with them. A French aeroplane having brought me to the Agordat airfield, I reached the area to the east of Keren where our brigade, joined on to an Indian divison, formed the left of the Allied positions. Our troops were magnificent. After Kub-Kub they had taken a notable part in the victory of Keren, by smashing and over-running the right flank of the Italians. Lieutenant-Colonel Génin, who had distinguished himself in the operation, was presented to me. To join us from Algiers, he had just crossed Africa and, no sooner arrived, had rushed into the fight: "You've seen now, Génin. What do you think?" "Ah! if they could all see, on the other side, there'd be no more question!"

On the morrow of my visit, while General Platt started the follow-up, the Commander of the French Brigade led his men towards Massawa, the capital and redoubt of Eritrea. Once Montecullo and the Umberto fort had been stormed by our men, on April 7th, the Legion entered Massawa like a whirlwind, pell-mell along with a rabble of routed Italians, rushed to the port, seized the Admiralty and gave Colonel Monclar the honour of receiving the surrender of the Commander of the enemy fleet in the Red Sea. In all, the French detachment had taken more than 4,000 prisoners in battle and received at Massawa the surrender of 10,000 more.

Henceforth the fragments of the Italian forces, thrown back into Abyssinia, no longer operated except in sporadic actions. But the fact that French Somaliland remained outside the struggle baulked France of the decisive part which her forces might have played by marching directly along the railway from Jibuti to Addis Ababa, whither the Negus was to return. I could only accept the deplorable consequences. It was elsewhere that the Free French forces would now have to be brought to bear,—both those who had just been engaged and those that were rushing up to be so. Palewski would remain on the spot as political and military delegate, keeping at his disposal a battalion and a few aircraft.

Cairo, where I landed on April 1st, was where the heart of the war was beating,—but a shaky heart. The situation of the British and their Allies there was indeed clearly unstable, not only because of military events, but also since they were on soil undermined by political currents, in the midst of populations who were watching, without taking part in, the battle between Western nations and were ready, whatever happened, to profit from the spoils of the vanquished.

These conditions gave a most complex character to the conduct of the war in the Middle East. General Wavell, the British Commander-in-Chief, by good fortune very highly gifted both with judgment and with coolness, moved in the midst of multiple contingencies, many of which had only an indirect relation to strategy. Besides, this strategy itself was as uneasy as could be. At the beginning of April, Wavell was carrying on a battle on three fronts painfully supplied over immensely long lines of communications.

In Libya, after handsome successes which had brought the British to the threshold of Tripolitania, it had been necessary to withdraw. Cyrenaica, except Tobruk, was about to be lost. The command, for all its quality, the troops, for all their courage, had not yet finished their apprenticeship in this desert struggle, so mobile and rapid over vast spaces without cover, so exhausting with the chronic thirst and fever, under the fiery sun, in

the sand, among the flies. Rommell was busy reversing fortune
at the very moment when the London Government was
ordering Wavell to strip his battle corps by sending an
important fraction of his forces to Greece. On the Hellenic
front things were not going well, either. It is true that the
victories in Eritrea and Abyssinia brought some consolation.
But alarming signs were making their appearance in the Arab
countries. Iraq was growing restless. Egypt remained enigmatic. On the subject of Syria the Germans were opening
disquieting dealings with Vichy. In Palestine the latent conflict between Arabs and Jews made many precautions necessary.

To the many difficulties accumulated round Wavell there
was added that of interference. There were the telegrams
from London. For Mr. Churchill, impatient and expert, never
ceased to ask for explanations and give directives. Apart from
the visits of Mr. Eden, first as Minister of War, and then, in
April, 1941,—when I met him in Cairo,—as Secretary of
State for Foreign Affairs, there were the interventions of the
Ambassador, Sir Miles Lampson, who was invested, in virtue
of his qualities and of the force of circumstances, with a sort
of permanent mission of co-ordination. There was the fact that
the Army in the Middle East consisted largely of contingents
from the Dominions—Australia, New Zealand, South Africa,
—whose Governments watched jealously the use made of
their forces, and also of the Indian troops which it was necessary to use without seeming to abuse. In short, Wavell exercised his command only through all sorts of political trammels.

I must say that he suffered them with a noble serenity.
To the point of keeping his headquarters in Cairo, where they
hemmed him in on all sides. It was in the heart of that teeming
city, in the tumult and dust, between the walls of a small
office overheated by the sun, that he was continually assailed
by interventions outside his normal domain as a soldier. And
here came I, troublesome and pressing, fully determined to
resolve on behalf of France problems which involved the
British and, first of all, their Commander-in-Chief.

I went over our prospects with General Catroux. The
essential thing for us was what would happen to Syria and in

the Lebanon. Sooner or later we would have to go there. As soon as we were there, France would have a chance of bringing an important contribution to the common effort. Otherwise, with this chance lost, the position of France would likewise be lost. For, supposing that the Axis won, it would dominate there as elsewhere. If the opposite happened, the English would take our place. The authority of Free France must therefore be extended to Damascus and to Beirut, as soon as events should offer the opportunity.

But when I reached Cairo the opportunity was not in sight. There was no hope of the authorities and army of the Levant themselves breaking the maleficent spell which held them enchained. The movement which, at the end of June, 1940, was thrusting whole columns in the direction of Palestine, had changed to a waiting game. Besides, the demobilisation of many officers and men, decreed by Vichy after its armistices, had brought them back to France. In addition, among the military and civil servants who remained active, Vichy had repatriated, or even placed under arrest, a number of " Gaullists." In short, the movement hoped for at the time of General Catroux's arrival in Cairo had not materialised, and our informants in Beirut and Damascus did not lead us to think that it was likely to materialise very soon.

The same inclination to give in was silting up the French squadron at Alexandria. Ever since Admiral Godfroy had concluded the agreement with Andrew Cunningham neutralising his ships, the battleship *Lorraine*, the cruisers *Duguay-Trouin*, *Duquesne*, *Suffren* and *Tourville*, the destroyers *Basque*, *Forbin* and *Fortuné*, and the submarine *Protée*, had remained at anchor in the port. A few from among the officers and crews joined us at intervals. But the others, obeying Vichy's orders, spent this time of war in proving to one another that the best way of serving invaded France consisted in not fighting. One April day, as I crossed the harbour of Alexandria to visit Admiral Cunningham on his flagship, I was able to see—and it wrung my heart—the fine French ships somnolent and useless in the midst of the British fleet with its decks cleared for action.

Unable, however, to admit that the course of the battle in the Mediterranean might have no effect on the state of mind of the leaders in Africa and the Middle East, we had tried to make contact with them. In November Catroux sent Weygand a neighbourly letter. Slight as were my illusions, I had approved this step. I myself broadcast several explicit appeals, declaring in particular, on 28th December, 1940: " All French leaders, whatever their mistakes, who may decide to draw the sword which they have sheathed, will find us at their side with no desire to exclude them and no ambition. If French Africa arises—at last!—to make war, we shall join it with our part of the Empire."

In January, having consulted the members of the Defence Council about the attitude we would have to take if by chance Vichy should re-enter the struggle, I found them, like me, in favour of union. On February 24th I had written to General Weygand in the same sense, in spite of the disagreeable fate to which he had consigned me and the discourteous reception he had given to my preceding missive. I urged Weygand to seize this last opportunity which was being offered him to resume the struggle. I proposed that we should unite, making it plain to him that, if he consented, he could count on my respect and co-operation. At the same time, Catroux missed no chance of sending tempting signals to Admiral Godfroy. Lastly, in November, he had written to M. Puaux, High Commissioner in the Levant, to General Fougère, over-all commander of the troops, and to General Arlabosse, his second-in-command, if only to make the beginnings of some sort of liaison with them.

But these many attempts had produced no result. To our emissaries Weygand replied, now that " de Gaulle ought to be shot," now that " he himself was too old to make a rebel," now that " with two-thirds of France occupied by the enemy and the remaining third by the Navy—which was even worse, —and with Darlan having him perpetually spied upon, he could do nothing, even if he had wanted to." As for Admiral Godfroy, he received General Catroux's messages with politeness, but did nothing about them. Lastly, from Beirut,

Arlabosse sent Catroux an impeccable but chilling reply. Besides, at the end of December, after the air accident to Chiappe, Ambassador Puaux was replaced by General Dentz, an extremely conventional general officer who was ready to apply strictly the orders given him by Darlan. Not long afterwards Fougère in his turn was relieved, and the command of the troops passed to General de Verdilhac.

In these conditions we could not think of entering Syria unless the enemy himself was setting foot there. Meanwhile the only thing to be done was to collect Legentilhomme's troops and place them at the disposal of Wavell, for him to engage them in Libya. That is what I arranged with the British Commander-in-Chief. At the same time I settled with Air Marshal Longmore the organisation and use of our small air force.

I must say that our soldiers, as they gradually arrived, made the best possible impression. In that quivering Middle East, where age-long echoes reverberated the renown of France, they felt that they were champions. The Egyptians, as it happened, gave them a particularly warm welcome,—not, perhaps, free from the intention that their graciousness towards the French should contrast with the coldness they were displaying to the British. I had myself made agreeable contacts with Prince Mohamed Ali, the King's uncle and heir, as well as with Sirry Pasha, the head of the Government, and with several of his Ministers. As for the Frenchmen resident in Egypt —scientists, members of the teaching profession, specialists in antiquities, churchmen, business men, traders, engineers and employees of the Canal,—most of them were warmhearted and active in aiding our troops. Already on June 18th they had, on the initiative of Baron de Benoist, Professor Jouguet and MM. Minost and Boniteau, formed an organisation which at once became one of the pillars of Free France. Nevertheless, some of our compatriots were holding aloof from the movement. Sometimes, in the evening, when I went for a short walk in the Cairo zoological gardens and passed in front of the French Legation, which stood opposite them, I could see, appearing at the windows, the strained faces of those who were not joining us, yet whose gaze followed General de Gaulle.

Thus, during the two weeks spent in the Sudan, Egypt and Palestine, certain things had been made clear. But the main thing remained to be done, and for the moment I could do nothing about it. I then went back to Brazzaville. It was in fact necessary, in any case, to push on with the organisation of our Equatorial block. If the Middle East were destined to be lost, that would become the breakwater of Allied resistance; if not, we would have there a base for some future offensive.

My tour of inspection took me once more to Duala, Yaunde, Marua, Libreville, Port-Gentil, Fort-Lamy, Moussoro, Faya, Fada, Abéché, Fort-Archambault, Bangui and Pointe-Noire. Many things were lacking there, but order and goodwill were not among them. The governors—Cournarie in the Cameroons, Lapie in the Chad, Saint-Mart in Ubangi, Fortuné in the Middle Congo, Valentin-Smith in the Gabon (where he had just replaced Parant, killed on service in an air accident)—were commanding and administrating in that atmosphere in which no doubts are felt, and which envelop the French whenever by chance they are at one in serving a great cause. In the military field it was to the preparation of Leclerc's Saharan column that I gave first priority. I had him sent from England all the officers and N.C.O.s still there, as well as all the appropriate material that the English consented to supply. But from the end of April it was clear to me beyond doubt that, from one day to the next, it was in the Levant that we would have to act.

In fact, the Germans were debouching upon the Mediterranean. On April 24th Anglo-Hellenic resistance collapsed, while the Yugoslavs also had just succumbed. Doubtless the British would try to hang on in Crete. But would they be able to hold? It seemed to me obvious that, starting from the shores of Greece, the enemy would, in the near future, bring to bear at least air squadrons on Syria. Their presence in the midst of the Arab countries would arouse there an agitation which might serve as a prelude to the arrival of the Wehrmacht. At the same time, from their airfields of Damascus, Rayak and Beirut, 300 miles from Suez and Port Said, the German aircraft would easily bombard the Canal and its approaches.

In this matter Darlan was powerless to reject Hitler's demands. But I did indulge in the hope that, should the leaders and soldiers of the Levant see the machines of the Luftwaffe landing on their bases, many of them would refuse to submit to their presence and to cover it with their arms. In this case we would have to be ready to give them a hand at once. I therefore worked out my directives about the action to be undertaken. It would involve thrusting General Legentilhomme's small division straight at Damascus, as soon as the appearance of the Germans should provoke among our compatriots the movement which seemed probable. Catroux for his part prepared to make, on this hypothesis, all the contacts possible, with Dentz himself if need be, so as to establish the common front of Frenchmen against the invader of France and Syria.

But these plans did not meet with the agreement of the British. General Wavell, absorbed by his three battle fronts, did not intend to see a fourth opened for him, at any price. Also, not wishing to believe the worst, he said he was sure, on the strength of the reports of the British Consul-General at Beirut, that Dentz would resist the Germans if the case arose. At the same time the London Government was making efforts to coax Vichy. So it was that, in February, the British Admiralty had, in spite of my protests, accorded free passage to the steamer *Providence*, which was transporting from Beirut to Marseille some compulsorily repatriated " Gaullists." So it was that, at the end of April, a commercial treaty was concluded with Dentz, assuring food supplies to the Levant. So it was that negotiations, opened by Governor Noailhetas with a view to the same result for Jibuti, were going on at Aden.

The information reaching us from France led me to think that American influence had something to do with these attempts at " appeasement." It was reported to me that Pétain and Darlan were prodigal of their overtures towards Admiral Leahy, the Ambassador at Vichy, while at the same time they were secretly agreeing to Hitler's demands. Roosevelt, influenced in his turn by Leahy's telegrams, was pressing the English to be lenient. The more necessary it seemed to me to prepare for action in the Levant, the less our Allies were disposed to it. On May 9th Spears advised me, from Cairo, that no operation there was " contemplated for the moment " for the Free French, that there would be " disadvantage " in my coming to Egypt and that the best thing would be to go back to London.

Convinced that temporisation might well cost us dear, I thought it my duty to impress the English in my turn. On May 10th I telegraphed to Cairo, to the British Ambassador and to the Commander-in-Chief, to protest on the one hand against the " unilateral decisions taken by them on the subject of the supply of foodstuffs to the Levant and Jibuti," on the other hand against the " delays caused to the concentration of the Legentilhomme division within reach of Syria at a time when the arrival of the Germans there was daily more probable." I made it plain that, in these conditions, I had no intention of going to Cairo in the near future, that I was letting matters there follow their course, and that it was in the Chad that I would henceforth bring the French effort to bear. Then I let London know that I was recalling General Catroux from Cairo, since his presence there was becoming useless. Finally, as the excellent Mr. Parr, the British Consul-General at Brazzaville, brought me messages sent by Mr. Eden to justify the policy of appeasement towards Vichy, I dictated to him a reply condemning this policy with all the more vigour because I had just heard of the interview between Darlan and Hitler at Berchtesgaden, of the conclusion of an agreement between them, and finally of the landing of German aeroplanes at Damascus and Aleppo.

For the enemy, too, was playing for high stakes. At his instigation Rashid Ali Kilani, the head of the Iraqi Government, opened hostilities in the first days of May. The English were besieged on their airfields. On May 12th the Luftwaffe machines arrived in Syria and from there reached Baghdad. On the day before, the Vichy authorities had sent to Tel

Kotchek, on the Iraqi frontier, the war material which the Italian armistice commission had previously made them place under its control. These arms were evidently intended for Rashid Ali. Dentz, from whom the British demanded an explanation, answered evasively, without, however, denying the facts. He added that if he received the order from Vichy to let the German troops disembark, he would not fail to obey, —which amounted to saying that the order had already been given. It has since become known, in fact, that the beaches where the enemy was to land had been already assigned.

The London Cabinet judged that, in these conditions, it was better to come round to my way of thinking. The reversal was sudden and complete. As from May 14th Eden, on the one hand, and Spears—who was still in Egypt—on the other, told me so, straight out. Finally, a message from Mr. Churchill asked me to go to Cairo and not to withdraw Catroux, seeing that action was imminent. Very satisfied with the attitude adopted by the British Prime Minister, I answered him warmly and, for once, in English. I could not, however, fail to draw the unavoidable conclusions about the behaviour of our allies in this affair. As for General Wavell, his Government had ordered him to undertake the action planned by us in Syria. I found him resigned to doing so, when I arrived in Cairo on May 25th. It is true that the loss of Crete and the disappearance of the Greek front lightened, for the moment, the burdens of the Commander-in-Chief.

Meanwhile, in Syria itself, things were not turning out as we had hoped. Catroux had, for one moment, believed that he could carry out our plan and march on Damascus with the Free French forces alone. But it soon became necessary to realise that the collusion between Vichy and the enemy was arousing no mass movement among the Levant troops. On the contrary, these were taking up positions on the frontier, to resist the Free French and the Allies, while behind them the Germans could move about as they wished. As Dentz had available more than thirty thousand men, well provided with artillery, aircraft and armour, without counting the Syrian and Lebanese troops, our first project of marching on Damascus with our six thousand infantrymen, our eight guns and our ten tanks, supported by our two dozen aircraft and taking advantage of the help we dreamed of finding on the spot, could not be applied as it was. The British would have to join in, and a pitched battle lay ahead.

At least we were anxious to reduce its desperate character and its length as far as possible. It was a question of the resources used. Our friends at Beirut and Damascus sent word to us. " If the Allies enter Syria from all directions and in large numbers, there will only be a show of resistance for honour's sake. If, on the contrary, the Levant troops find themselves up against forces that are mediocre in numbers and material, their professional pride will come into play and the battles will be harsh." Accompanied by General Catroux, I had many interviews on this subject with Wavell. We pressed him to go into the Levant not only from the south, starting from Palestine, but also from the east, starting from Iraq, where, in fact, the British were engaged in reducing Rashid Ali. We asked the Commander-in-Chief to operate with four divisions, one of them armoured, and to deploy a large section of the Royal Air Force in the Syrian sky. We insisted that he should give Legentilhomme's troops what they chiefly lacked: means of transport and artillery support.

General Wavell was certainly not without strategical intelligence. In addition, he wanted to satisfy us. But, absorbed as he was by the Libya operations and harassed, no doubt, by Mr. Churchill's comminatory telegrams in which he saw the effect of our own insistence, he met our plain speaking with a negative courtesy. Nothing could persuade him to devote more than a strict minimum of forces to the Syrian affair. All he would put into the field, under General Wilson's orders, was an Australian division and a cavalry brigade marching along the Tyre-Sidon coastal road, an infantry brigade making for Kuneitra and Merdjayoun, and a Hindu brigade lent to Legentilhomme, who was to bear down on Damascus through Deraa. Wavell added, later, two Australian battalions. Lastly, a Hindu detachment eventually, as a last resort, went into action from Iraq. The whole was supported by about sixty

*General de Gaulle in Cairo with General Wavell (left) and
General Catroux (second from right), April 1941*

aircraft, while various warships accompanied the land operations along the coast. In all, the Allies engaged less forces
than would be opposed to them. And yet on this inadequate
basis we had to act and go through with it. The final decision
was taken. The tragedy was about to begin.

On May 26th I had been to inspect the Free French troops
at Kistina, concentrated now, but still ill-provided. Legentilhomme paraded for me seven battalions, a tank company, a
battery, a squadron of Spahis, a reconnaissance company and
supporting services. It was on this occasion that I bestowed
the first Crosses of Liberation earned in Libya and Eritrea.
In making contact with the officers and men, I realised that
they were in exactly the same state of mind as I was: grief and
disgust at having to fight Frenchmen, indignation with Vichy
for leading astray the discipline of the troops, and conviction
that it was necessary to march, to make sure of the Levant
and turn it against the enemy. On May 21st Colonel Collet,
who commanded the group of the Circassian squadrons, an
officer of high value and legendary bravery, crossed the
frontier and joined us with part of his troops. On June 8th
Free French and British advanced, waving the Allied flags,
with orders, given jointly by Wavell and Catroux, to use their
weapons against those who should fire on them. A radio
station had been set up in Palestine, and had for weeks been
broadcasting, with the voices of Captains Schmittlein, Coulet
and Repiton, friendly exhortations to our compatriots, in
whom we hoped, from the bottom of our hearts, not to find
adversaries. Nonetheless, we had got to get through. In a
public declaration I left no doubt on this point.

I was, indeed, all the more resolved to push things to a
conclusion, and quickly, since many signs led us to expect an
offensive by Vichy, and perhaps by the Axis, against Free
French Africa. According to our information, Hitler had
demanded of Darlan, during their interviews at Berchtesgaden
on May 11th and 12th, not only that the Syrian aerodromes and
ports should be placed at Germany's disposal, but also that
his troops, aircraft and ships should be able to use Tunis,
Sfax and Gabès, and, moreover, that the Vichy forces should

reconquer the Equatorial territories. Certainly our informants added that Weygand had refused to allow the Germans to have access to Tunisia and start an offensive against the Free French territories, alleging his subordinates would not obey him. But if Hitler's plan was firmly decided on, what weight would a protest from Weygand possess, when in the last resort, and failing the willingness to fight, all he would have to set against it, in the Marshal's councils, was an offer of resignation?

We were therefore holding ourselves in readiness to reply to an attack. Larminat, taking advantage of the impression made by the arrival of German aircraft in Syria upon certain elements in the Ivory Coast, Dahomey, Togoland and the Niger, was preparing to march in at the first opportunity. I had myself given him instructions on the line of conduct to follow. At the same time the British Government, when I asked it what it would do if Vichy, with or without immediate assistance from the Germans, were to attempt to act, for instance, against the Chad, replied in a message to me from Mr. Eden that it would help us to resist by all means in its power. Lastly, we had done what was required to interest the Americans directly in the security of Free French Africa. On June 5th I handed to the United States Minister in Cairo a memorandum bringing out the fact that Africa would one day have to be an American base for the liberation of Europe and proposing to Washington that it should without delay establish air forces in the Cameroons, the Chad and the Congo. Four days later the United States Consul at Léopold-ville went to see Larminat, asked him on behalf of his Government if he considered that French Equatorial Africa was threatened and, on the High Commissioner's affirmative answer, invited him to let him know what direct aid he would wish America to give him, especially in armaments. In spite of everything, and of all the precautions we had managed to take to defend the Equatorial bastion in case of need, I was very impatient, faced as I was by the prospect of a major effort by the Axis and its collaborators in Africa, to see the Levant shut against the Germans and cut off from Vichy.

While British and Free French were preparing to act together there on the military field, their political rivalry was taking shape behind the façade. In Allied staff circles, around the Cairo Embassy, in close touch with the British High Commissioner's office at Jerusalem, in the communications made by the Foreign Office to Cassin, Pleven and Dejean and passed on by them from London to me, and through the columns of the inspired newspapers, notably the *Palestine Post*, we could perceive the quivering activity of a specialised personnel which saw opening—at last!—in Syria—the prospect of realising plans of action long since prepared. Events were about to put Great Britain in possession of such a hand of trumps, political, military and economic, that she would certainly not refrain from playing them on her own account.

All the more since, once installed at Damascus and Beirut, it would be impossible even for us to maintain the "status quo ante " there. The shocks caused by the disaster of 1940, Vichy's capitulation and the activity of the Axis made it imperative for Free France to take up towards the Levant States a new position, answering to developments and to the forces emerging. It seemed to us, indeed, that, once the war was over France would not keep the mandate. Even supposing she still wished to do so, it was clear that the movement of the Arab peoples and international necessities would not allow her to do so. Now, only one régime could, *de jure* and *de facto*, be substituted for the mandate, and that was independence,—historical precedence and the interests of France being, however, safeguarded. That had, indeed, been the purpose of the treaties concluded by Paris in 1936 with the Lebanon and Syria. These treaties, although their ratification had been postponed, constituted facts which good sense and the circumstances forbade us to ignore.

We had therefore decided that, at the moment of going into Syrian and Lebanese territory, Free France would declare its determination to put an end to the régime of the mandate and to conclude treaties with the now sovereign States. As long as the war lasted in the Middle East, we would naturally keep the mandatory's supreme power in the Levant, together with its obligations. Lastly, since the territory of Syria and the Lebanon was part and parcel of the Middle East theatre of operations, over which the English possessed, compared to us, an enormous superiority in resources, we would consent to the British military command exercising the strategic direction over the whole against the common enemies.

But it was at once evident that the English would not be content with that. Their game,—settled in London by firmly established services, carried out on the spot by a team without scruples but not without resources, accepted by the Foreign Office, which sometimes sighed over it but never disavowed it, and supported by the Prime Minister, whose ambiguous promises and calculated emotions camouflaged what was intended, aimed at establishing British " leadership " in the whole Middle East. British policy would therefore endeavour, sometimes stealthily and sometimes harshly, to replace France at Damascus and at Beirut.

The procedure to be employed by this policy would be that of going one better—letting it be thought that every concession granted by us to Syria and the Lebanon was granted thanks to England's good offices, egging the local rulers on to formulate increasing demands and, lastly, supporting the acts of provocation to which it was bound to lead them. At the same time efforts would be made to use the French as foils,—to raise up local and international opinion against them, and so to divert popular reprobation from British encroachments in the other Arab countries.

Hardly had the decision to go into Syria been taken in common when already the British let their intentions be seen. As Catroux was preparing his declaration announcing independence, Sir Miles Lampson requested that the proclamation should be made both in the name of England and in that of Free France. I opposed this, naturally. The Ambassador then insisted that the text should mention the British guarantee given to our promise. I rejected this request, on the ground that the word of France had no need of a foreign guarantee. Mr. Churchill, when he telegraphed to me on June 6th to express his friendly wishes on the eve of the advance, insisted on the importance of this famous guarantee. I replied to these good wishes, but not to this claim. It was easy to see that our partners wanted to create the impression that, if the Syrians and Lebanese received independence, they would owe it to England, and so to place themselves in the position of arbiters between us and the Levant States in the next phase. In the end Catroux's declaration was as it should be. But as soon as it had been made, the London Government published another, separately and in its own name.

The memories evoked in me by the campaign we had been obliged to open are cruel ones. I can still see myself coming and going between Jerusalem, where I had fixed my head-quarters, and our brave troops as they advanced towards Damascus, or else going to visit the wounded in the Franco-British ambulance unit of Mrs. Spears and Dr. Fruchaut. As I heard, gradually, how many of our men, and of the best, were left on the field,—how, for instance, General Legentil-homme had been severely wounded, how Colonel Génin and Capitaine de Corvette Détroyat had been killed, how Commandants de Chevigné, de Boissoudy, and de Villoutreys had been badly hit,—and how, on the other side, many good officers and men were falling bravely under our fire,—how, on the Litani on June 9th and 10th, before Kiswa on the 12th and round about Kuneitra and Ezraa on the 15th and 16th, violent fighting had mingled the French dead from both camps and those of their British Allies,—I felt, towards those who were opposing us on a point of honour, mixed emotions of esteem and commiseration. At a time when the enemy held Paris under his boot, was attacking in Africa and was infiltrating into the Levant, this courage shown and these losses borne in the fratricidal struggle imposed by Hitler upon leaders who had fallen under his yoke made on me an impression of horrible waste.

But the more tightly sorrow gripped, the firmer I grew in the determination to persevere. The same was true, indeed, of the soldiers of Free France, of whom, practically speaking, none was to weaken. The same was true, likewise, of all our compatriots in Egypt who, meeting in Cairo for the first anniversary of June 18th, responded to my address with unanimous acclamations.

On that day there was reason to believe that Dentz was on the point of putting an end to this odious struggle. Already, indeed, it no longer offered him any hope. In fact, Benoist-Méchin, sent by Vichy to Ankara to obtain permission for reinforcements to be sent to the Levant across Turkey, had met with a refusal. At the same time, the rout of Rashid Ali in Iraq and his flight to Germany on May 31st opened to the Allies the gates of Syria by way of the desert and the Euphrates. All at once the Germans seemed no longer in a hurry to get fresh forces through into Arab countries. On the contrary, the aircraft they had sent there were brought back to Greece. The only reinforcements that had reached the Levant since the start of the fighting were two French air squadrons, which had come from North Africa via Athens, where the Germans had welcomed them and refuelled them. And now there reached us from Washington the news that M. Conty, political director of the Levant High Commissioner's office, had on June 18th begged the American Consul-General at Beirut to ask the British, as a matter of urgency, what terms they themselves and the " Gaullists " would require for a cessation of hostilities.

As early as June 13th, foreseeing what would follow and by way of precaution, I had made known to Mr. Churchill what were the bases on which, in my view, the future armistice should be concluded. In the course of the meeting held on June 19th at Sir Miles Lampson's, at which Wavell and Catroux were present, I drew up in the same sense the text of the terms which appeared to me acceptable for ourselves and suitable for those who were fighting against us. " The arrangement," I wrote, " must be based on: honourable treatment for all members of the armed forces and all officials; a guarantee given by Great Britain that, as far as she is concerned, the rights and interests of France in the Levant will be maintained; and the representation of France in the Levant to be the responsibility of the Free French authorities." I specified that

" all members of the armed forces and officials who may desire it shall be able to remain, and likewise their families, the others being repatriated later." But I added that " all possible steps should be taken by the Allies that this choice may be really free." Finally, in order to counter the rumours which Vichy was spreading, I declared that " never having brought to judgment those of my army comrades who have fought against me in obedience to orders received by them, I had no intention of doing so in the present case." These are, in essence, the provisions which, adopted there and then by the British, were at once telegraphed to London to be passed on to Washington and, from there, to Beirut.

I was disagreeably impressed, therefore, next day when I came to know the exact text which the British Government had finally sent, and which did not resemble the one to which I had subscribed. Free France was not even mentioned in it, as though it were to England that Dentz was being asked to hand over Syria! There was not a word, either, about the precautions which I was anxious to take to prevent the members of the armed forces and officials in the Levant from being repatriated wholesale and compulsorily; and it was vital for me to hold on to these as much as possible. I therefore sent Mr. Eden a formal protest, and warned him that for my part I was adhering to the conditions of June 19th and not recognising any others. This reservation was to have its importance, as will be seen later.

Why did the Vichy authorities wait more than three weeks before carrying out their own intention of negotiating the end of the struggle? Why was it necessary, on this account, to go on for so long with fighting which could alter nothing except the total of the losses? The only explanation I can find is in the start of the German offensive in Russia. On June 22nd, the morrow of the day on which the United States Consul at Beirut handed Great Britain's reply to the High Commissioner, Hitler launched his armies in the direction of Moscow. He had an obvious interest in the largest possible fraction of the forces opposed to him being tied up in Africa and Syria. Rommel was looking after this on one side. It was necessary that the unfortunate French forces of the Levant should do as much on the other.

Meanwhile on June 21st, after a sharp engagement at Kiswa, our troops entered Damascus. Catroux proceeded there at once. I arrived there on the 23rd. In the night that followed, German aircraft came and bombarded the town, killing some hundreds of people in the Christian quarter and demonstrating in this way their co-operation with Vichy. But hardly were we on the spot before there reached us, from all sides,—notably from the Hauran, the Jebel ed Druz, Palmyra and Jezireh,—disquieting news about the behaviour of the British. There was no time to be lost if we wished to show that Vichy's discomfiture did not mean the retirement of France, and to affirm our authority.

On June 24th I appointed General Catroux delegate-general and plenipotentiary in the Levant and defined for him, by letter, the purpose of his mission: " To direct the re-establishment of an internal and economic situation as close to the normal as the war may permit; to negotiate, with the qualified representatives of the population-groups, treaties instituting the independence and sovereignty of the States, and at the same time the alliance of these States with France; to ensure the defence of the territory against the enemy, and to co-operate with the Allies in the operations of war in the Middle East." Until such time as the future treaties would enter into force, General Catroux was assuming " all the powers and all the responsibilities of the High Commissioner of France in the Levant." As for the negotiations to be opened, they were to be so " with governments approved by assemblies really representative of the people as a whole, and called together as soon as possible; the point of departure for the negotiations being the treaties of 1936." Thus " the mandate entrusted to France in the Levant would be brought to its due conclusion and the work of France continued."

During my stay at Damascus, I received all the political, religious and administrative notabilities who were there, and there were many. Through the usual Oriental prudence it was possible to see that the authority of France was without dispute recognised in us personally, that the failure of the German plan for gaining a footing in Syria was put down largely to our credit, and finally that everyone expected from us, and from no one else, the re-starting of the machinery of State and the setting up of a new government. General Catroux, who had a profound knowledge of men and affairs in that country, saw to it that order, food supplies and health services were ensured, but took his time over appointing ministers.

The tragedy, indeed, was ending. On June 20th Legentil-homme, who in spite of his severe wound had never given up commanding his troops, seized Nebeck and, on the 30th, repulsed a final counter-attack there. A Hindu column from Iraq crossed the Euphrates on July 3rd by the Deir-ez-Zor bridge, left intact through some chance which I can safely call well arranged, and made progress towards Aleppo and towards Homs. Along the coastal road the British reached Damour on the 9th, and farther to the east, Jezzin. On July 10th Dentz sent his warships and aircraft to Turkey, where they were interned. He then asked for a cease-fire, which was granted immediately. It was agreed that the pleni-potentiaries should meet three days later, at Saint John of Acre.

Many signs led me to think that the outcome of this meeting would not be in conformity with the interests of France. It was true that I had warned Mr. Churchill on June 28th " of the extreme importance which England's behaviour towards us in the Middle East would have from the point of view of our alliance." It was true that I had obtained agreement that General Catroux should be present at the negotiations. It was true that our delegates in London had received from myself clear indications as to the way in which our authority should be established in the Levant, for them to make use of in their conversations. But the terms already formulated by Mr. Eden for the armistice with Dentz, the mood which prevailed in the British services, and the fact that the loyal Wavell had just left Cairo, having been appointed Viceroy of India, and that his successor, Auchinleck, was not yet installed there,—which left the field clear for the passions of the " arabophiles,"—made it impossible for me to doubt that the arrangement would leave much to be desired. In point of fact the armistice was to be concluded by Wilson with Verdilhac. My only means of limiting the damage was to gain space and height, to reach some cloud and from there swoop down upon a convention which would not bind me, and which I would tear up as far as I could.

The cloud was Brazzaville. I stayed there, while at Saint John of Acre the act was drawn up, whose substance and form went beyond my worst fears.

In fact, the text of the agreement amounted to a pure and simple transference of Syria and the Lebanon to the British. Not a word about the rights of France, either for the present or for the future. No mention of the Levant States. Vichy was abandoning everything to the discretion of a foreign power, and sought to obtain only one thing: the departure of all the troops, and likewise of the maximum number of French officials and nationals. In this way de Gaulle would be, as far as possible, prevented from increasing his forces and from preserving the position of France in the Levant.

By signing this capitulation, Vichy showed itself faithful to its wretched vocation. But the English were apparently lending themselves to it with all their ulterior motives. Obviously ignoring, even in matters of form, their Free French allies, whose initiative and co-operation had powerfully helped them to gain the strategic aim, they seemed to be taking advantage of Vichy's supineness in order to try to gather under the grasp of their military Command the authority which Dentz was handing over to them at Beirut and at Damascus. They were, moreover, ready to let the Levant troops go as soon as possible. These, according to the convention, would be concentrated under the orders of their leaders and embarked on the ships which Darlan would send. What was more, the Free French were forbidden to make contact with them and to try to win them over. The material which they would leave behind would be handed over to the English alone. Finally, the so-called " special,"—that is to say, Syrian and Lebanese—troops, who had always showed themselves faithful to France, so much so that Vichy had not dared to use them against us in the recent engagements, were to be placed, without more ado, under British command.

Before I even knew the details, and taking as my basis the naturally sugared indications given by the London radio, I let it be known that I repudiated the Saint John of Acre convention. After which, I left for Cairo, making it plain to the British governors and military leaders at each stage of my journey how serious the matter was. I did so at Khartoum to the Governor-General of the Sudan, at Kampala to the Governor, at Wadi Halfa to the Manager of the Club, so as to have myself preceded by alarming telegrams. On July 21st I made contact with Mr. Oliver Lyttleton, Minister of State in the British Government, who had just been sent by it to Cairo, there to group under his authority all British affairs in the Middle East.

" Captain " Lyttleton, an amiable and thoughtful man with a lively and open mind, had manifestly no desire to begin his mission with a catastrophe. He welcomed me with some embarrassment. I tried to avoid explosions and, casing myself in ice, told him, in substance, this:

" Thanks to a campaign which we have just carried through together, we have managed to gain ourselves a notable strategic advantage. The mortgage which, in the Levant, Vichy's subordination to Germany made such a burden on the Eastern theatre of operations is now liquidated. But the agreement you have just concluded with Dentz is, I must tell you, unacceptable. The authority in Syria and the Lebanon cannot pass from France to England. It belongs to Free France, and to her alone, to exercise it. She must render account for it to France. At the same time, I need to bring over as many as possible of the French troops who have just been fighting against us. Their rapid and wholesale repatriation, as also the fact of their being kept all together and in isolation, deprive me of all means of acting upon them. In short, the Free French cannot consent to be kept away from a French source of reinforcements, and, above all, they do not admit that our common effort should end in establishing your authority at Damascus and Beirut."

"We have no such intention," replied Mr. Lyttleton. "Great Britain is pursuing no aim in Syria and the Lebanon other than to win the war. But that implies that the internal situation there should not be troubled. Therefore it seemed to us necessary that the Levant States should receive independence, which England has guaranteed to them. At the same time, as long as the war lasts, the military Command has over-riding powers as regards public order. Decisions on the spot therefore belong to it in the last resort. As for the technical conditions adopted by Generals Wilson and de Verdilhac for the withdrawal and embarkation of the French troops, they also answer to our anxiety to see that things pass off in an orderly fashion. Lastly, we do not understand why you should not trust us. After all, our cause is common."

"Yes," I resumed, "our cause is common. But our position is not, and our action may cease to be. In the Levant, France is the mandatory power, not Great Britain. You speak of the independence of the States. But we alone are qualified to give it to them, and in fact are giving it them, for reasons and on terms of which we are alone judge and alone responsible. You can certainly give us your approval from outside. It is not for you to meddle with it inside. As for public order in Syria and the Lebanon, that is our affair, not yours."

"All the same," said Mr. Lyttleton, "you recognised the authority of the British High Command by our agreement of August 7th, 1940."

"I have," I replied, "in fact recognised the right of that Command to give directives to the Free French Forces, but only in strategic matters and against the common enemy. I never intended that this prerogative should extend to sovereignty, policy or administration in territories for which France has the responsibility. When, one day, we land on French soil proper, will you invoke the rights of the High Command in order to claim to govern France? Also, I must repeat to you that I am anxious to have contacts made with the elements who were under Vichy's orders. This, indeed, is to your advantage as well. For it would be strictly absurd to send back, without more ado, troops who have been warmed up by fighting and whom we shall meet again one day, in Africa or elsewhere. Lastly, the war material and the command of the special troops must belong to Free France."

"You have made known to me your point of view," Mr. Lyttleton then said. "As regards our reciprocal relations in Syria and the Lebanon, we can discuss them. But as far as the armistice convention is concerned, it is signed. We must apply it."

"That convention does not bind Free France. I have not ratified it."

"Well, what do you intend to do?"

"This: To obviate all ambiguity as regards the rights which the British Command seems to wish to exercise in Syria and the Lebanon, I have the honour to inform you that the Free French Forces will no longer be dependent on that Command as from July 24th,—that is, in three days' time. Moreover, I am ordering General Catroux to take in hand immediately the authority over the whole extent of the territory of Syria and the Lebanon, whatever opposition he may meet with from any quarter. I am giving the Free French Forces the order to enter into contact, as best they may, with all other French elements and to take control of their war material. Finally, the reorganisation of the Syrian and Lebanese troops, which we have already begun, will be actively pursued."

I handed Captain Lyttleton a note prepared in advance, laying down these conditions. As I took my leave, I said to him:

"You know what I myself and those who follow me have done and are doing for our alliance. You can therefore measure how great our regret would be if we were forced to see it deteriorate. But neither we nor those who, in our country, turn their hopes towards us, could admit that the alliance should work to the detriment of France. If, by ill-fortune, the case should arise, we would prefer to suspend our engagements with regard to England. In any event, indeed, we shall pursue the fight against the common enemy with the means in our power. I intend to proceed to Beirut in three days. Between now and then I am ready for any negotiation which might seem to you desirable."

I left Lyttleton who, under a cool exterior, seemed to me disturbed and uneasy. I was myself somewhat deeply moved. That afternoon I confirmed to him by letter that the subordination of the Free French Forces to the British Command was ceasing on the 24th at midday, but that I was ready to settle with him the new lines for military collaboration. Finally I telegraphed to Churchill as follows: " We regard the Saint John of Acre convention as being opposed, in its substance, to the military and political interests of Free France, and as being, in its form, extremely painful to our dignity. . . . I hope you may feel personally that such an attitude on the part of Great Britain, in a matter which is vital for us, aggravates my difficulties considerably and will have consequences which I consider deplorable, from the point of view of the task I have undertaken."

It was England's turn to speak. She did so in the direction of concession. That very evening Mr. Lyttleton, having asked to see me again, spoke to me in the following terms:

" I agree that certain appearances may have given you the idea that we wanted to take the place of France in the Levant. I assure you that it is mistaken. To dispel this mis-understanding, I am ready to write you a letter guaranteeing our complete disinterestedness in the political and admini-strative field."

" That," I replied, " would be an auspicious statement of principle. But there remains the Saint John of Acre con-vention, which goes against it in an unfortunate way and which, what is more, threatens to lead to incidents between your people, who are applying it, and mine, who do not accept it. There remains also your proposed extension of the com-petence of your military Command in the Levant, an extension incompatible with our position."

" Would you perhaps have some proposal to make to us on these two questions? "

" On the first I can see no issue other than an immediate

agreement between us on the subject of the ' application ' of
the armistice convention, correcting in practice what is
vicious in the text. As for the second question, what is necessary
and urgent is that you should undertake to limit the com-
petence of your Command in Syrian and Lebanese territory
to the military operations against the common enemy."

" Give me a chance to think it over."

The atmosphere was improving. After various to-ings and
fro-ings we reached, to begin with, on July 24th an agreement
" interpretative " of the Saint John of Acre convention,—an
agreement negotiated by General de Larminat and Colonel
Valin on our behalf. In it the English declared themselves
ready to let us make contacts with the Levant troops so as to
find those among them who would come over to us, recognised
that the war material belonged to the Free French Forces,
and gave up the claim to take the Syrian and Lebanese troops
under their control. It was also understood that " if a substantial violation of the armistice convention by the Vichy
authorities became a fact, the British forces and the Free
French Forces would take all measures they might consider
useful to bring the Vichy troops over to Free France." As
several " substantial violations " had already been reported,
there was reason to believe,—as Mr. Lyttleton himself assured
me,—that in the end the whole matter of the destination of
the troops would be reconsidered.

I had no doubt of the British Minister's goodwill. But
what were General Wilson and his arabophil team going to
do, in spite of the agreements concluded? To try to make
sure that they would behave properly, I telegraphed afresh
to Mr. Churchill, urging him " not to let an entire army, with
its units still in formation, be handed over again to Vichy, to
dispose of." " I must report to you," I added, " that it seems
to me in accordance with elementary security to suspend the
repatriation of Dentz's army, and to let the Free French
proceed as they mean to do in order to bring back into the
path of duty these poor troops led astray by enemy propaganda."

Next day, the 25th, Mr. Oliver Lyttleton, Minister of

State in the British Government, wrote to me, in the name of his country:

". . . We recognise the historic interests of France in the Levant. Great Britain has no interest in Syria or the Lebanon except to win the war. We have no desire to encroach in any way upon the position of France. Both Free France and Great Britain are pledged to the independence of Syria and the Lebanon. When this essential step has been taken, and without prejudice to it, we freely admit that France should have the dominant privileged position in the Levant among all European nations. . . . You will have seen the recent utterances of the Prime Minister in this sense and I am glad to reaffirm them now."

In the same letter Mr. Lyttleton declared his acceptance of the text of an agreement which I had given him, concerning co-operation between the British and French military authorities in the Middle East. It said in effect that the English would have no right to interfere in the political and administrative fields in the Levant, in return for which we agreed that their Command should exercise the strategic leadership,—under certain well-defined conditions, indeed.

That same day I left for Damascus and Beirut.

At the solemn entry of the leader of Free France into the Syrian capital, that great city which, till then, had been concerned to show its coldness towards the French authority on every occasion, was moved by an enthusiasm plain to see. A few days later, speaking in the University precincts to the country's most eminent men, who were there together with the members of the Syrian Government, I met with obvious assent as I defined the aim which France, from that time on, had set before herself in the Levant.

It was on July 27th that I arrived at Beirut. The French and Lebanese troops lined the streets, while the population, massed in the open, applauded without stint. Passing through the Place des Canons, which rang with enthusiasm, I proceeded to the Petit Sérail, where I ceremonially exchanged speeches full of optimism with the head of the Lebanese Government, M. Alfred Naccache. Then I moved on to the

Grand Sérail, where the leading Frenchmen were assembled. The majority had given their support, and often their confidence, to the system established by Vichy. But as I made contact with them I realised, once more, how strongly accomplished facts, when they have right behind them, influence men's attitudes and even their convictions. Officials, notables and churchmen all assured me of their loyalty and promised me to bring unreserved devotion to the service of the country under the new authority. I must say that, with few exceptions, this undertaking was kept. Almost all the Frenchmen who remained in the Lebanon and in Syria continued to show themselves—in the midst of the most difficult circumstances— ardently united within Free France, fighting as it was to liberate the country and at the same time to assume the rights and duties of France on the spot.

It was in fact most urgent to assert these rights and duties. Hardly had I reached Beirut when I realised, without surprise, how little account General Wilson and the political agents assisting him under cover of uniform took of the agreements concluded by me with Lyttleton. As regards both the carrying out of the armistice and the behaviour of the British in Syria and the Lebanon, everything was going on as though nobody owed us anything.

Dentz, in full agreement with the English, had concentrated his troops in the region of Tripoli. He was still commanding them. The units, with their leaders, their arms and their flags, were encamped side by side, showered by Vichy with decorations and mentions in despatches, receiving no information except what came to them through the channel of the hierarchy, and basking in an atmosphere of imminent repatriation. Indeed the ships, which were to take them away wholesale, were already announced from Marseille, for Darlan was not wasting a day before getting them on their way, nor the Germans before letting them leave. Meanwhile, in obedience to Dentz's orders, which the British armistice commission and the police posts were enforcing integrally, the officers and ranks found themselves forbidden to have any relations with their Free French comrades, nor had these any chance of getting in touch with them. In such conditions few came over. Instead of the honest influence which we claimed the right to exercise on the mind and conscience of men placed, as individuals, in a position to hear us and to choose, there would merely be an operation of collective embarkation applied to an army still in formation, kept in an atmosphere of rancour and humiliation and with no desire other than to leave, as soon as possible, the theatre of its useless sacrifices and bitter efforts.

While the undertakings made to us by the British Government about the interpretation of the Saint John of Acre armistice remained thus a dead letter, it was exactly the same with regard to Great Britain's political disinterest in Syria and the limits of its military Command's authority. While at Damascus and Beirut the encroachments kept a certain appearance of discretion, they displayed themselves openly, on the contrary, in the most sensitive regions, at which the ambitions of England or of her Husseinist vassals had always aimed.

In Jezireh Commandant Reyniers, General Catroux's delegate, was treated as a suspect by the British forces on the spot and prevented from re-forming the Assyro-Chaldean battalions and the Syrian squadrons, which had been provisionally dispersed. At Palmyra and in the desert Mr. Glubb, known as " Glubb Pasha," the English commander of the " Transjordanian Force," was rampant, endeavouring to win the Beduin tribes over to Emir Abdullah. In the Hauran the English agents were bringing pressure upon the local chieftains to make them also recognise the authority of Abdullah and pay taxes to him. Alarming reports came from Aleppo, as also from the tribal state of the Alawis.

But it was in the Jebel ed Druz, above all, that the British showed their intentions openly. And yet no fighting had taken place there, and it had been agreed between Catroux and Wilson that the allied troops should not penetrate there before a joint decision had been taken. It is easy to judge of our state of mind when we heard that a British brigade was installing itself there, that the Druz squadrons were being compulsorily taken in charge by the English, that certain chieftains, who had been summoned and promised immunity by Mr. Bass, known as " Commodore Bass," were declaring that they rejected French authority, that at Suweida the " Maison de France," the residence of our delegate, had been made by force into the seat of the British Command and, finally, that the latter had, in the presence of the troops and population, hauled down the Tricolour flag on it and hoisted the Union Jack.

It was essential to react at once. General Catroux, with my agreement, gave Colonel Monclar on July 29th the order to preceed immediately to Suweida with a strong column, re-take possession of the Maison de France and recover the Druz squadrons. Wilson, duly warned, sent me a somewhat threatening message urging me to stop the column. I answered " that it had already reached its destination, . . . that it was open to him, Wilson, to settle with Catroux—who had proposed this to him,—the question of the stationing of British and French troops in the Jebel ed Druz, . . . that I considered his menacing allusions regrettable, . . . but that, while I remained ready for frank military co-operation, the sovereign rights of France in Syria and the Lebanon and the dignity of the French Army must be kept free from all injury."

At the same time Monclar, having arrived at Suweida, was told by the Commander of the British brigade that " if there had to be a fight, they would fight," and replied with an affirmative. Things did not go so far. On July 31st Monclar was able to instal himself at the Maison de France, ceremonially replace the tricolour upon it, quarter his troops in the town and re-form the group of Druz squadrons under the orders of a French officer. Shortly afterwards the British forces left the region.

But, to set against one incident that was settled, many others kept arising everywhere. Wilson, even, announced that he was going to establish what he called " martial law " and take over all powers. We warned him that, in this case, we would oppose our powers to his, and it would mean rupture. Lyttleton, though kept posted, abstained from intervening. On hearing the rumour that Catroux was about to open discussions at Beirut and Damascus with a view to the future treaties, the British Minister of State even wrote to him direct to ask, as something to be taken for granted, that Spears should be present at these negotiations. This persistent claim to meddle in our affairs, and the incessantly multiplying encroachments, were now reaching the limit of what we could tolerate. On August 1st I telegraphed to Cassin to go and see Mr. Eden and tell him, from me, " that meddling by England was leading us to the gravest complications, and that the doubtful advantages which British policy could derive, in the Levant, from this forgetfulness of the rights of France would be decidedly mediocre in comparison with the major disadvantages which would result from an open quarrel between Free France and England."

Open quarrel? London did not want that. On August 7th Mr. Lyttleton came to visit me at Beirut and spent the day at my residence. This was the occasion of a conference which one might have thought decisive,—if anything, in the Middle East, ever was so for the British. The Minister agreed frankly that the British military were not carrying out our agreements of July 24th and 25th. " In that there is no more," he affirmed, " than a delay to be attributed to faults of transmission and, perhaps, of understanding, which I keenly regret and to which I mean to put an end." He appeared surprised and displeased at the incidents created by the English agents, of which Catroux gave chapter and verse. He declared that Vichy was violating the armistice convention; that, for example, the 52 British officers who had been made prisoner in the recent fighting and were supposed to be given up without delay, had not yet been so, and that it was not even known where they had been put; that, in consequence, Dentz was about to be transferred to Palestine, and that all facilities would henceforth be given us for winning people over.

I did not conceal from Lyttleton that we were outraged by the manner in which our allies were practising co-operation. " Rather than continue like this, we prefer," I told him,

" to go our own way while you go yours." When he complained, in his turn, citing the obstacles we were creating to the British Command, I replied, on the lines of what Foch in person had once taught me, that there could be no such thing as a valid inter-allied Command that was not disinterested and that, whatever he, Lyttleton, might say to me or write to me in all good faith, that was not the case here with the British. As for invoking, as Wilson was doing, the necessity of the defence of the Levant in order to usurp authority in the Jezireh, at Palmyra and in the Jebel ed Druz, this was merely a bad excuse. The enemy was now a long way away from the Jebel ed Druz, from Palmyra, from the Jezireh. If it was wise to provide for the possibility of the Axis menace weighing on Syria and the Lebanon anew, the proper way to prepare for that was a common defence plan between French and British, not an English policy of encroachments on our domain.

Mr. Lyttleton, anxious to end his visit on some note of harmony, caught the " defence plan " ball. He suggested bringing in General Wilson, whom I had been unwilling to have come to our meeting, to discuss it. I replied in the negative, but agreed that Wilson should see Catroux outside Beirut to get a draft worked out. Their meeting took place next day. Practically nothing came of it: a proof that, on the English side, as far as the Levant was concerned, something quite other than an offensive by the Germans was in mind. However, the Minister of State, to mark his goodwill, had handed me, before leaving, a letter which repeated the assurances already given on the subject of Great Britain's political disinterestedness. In addition, Mr. Lyttleton had stated to me verbally that I would be satisfied by the practical results of our interview.

As so many shocks had not shattered Free France, I was prepared to believe that one might, in fact, count on a respite from our difficulties. Nonetheless I had seen enough to be sure that, sooner or later, the crisis would begin again. But sufficient unto the day is the evil thereof. To formulate the conclusion of this temporarily overcome trial, I sent to the delegation in London, which was alarmed at my attitude, messages recapitulating its phases and drawing this moral: "Our greatness and our strength consist solely in intransigence concerning the rights of France. We shall have need of this intransigence up to the Rhine, inclusive."

At any rate, from that moment things took a different turn. Larminat was able, with his staff, to visit those units which were not yet embarked and to make the last-moment appeal to officers and men. Catroux had the opportunity of seeing certain officials whom he personally wanted to keep. I myself received many visits. In the end those who came over amounted to 127 officers and about 6,000 N.C.O.s and men, or one-fifth of the strength of the troops in the Levant. In addition, the Syrian and Lebanese elements, totalling 290 officers and 14,000 men, were at once reconstituted. But 25,000 officers, N.C.O.s and men of the French Army and Air Force were finally torn away from us, whereas the great majority would, without any doubt, have decided to join us if we had had the time and the means to enlighten them. For those Frenchmen who were returning to France with the permission of the enemy, so giving up the possibility of returning there as fighters, were, I knew, submerged in doubt and sadness. As for me, it was with my heart wrung that I gazed at the Vichy transports lying in the harbour and saw them, once loaded, disappear out to sea, taking with them one of the chances of our country.

At least those that remained to her, out there, could now be made to yield results. General Catroux applied himself to this most actively. Possessing the sense of the greatness of France and the taste for authority, skilful at handling men, especially those of the Middle East, whose subtle and passionate games he readily saw through, as sure of his own value as he was devoted to our great enterprise and to the man at its head, he was destined to guide the policy of France in the Levant with much dignity and distinction. If I came to think that his desire to charm and his leaning towards conciliation were not always suitable to the kind of sword-play which was imposed on him, if, in particular, he was late in discerning the full depths of malice in the British design, I never ceased to recognise his great merits and his high qualities. In a situation rendered exceptionally unpromising by appalling initial conditions—the lack of resources, and the obstacles reared up on every side,—General Catroux did France good service.

He had, to begin with, to organise from top to bottom the representation of France, which the departure of most of the " authoritative " officials and of the majority of the political officers had suddenly and everywhere reduced almost to nothing. Catroux took as his secretary-general Paul Lepissié, who had come to us from Bangkok, where he was French Minister. He delegated General Collet and M. Pierre Bart respectively to the Syrian and Lebanese Governments. At the same time MM. David, later Fauquenot, at Aleppo, de Montjou at Tripoli, Dumarçay at Sidon, Governor Schoeffler and later General Monclar among the Alawis, and Colonels Brosset in the Jezireh, des Essars at Homs and Oliva-Roget in the Jebel ed Druz, were to ensure our presence and our influence in each of the regions.

I must say that the populations showed warm approval of us. They saw in Free France something gallant, surprising and chivalrous which seemed to them to correspond to what was, in their eyes, the ideal persona of France. Besides, they felt that our presence warded off the danger of a German invasion from their territory, assured them of a future in the economic field and imposed a limit on the abuses of their feudal lords. Lastly, our generous announcement of their independence never ceased to move them. The same manifestations which had occurred at the moment of my entry into Damascus and Beirut were renewed, a few days later, at Aleppo, at Latakia, at Tripoli, and in many towns and villages of that marvellous land, where every site and every locality, in its drama and poetry, is as it were a witness of history.

But while the feelings of the people showed themselves clearly favourable, the politicians yielded less frankly. Here what was most urgent, in each of the two States, was to invest a Government capable of assuming the new duties we were about to transfer to it, especially in the fields of finance, economics and public order. We intended, in fact, to reserve to the mandatory authority merely the responsibility for defence, for foreign relations and for the " interests common " to the two States: currency, customs, supply,—all fields in which it was as impossible to hand over at once as it was to separate Syria and the Lebanon on the spur of the moment. Later, when the evolution of the war made it possible, elections would be held, from which complete national authorities would issue. Pending this stage, the setting-to-work of governments with enlarged prerogatives was already bringing clan passions and personal rivalries to the boiling point.

In Syria the situation, from this point of view, was particularly complicated. In July, 1939, when Paris finally refused to ratify the 1936 treaty, the High Commissioner had been led to set aside the President of the Republic, Hachem Bey Atassi, and to dissolve Parliament. We found in the saddle at Damascus, under the direction of Khaled Bey Azem, who indeed was a valuable and well-thought-of man, a ministry which confined itself to dispatching business without taking on the character of a national Government. I had at first hoped to be able to re-establish in Syria the previous state of things. At first President Hachem Bey and, with him, the head of his last government, Djemil Mardam Bey, and M. Fares El Koury, President of the dissolved House, had shown themselves ready in principle for this, in the course of the conversations I had with them in the presence of General Catroux. But although they were, all three, experienced politicians, patriots devoted to their country and men desirous of conciliating French friendship, they did not seem to discern in all its amplitude the historic opportunity, now presented to them, of setting Syria on the road to independence in full agreement with France and by overcoming misgivings and grievances in one great impulse. I found them too careful, to my way of thinking, of juridical formalities, and too sensitive to the suggestions of a punctilious nationalism. However, I invited General Catroux to pursue the conversations with them and to turn towards a different solution only if their reservations were really preventing us from getting anywhere.

In the Lebanon we were able to move faster, though what

we met with was not the ideal. The President of the Republic, Emile Eddé, an unshakeable friend of France and a seasoned statesman, had voluntarily resigned three months before the campaign which brought us to Beirut. He had not been replaced. At the same time, the duration of the Parliament's mandate had long expired. From the point of view of principles and of the Constitution, we had a clean slate before us. But the same could not be said of the struggles of the political clans. A desperate rivalry set against Emile Eddé another eminent Maronite, M. Bechara El Koury. Inured to the twists and turns of Lebanese affairs, he grouped around him numerous partisans and various interests. " Eddé has had the position already," M. Koury told me; " it's my turn to be President! " Lastly, Riad Solh, the passionate leader of the Sunnite Moslems, waving the standard of Arab nationalism round about the mosques, alarmed the two competitors without, however, making them agree.

We judged, in these circumstances, that it was better to raise to the supreme rank the man whom we found in the saddle, at the head of the Government,—M. Alfred Naccache, who was less brilliant than any of the other three, but capable, esteemed and a man whose presence at the head of the State in a transitional situation ought not, it seemed to us, to provoke vehement opposition. That, indeed, was only partly true. For, while Emile Eddé adapted himself generously to our momentary choice and Riad Solh avoided embarrassing the man who was carrying the burden, M. Bechara El Koury went at him full tilt with intrigues and cabals.

Pending the free consultation of the people, this political situation at Damascus and Beirut was in no way disquieting in itself. Public order was in no danger. The administration did its job. Opinion accepted straightaway the postponement of the elections due to the *force majeure* of war. In short, the transition period between the mandate régime and that of independence could and would, no doubt, pass off very peacefully, if British intervention did not systematically seek in it pretexts and opportunities.

Now, while Mr. Lyttleton, at Cairo, absorbed himself in

the problems raised by the supplying of the Middle East, and
while General Wilson disappeared, together with his martial
law and direct encroachments, Spears was installing himself
at Beirut as head of the British liaison services, to become, in
January, British minister plenipotentiary to the Syrian and
Lebanese Governments. He had some incomparable trump
cards: the presence of the British Army; the multifarious
activity of the Intelligence agents; the mastery of the economic
relations of the two countries, which lived on exchanges;
support in all capitals from the leading diplomatic service in
the world; great propaganda resources; official backing
from the neighbouring Arab States,—Iraq and Transjordania
where Husseinite princes reigned, Palestine whose British
High Commissioner constantly displayed alarm as to the
repercussions among the Arabs in his territory of the " oppression " suffered by their Syrian and Lebanese brothers, and,
lastly, Egypt where the stability of the Ministers in power and
the ambition of those who aspired to reach it had alike no
real chance except with British blessing.

In the permeable, intrigue-ridden, venal medium which
the Levant laid open to England's plans, the game, with such
cards, was easy and tempting. Only the prospect of a rupture
with us and the necessity of conciliating the feelings of France
could impose on London a certain moderation. But the same
prospect and the same necessity similarly restricted our own
freedom of action. The moral and material damage which
separation from Great Britain would entail for us was bound,
obviously, to make us hesitate. Besides, would not Free France,
as she grew larger, lose some of that concentrated firmness
which had made it possible for her to win this time by staking
all on one throw? How, lastly, could we reveal to the French
people the behaviour of its allies when, in the abyss where it
was plunged, nothing was more vital than to arouse its confidence and hope in order to lead it into the fight against the
enemy?

In spite of everything, the fact that our authority was
being set up in Syria and the Lebanon brought considerable
reinforcement to the camp of liberty. From now on, the Allies'

rear in the Middle East was solidly protected. It was no longer possible for the Germans to get a footing in the Arab countries, except by undertaking a large-scale and dangerous expedition. Turkey, whom Hitler hoped to harass sufficiently to make her join the Axis and serve it as a bridge between Europe and Asia, was no longer in danger of being invested and would therefore grow firmer. Finally, Free France was in a position to put increased forces into the field.

In this connection, we decided to hold the Levant territories with the Syrian and Lebanese troops, a fixed coastal defence entrusted to our Navy and a reserve formed by a French brigade, the whole placed under the orders of General Humblot. At the same time we organised two strong mixed brigades and an armoured group with the corresponding services, to go and fight elsewhere. General de Larminat, replaced in his function of High Commissioner at Brazzaville by Médecin-Général Sicé, was given command of this mobile force, whose effectives, alas! were limited, but whose fire-power was great, thanks to the war material we had just taken in the Levant. On my way back through Cairo I saw General Auchinleck, the new Commander-in-Chief. " As soon as our forces are ready," I told him, " we shall place them at your disposal, provided it is to fight." " Rommel," he replied, " will certainly see to it that I shall find the opportunity."

But while in the Mediterranean the war was about to become concentrated on the borders of Egypt and Libya, in better conditions for us and for our allies, it was setting fire to immense expanses of Europe from the Baltic to the Black Sea. The German offensive in Russia was progressing with immense rapidity. And yet, whatever the initial successes of Hitler's armies, Russian resistance was strengthening, day after day. On the political plane as on the strategic, these were events of an incalculable bearing.

Because of them, America saw offered to her a chance for decisive action. No doubt it had to be expected that Japan would soon undertake in the Pacific a diversion of great scope which would reduce and retard the intervention of the United States. But this intervention, aimed at Europe and at Africa, was henceforth certain, since a gigantic adventure now absorbed the main part of the German strength in the distances of Russia, since at the same time the British, with the help of the Free French, had been able to make sure of solid positions in the Middle East and since, finally, the turn taken by the war was bound to awake hope, and so a fighting spirit, in the oppressed peoples.

What I had to do now was, as far as possible, to influence Washington and Moscow, to push on towards the development of French resistance, to inspire and guide the mobilisation of our resources throughout the world. For that, I needed to return to London, the centre of communications and capital of the war. I arrived there on September 1st, foreseeing, after my recent experiences, what the ordeals of the enterprise would be like up to the last day, but convinced, from now on, that victory lay at the end.

VII. THE ALLIES

I n the world's eyes Free France, at the approach of its second winter, was no longer the astonishing escapade which had been received at first with irony, pity or tears. Its reality—political, martial and territorial—was now to be seen on all sides. From now on, what it needed was to debouch on to the diplomatic plane, clear the space which belonged to it in the midst of the Allies, appear there as belligerent and sovereign France, whose rights must be respected and whose share of victory reserved. In these matters, I was prepared to submit to periods of transition. But I was neither willing nor able to concede anything as regards the substance. Besides, I was impatient to reach results and to acquire the position before the decisive collision should have settled the outcome of the war. There was therefore no time to lose, especially with the Great Powers: Washington, Moscow and London.

The United States bring to great affairs elementary feelings and a complicated policy. This was the case in 1941 with their attitude towards France. While in the depths of American opinion the enterprise of General de Gaulle aroused passionate response, the whole fringe of officialdom persisted in treating it with coldness or indifference. As for the officials, they kept their relations with Vichy unchanged, claiming thus to be wresting France from German influence, preventing the fleet from being handed over, maintaining contact with Weygand, Noguès and Boisson, whom Roosevelt expected one day to open to him the gates of Africa. But, with an astonishing self-contradiction, the policy of the United States, while keeping diplomatic relations with Pétain, held aloof from Free France

213

on the pretext that it was impossible to prejudge what government the French nation would give itself when it was liberated. At bottom, what the American policy-makers took for granted was the effacement of France. They therefore came to terms with Vichy. If, nonetheless, at certain points of the world they contemplated collaborating with this or that French authority as the struggle might dictate, they intended that this should only be by occasional and local arrangements.

These conditions made agreement with Washington difficult for us. Besides, the personal equation of the President affected the problem with a factor that was the opposite of favourable. Although Franklin Roosevelt and I had not yet been able to meet, various signs made me aware of his reserve towards me. I wanted, nonetheless, to do everything possible to prevent the United States, then about to enter the war, and France, for whom I was ready to answer that she had never left it, from following divergent paths.

As for the form of the relations to be established—a subject which the politicians, diplomats and publicists were to discuss to their hearts' content,—I must say that to me at that time it was almost a matter of indifference. I attached much more importance to the reality and content of the relations than to the successive formulæ which the jurists of Washington would drape about the " recognition." At the same time, in face of America's enormous resources and the ambition of Roosevelt to make law and dictate rights throughout the world, I felt that independence was well and truly at stake. In short, while I wanted to try to reach an understanding with Washington, we must do so on practical foundations and yet standing on our own feet.

During the heroic period of the first months of Free France, Garreau-Dombasle and Jacques de Sieyès had served me most usefully as spokesmen. It was now a matter of negotiating. I instructed Pleven to begin the approaches. He knew America. He was skilful. There was nothing he did not know of our own affairs. As early as May, 1941, I had laid down this mission for him as follows: " Settling the establishment of our permanent and direct relations with the State Department, the economic relations of Free French Africa and Oceania with America and the direct purchases by us of material useful for the war; setting on foot our information and our propaganda services in the United States; forming our committees there and organising the assistance of American well-wishers." Pleven had left at the beginning of June and was not arriving empty-handed. In fact we were offering the United States, immediately, the possibility of installing their air forces in the Cameroons, the Chad and the Congo, Africa being marked out in advance to serve them as a base for approaching Europe when the day came on which they would have to take armed action. In addition, in face of the Japanese menace, the assistance of the Pacific islands over which the Cross of Lorraine was flying would have considerable importance for them.

In fact, the American Government was not slow to ask for the right to use certain of our African bases, and later those in the New Hebrides and New Caledonia, for its aircraft. Not being yet belligerent, it did so on behalf of " Pan-American Airways," but without there being any possible doubt as to the significance of its step.

As the United States saw approaching them the date when war would fall due, Washington showed us more attention. In August a liaison mission directed by Colonel Cunningham was sent to the Chad. In September Mr. Cordell Hull stated publicly that there was a community of interests between the United States and Free France. " Our relations with this group," he added, " are very good in all respects." On October 1st, Pleven was received officially at the State Department by the Under-Secretary of State, Sumner Welles. On November 11th President Roosevelt, in a letter to Mr. Stettinius, extended the benefit of " Lend-Lease " to Free France because " the defence of the territories rallied to Free France was vital for the defence of the United States." At the end of the same month Weygand, recalled from Algiers, took with him an American illusion, and Washington did not yet know by what other to replace it. Meanwhile, Pleven having returned to London to serve as a member of the National Committee which I had just set up, Adrien Tixier, the director of the International Labour Office, became head of our delegation, with the agreement of the State Department. Lastly, in London itself, regular relations had been established between us and Mr. Drexel Biddle, Ambassador of the United States to the refugee Governments in Great Britain.

While the first official relations were thus being drawn together, various changes became noticeable in the press and radio, hitherto malevolent about us, when not silent. At the same time there were signs among the French émigrés, some of whom were men of note, of the desire to link themselves with those who were upholding the flag. So it was that, when Professor Focillon founded the French Institute at New York, grouping together the leading scientists, historians and philosophers, he obtained the agreement of his colleagues that he should ask General de Gaulle to recognise its establishment by decree.

On December 7th the attack on Pearl Harbour hurled America into the war. One might have thought that, from that moment, American policy would treat the Free French, who were fighting its own enemies, as allies. Nothing of the sort happened, however. Before Washington finally made up its mind to do so, many painful ups and downs would have to be endured. So it was that, on December 13th, the American Government requisitioned in its ports the liner *Normandie* and thirteen other French ships, without consenting to treat with us, or even to talk with us, about the use to be made of them or the arming of them. A few weeks later, the *Normandie* went up in flames, in lamentable circumstances. In the course of December the Declaration of the United Nations was negotiated, then signed by twenty-six governments, of whom we were not one. The strange, not to say troubling, nature of the attitude of the United States towards us was to be revealed, indeed, by an incident almost insignificant in itself, but which was given serious importance by the official reaction of Washington. Perhaps, on my side, I had provoked it in order to stir up the bottom of things, as one throws a stone into a pond. This was the rallying of Saint Pierre and Miquelon.

We had thought of this since the beginning. It was, indeed,

scandalous that, quite close to Newfoundland, a small French archipelago, whose population was asking to join us, should be kept in obedience to Vichy. The British, haunted by the idea that, right on the route of the big convoys, the German submarines might one day receive assistance thanks to the radio station at Saint Pierre, wished it to be rallied. But, according to them, Washington's agreement was necessary. As for me, I considered this agreement desirable, but not indispensable since this was merely an internal French affair. Indeed I was all the more determined to gain control of the archipelago when I saw Admiral Robert, Vichy's High Commissioner for the Antilles, Guiana and Saint Pierre, treating with the Americans,—the end of which could only be the neutralisation of these French territories under Washington's guarantee. Hearing in December that, in point of fact, Admiral Horne had been sent by Roosevelt to settle with Robert the terms for the neutralisation of our possessions in America, and of the ships there, I decided to act at the first opportunity.

This opportunity presented itself in the form of Admiral Muselier. As he was to go to Canada to inspect the submarine cruiser *Surcouf*, then stationed at Halifax, together with the French corvettes on convoy escort duty, I arranged with him that, in principle, he should carry out the operation. In fact, on December 12th, having grouped the corvettes *Mimosa*, *Aconit* and *Alysse* around the *Surcouf*, he held himself ready to move on to Saint Pierre and Miquelon. But he thought it right, on his own, to ask the Canadians and Americans at Ottawa for their assent beforehand. The secret was thus out. I found myself obliged to warn the British in order to avoid the appearance of concealment. To Muselier Washington sent the answer " No! " through its Minister at Ottawa, and the Admiral assured him that from that moment he was giving up the idea of going to the islands. To me the London Government wrote that, for its part, it raised no obstacle, but that, given American opposition, it requested that the operation should be postponed. In these circumstances, and barring some new fact, we would have to resign ourselves to this.

But the new fact did arise. A few hours after replying to me, the Foreign Office let us know—was it not intentional?—that the Canadian Government, in agreement with the United States if not at their instigation, had decided to land at Saint Pierre, with consent or by force, the staff necessary to take over the radio station. We at once protested in London and Washington. But as soon as a foreign intervention on French territory was in question, no hesitation seemed to me permissible. I gave Admiral Muselier the order to win Saint Pierre and Miquelon over at once. He did so on Christmas Eve, in the midst of the greatest enthusiasm from the inhabitants, without a shot having to be fired. A plebiscite gave Free France a crushing majority. The young people at once joined up. The men in their prime formed a detachment to ensure the defence of the islands. Savary, appointed as administrator, replaced the Governor.

One might have thought that this small operation, carried out so happily, would have been ratified by the American Government without any shock. The most to be normally expected was a little ill-humour in the offices of the State Department. But no, it was a real storm that broke in the United States. Mr. Cordell Hull himself began it with a communiqué in which he announced that he was interrupting his Christmas holidays and returning in haste to Washington. "The action taken by three so-called Free French ships at Saint Pierre-Miquelon," the Secretary of State added, "was an arbitrary action contrary to the agreement of all parties and certainly without the prior knowledge or consent of the United States Government." He ended by declaring that his Government had "inquired of the Canadian Government as to the steps that Government is prepared to take to restore the *status quo* of these islands."

In the United States, for three weeks, the tumult in the Press and the emotion of public opinion went beyond all imaginable limits. This was because the incident suddenly offered the American public the opportunity of manifesting its preference as between an official policy which was still based on Pétain and the feeling of many which was inclining towards de Gaulle. As for us, the end having been attained, we now aimed at bringing Washington to a more just understanding of things. As Churchill was at Quebec, in conference with Roosevelt, I telegraphed to the Prime Minister to warn him of the bad effect produced on French opinion by the State Department's attitude. Churchill replied that he would do all he could to see that the affair was settled, although he referred to favourable developments as being held up by it. At the same time Tixier, on my behalf, handed appeasing messages to Mr. Cordell Hull, while Roussy de Sales used his credit with the American Press for the same purpose and we tried to enlist Mr. W. Bullitt, the last United States Ambassador to the Republic, who was then in Cairo.

The Washington Government, faced by much criticism in its own country and tacit disapproval from England and Canada, could in the end only accept the accomplished fact. However, before consenting to this, it tried intimidation, using the British Government as intermediary. But this intermediary was itself not very convinced. Mr. Eden saw me twice on January 14th and put up a show of insisting that we should agree to the islands being neutralised, to the administration being independent of the National Committee and to a control by allied officials being established on the spot. As I refused such a solution, Mr. Eden announced to me that the United States was thinking of sending a cruiser and two destroyers to Saint Pierre. " What will you do then? " he asked me. " The allied ships," I answered, " will stop at the limit of territorial waters, and the American admiral will come to lunch with Muselier, who will be delighted." " But if the cruiser crosses the limit? " " Our people will summon her to stop in the usual way." " If she holds on her course? " " That would be most unfortunate, for then our people would have to open fire." Mr. Eden threw up his arms. " I can understand your alarm," I concluded with a smile, " but I have confidence in the democracies."

The only thing to do was to turn over the page. On January 19th Mr. Cordell Hull received Tixier and explained to him without bitterness the reasons for the policy he had pursued up to then. Not long afterwards he took cognizance of the reply I had had conveyed to him. On the 22nd Mr. Churchill, back in England, sent to ask me to call on him. I went with Pleven. The Prime Minister, with Eden beside him, proposed to us on behalf of Washington, London and Ottawa an arrangement according to which everything at Saint Pierre and Miquelon would remain as we had ordered it. In exchange, we were to let the three Governments publish a communiqué which would to some extent save the face of the State Department. " After which," the British Ministers told us, " no one will meddle in the business." We accepted the arrangement. In the end nothing was published. We kept Saint Pierre and Miquelon and none of the Allies bothered about it any more.

Moreover, whatever might be Washington's juridical position and feelings towards us, the entry of the United States into the war obliged them to co-operate with Free France. This was the case, immediately, with the Pacific where, by reason of the lightning advance of the Japanese, our possessions—New Caledonia, the Marquesas, Tuamotu, the Society Islands and even Tahiti—might from one day to the next become vital to allied strategy. Some of them were already being used as naval and air ports of call. In addition, New Caledonia's nickel was of great importance for armaments manufacture. The Americans soon saw the advantage which an understanding with us would present. This was true reciprocally, for if the need arose we would not be capable of defending our islands by ourselves. It was thus of set policy that our National Committee had decided in advance to give satisfaction to what the Americans would ask of us as regards our possessions in the Pacific Ocean, on the sole condition that they on their side would respect French sovereignty and our own authority there.

It was necessary, however, that this authority should be exercised on the spot in a satisfactory way. This would certainly not be easy in view of the extreme remoteness and dispersion of our islands, the shortage of resources and the character of the populations, who were certainly very attached

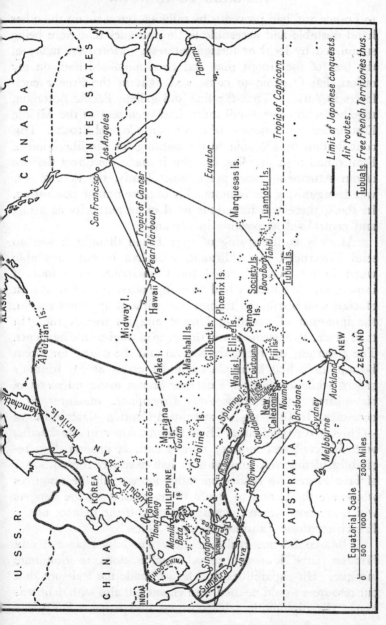

THE BATTLE OF THE PACIFIC

Legend:
——— Limit of Japanese conquests.
- - - Air routes.
Tubuais Free French Territories thus.

to France and had proved it by rallying, but were on the other hand unstable and accessible to the intrigues that were being stimulated by local or foreign interests. Moreover, many of the best of the troops that had been mobilised had, on my orders, left Oceania to come and fight in the Free French forces in Africa. Thus the fine and gallant Pacific Battalion, together with other small units, had been sent to the Middle East under the command of Lieutenant-Colonel Broche. This contribution by Oceania to the fighting for the liberation of France had high significance. But it made the direct defence of our settlements more precarious. Lastly, the state of war was disorganising the economic life of these remote possessions. In short, there was imperious need of an authority as strong and centralised as possible in Oceania.

As early as the spring of 1941 I had thought it wise to send Governor-General Brunot, who had become available when Leclerc had liberated the Cameroons, on a tour of inspection. But Brunot had come up, often violently, against officials who attributed to him, not without apparent reason, the intention of installing himself and his friends there in their place. Papeete had been the scene of tragi-comic incidents. The governor, the secretary-general and the consul for Great Britain there had been placed under arrest at M. Brunot's orders, while at Noumea Governor Sautot made no secret of his mistrust of the inspector. Exceptional measures were necessary. In July, 1941, I appointed Captain—later Admiral —Thierry d'Argenlieu as High Commissioner in the Pacific, with full civil and military powers and, as mission, " to re-establish definitively and without half-measures the authority of Free France, to render operative for war all the resources which are there, and to assure there, against all the dangers which are possible and perhaps imminent, the defence of the French territories in union with our Allies."

I had confidence in d'Argenlieu. His lofty character and firmness gave him the moral qualifications to dominate intrigue. His capabilities as a leader made me feel sure that our resources would be used with vigour but also with delibera-tion. His diplomatic talents would find scope. For while his nature and, if I may say so, his vocation,[1] led him to conceive of the action of Free France as a crusade, he thought, and rightly, that this crusade might as well be skilful. The light cruiser *Le Triomphant* and the sloop *Chevreuil* were placed at the disposal of the High Commissioner in the Pacific. He began by putting things in order once more in Tahiti. Orselli was appointed Governor there, while Brunot and his " victims " came to state their case in London. At the same time, with the situation in the Far East becoming graver day by day, d'Argenlieu saw his original mission augmented by that of co-ordinating the activities of our representatives in Australia, New Zealand and China as well as at Hong Kong, Singapore, Manila and Batavia. At the same time Escarra, who was already well known among the Chinese as an international jurist, proceeded to Chung King to make contact with Marshal Chiang Kai Shek and prepare for the establishment of official relations.

Suddenly, at the beginning of December, the Pacific caught fire. After the terrible surprise at Pearl Harbour, the Japanese landed in British Malaya, in the Netherlands East Indies and in the Philippines, and seized Guam, Wake and Hong Kong. By the beginning of January they were blockading a British army at Singapore, and it was soon forced to capitulate. At the same time they took Manila. MacArthur was besieged in the Bataan Peninsula. What I knew of this general made me esteem him highly. One day I went to call on John Winant, United States Ambassador in London, a diplomat of great intelligence and feeling, and spoke as follows: " As a soldier and an ally, I must tell you that the disappearance of MacArthur would be a great misfortune. There are only a few first-class military leaders in our camp. He is one of them. He must not be lost. But he is lost unless his Government gives him the order personally to leave Bataan by some combination

[1] After serving in the French Navy during the first world war, he joined the Carmelite Order in 1920. In 1932 he was chosen as Provincial of the Carmelite Order. In August, 1939, he was again called to the service of France and was placed on the staff of the Cherbourg sector. In June, 1940, he played an active part in the defence of the arsenal and was made prisoner. Having escaped to the French coast from the convoy taking him to Germany, he crossed the Channel and joined General de Gaulle. (Translator's note.)

of motor-boat and flying-boat. I think this order ought to be given him and am asking you to make General de Gaulle's opinion on this subject known to President Roosevelt." I do not know whether my approach did or did not contribute to the decision which was taken. In any case it was with great satisfaction that I heard, some time afterwards, that General MacArthur had managed to reach Melbourne.

As early, then, as the end of December New Caledonia was threatened,—and all the more so since it flanked Australia, a principal enemy objective. On December 22nd, indeed, Vichy, foreseeing the occupation of our islands in Oceania by the Japanese and wishing, no doubt, to try to regain authority there under cover of the invader, appointed Admiral Decoux as High Commissioner for the Pacific. By means of the Saigon radio he ceaselessly incited the population of New Caledonia to revolt against Free France. Meanwhile, d'Argenlieu, struggling in the midst of anxieties and difficulties, was sending me reports full of determination but free from any illusion. As for me, while assuring him of my certainty that he would save honour at least, I despatched to Noumea the few reinforcements available: cadres, naval guns, the auxiliary cruiser *Cap des Palmes* and, lastly, the *Surcouf*, whose submarine usefulness and wide radius of action would, it was hoped, find scope for themselves in the Pacific. Alas! On the night of February 19th, near the entrance to the Panama Canal, this submarine—the largest in the world—was run down by a cargo boat and sank with her commander, Capitaine de Corvette Blaison, and her crew of 130 men.

Meanwhile, under the pressure of events, co-operation with our allies was beginning to get organised. On January 15th the State Department sent our Washington delegation a memorandum laying down the undertakings into which the United States were entering with reference to " respect for our sovereignty in the French islands of the Pacific; the fact that the bases and installations which they would be authorised to establish there would remain the property of France; the right of reciprocity which would be recognised as belonging to France if the American bases were kept there after the war."

On January 23rd, Mr. Cordell Hull telegraphed to me that
" the American and British chiefs of staff appreciated the
importance of New Caledonia and were taking steps to ensure
its defence in accordance with the conditions laid down in
the memorandum of January 15th." The Secretary of State
graciously expressed " his hope that the splendid assistance
and the co-operation offered in the past by the French High
Commissioner would be continued in the future."

Practical measures followed these excellent moves. On
February 25th I was able to announce to d'Argenlieu that
General Patch, who had been appointed commander of the
American land forces in the Pacific, had received orders from
his Government to go to Noumea and there to reach agreement with him " directly and in the most friendly spirit " on
the organisation of the command. On March 6th the French
National Committee was invited to send its representative to
the " Pacific War Committee " which had been set up in
London, and on which delegates from Great Britain, New
Zealand, Australia and the United States sat for the purpose
of exchanging information and suggestions. On March 7th
the American Government asked us for, and obtained,
authorisation to establish bases in the Tuamotu Archipelago
and the Society Islands. Lastly, on March 9th, General Patch
arrived at Noumea, followed by considerable forces.

The French possessions in the Pacific had, from that
moment, some chance of escaping invasion. However, before
co-operation between our allies and us could work on the spot
as it should, a serious crisis was to arise and require sur-
mounting. At first, certainly, harmony reigned between
Patch and d'Argenlieu. But soon the presence of the American
forces, dollars and secret services in the midst of populations
disturbed by siege fever was to aggravate the latent causes of
agitation. Part of the militia, stirred by local ambitions, stole
away from the High Commissioner's authority and placed
itself under that of Patch, who committed the error of covering
this insubordination. At the same time Governor Sautot, who
found it hard to endure being subordinated to d'Argenlieu,
sought to acquire a personal popularity of which he might

make use. When, after exercising patience for some time, I summoned Sautot to London to give him a different post—and indeed one suitable to the services he had rendered,—he decided at first to obey, but then, giving as his reason " the discontent caused among the population by the order he had received," he took it upon himself to " postpone his departure."

Governor Sautot was nonetheless shipped away—with the proper formalities and the requisite firmness—to answer my summons, Montchamp being sent from the Chad to replace him and Colonel de Conchard despatched from London to command the troops. But there followed, at Noumea and in the bush, violent demonstrations openly encouraged by the attitude of the Americans. Having a foreboding of some unfortunate move, I had warned Washington and, at the same time, let Patch know that " we could not accept his interference in a French matter." But simultaneously I invited d'Argenlieu " to make the greatest efforts to re-establish personal relations of confidence with Patch and to show, if possible, some leniency towards a population which is obviously disturbed." After three days of incidents, good sense resumed its sway and d'Argenlieu all the levers of command. Indeed it was urgent, for on May 6th at Corregidor and on the 10th at Mindanao the last American forces in the Philippines had capitulated, while in the Coral Sea, which washes Australia on the north-east, a battle was beginning on which all depended, between the fleets of Japan and the United States. From one moment to another, Noumea might be attacked.

In face of the imminent peril, the population, condemning the recent disorders, drew together about the French authority. Various turbulent individuals were sent off to serve in Syria. Patch, on his side, went to see d'Argenlieu to excuse himself for the " misunderstandings " in which he had become involved. I telegraphed to the American general that he had my confidence and that of Free France provided he marched hand in hand with the High Commissioner of France. After which Americans and French went off together and resolutely to take up their battle stations. As things turned out, they did not have to defend themselves. For at that very moment the Japanese, beaten in the Coral Sea, were obliged to give up the idea of attacking Australia and New Caledonia.

In this way the war was forcing the United States to entertain closer and closer relations with us. It must be said that in their own country the national mood favoured this. At a time when the American people was inspired by its instinctive idealism to a crusading fervour and had decided to shoulder an immense and magnificent programme of arms production and mobilisation, the fighters of Free France could not fail to be popular. Politics were bound to feel the effects. In February, 1942, we were in a position to complete our delegation in Washington by a military mission, which I entrusted to Colonel de Chevigné. On March 1st, in a public statement, America recognised that " the French islands in the Pacific were under the effective control of the French National Committee, and that it was with the authorities exercising this control that the Government of the United States was dealing and would continue to deal." As for Equatorial Africa, the State Department declared, in a communiqué dated April 4th, that there, too, it recognised the authority of Free France, while a United States Consul-General was being appointed to Brazzaville with our exequatur. Since the United States were asking us for the right to use the aerodrome at Pointe-Noire for their heavy bombers, we gave them the authorisation on condition that they should first supply us with the eight Lockheed aircraft indispensable to our own communications. After a close negotiation the Lockheeds were delivered to us, and this made it possible for Colonel de Marmier to establish a French line between Brazzaville and Damascus and for the American aircraft to land and take off at Pointe-Noire. Between America and us the air had been cleared without our having ceased—far from it—to stand up for France.

While we were, step by step and not without trouble, reducing the diplomatic distance that separated Washington from Free France, we managed, in one leap, to create a relationship of alliance with Moscow. It must be said that, in this respect, the attack launched by Hitler simplified the procedure by placing Russia in mortal peril. At the same time, the Soviets realised the absurdity of the policy by which they had, in 1917 and in 1939, treated with Germany and turned their back on France and England. In the extreme disarray into which the invasion was plunging them, the rulers of the Kremlin were now seen to reverse their attitude immediately and without reserve. Whereas the Moscow radio had not ceased to hold forth against the " English imperialists " and " their Gaullist mercenaries " up to the very moment when the German tanks crossed the Russian frontier, the Moscow wavelengths were heard pouring forth encomia on Churchill and de Gaulle literally an hour afterwards.

In any case, for crushed France the fact that Russia was now thrown into the war opened up the greatest hopes. Unless the Reich succeeded in rapidly liquidating the army of the Soviets, it would make the enemy suffer a constant and terrible attrition. I had no doubt, obviously, that a victory in which the Soviets would have taken a major share might well, *ipso facto*, face the world with other perils later. These would have to be taken into account, even as we fought at their side. But I considered that, before philosophising, one must live, that is to say win. Russia offered the chance of doing so. At the same time her presence in the allied camp brought Fighting France a balancing element over against the Anglo-Saxons, of which I was determined to make use.

It was at Damascus, where I had gone after the entry of our troops into the town, that I heard, on June 23rd, 1941, of the opening of hostilities between Russians and Germans. My decision was made at once. As early as the 24th I telegraphed to the delegation in London the following instructions: " Without consenting to discuss at present the vices and even crimes of the Soviet régime, we must proclaim—like Churchill —that we are very frankly with the Russians, since they are fighting the Germans. . . . It is not the Russians who are crushing France, occupying Paris, Reims, Bordeaux and Strasbourg. . . . The German aircraft, tanks and soldiers which the Russians are destroying and will destroy will no longer be

there to prevent us from liberating France." Such is the tone
I ordered to be given to our propaganda. At the same time
I invited our delegation to go to M. Maisky, the Soviet
Ambassador in London, and tell him in my name: "The
French people is with the Russians against Germany. We
desire, therefore, to organise military relations with Moscow."

Cassin and Dejean saw M. Maisky, who immediately
showed himself as well disposed as could be wished. As for
practical consequences, the rupture of relations between
Vichy and Moscow, a rupture exacted by Hitler from Vichy,
was soon to make things easier. From Beirut, on August 2nd,
I invited Cassin and Dejean, therefore, to ask M. Maisky
" if Russia would be disposed to entertain direct relations with
us . . ., and if she would contemplate addressing a declaration
to us on the subject of her intention to help restore the independence and greatness of France,—adding to those words, if
possible, the word ' integrity.' "

The conversations resulted, on September 26th, in an
exchange of letters between M. Maisky and myself. The
Ambassador of the U.S.S.R. declared, in the name of his
Government, that it "recognised me as Leader of all the
Free French . . . that it was ready to enter into relations with
the French Empire Defence Council over all questions relative
to collaboration with the overseas territories placed under my
authority . . ., that it was disposed to lend aid and assistance
to the Free French for the common struggle . . ., and that it
was resolved to ensure the full and entire restoration of the
independence and greatness of France . . ." Nonetheless the
Soviets did not—any more than Great Britain had done in
the agreement of August 7th, 1940—mention our territorial
integrity.

Shortly afterwards, the Soviet Government accredited
M. Bogomolov as its representative to the National Committee.
M. Bogomolov came from Vichy, where for the last year he had
been Ambassador to Pétain. He adapted himself without any
embarrassment to the—to say the least—novel conditions in
which he was to serve. Never, however, did I hear from his
mouth any malevolent personal remark about those—Marshal

or Ministers—to whom he had just been representing his Government. In one of our conversations he even went out of his way to tell me this: " At Vichy I had leisure, and used it to wander incognito through the countryside, chatting with the good people. A peasant, who was ploughing, said to me one day: ' It's very sad that the French should have been beaten at the start. But look at this field! I can till it because they've managed to fix things up so that the Germans let me keep it. You'll see, soon they'll manage to fix things so that they clear out of France.' " I supposed that, by this fable in illustration of the theory of the shield and the sword, M. Bogomolov meant to show me that he had understood the French situation thoroughly and, at the same time, to explain to me the reasons for Soviet Russia's successive attitudes.

From that time onwards I saw M. Bogomolov often. In the steps he took and the things he said, to the utmost extent to which the crushing rigidity imposed on him allowed him to show himself human, he did so. Stiff, on his guard, all of a piece when he was making or receiving an official communication, this man of real culture showed himself, in other circumstances, winning and relaxed. In his judgments of people and things he could be humorous, even going so far as to smile. I must say that by my contact with him I became convinced that, while the Soviet rule encased the personality of its servants in an iron mask without a chink, it was unable to prevent there being still a man underneath.

For our part, we had sent General Petit to Moscow as military liaison. The Soviets had at once shown that they were predisposed to treat him graciously and with consideration: staff conferences, a visit to the front, reception by Stalin himself. I had occasion, indeed, to wonder, later, if the purpose of their advances to Petit was merely professional. In any case the reports which came from various sources gave the impression that the Russian armies, at first broken by the German offensive, were gradually recovering, that the people, in its deep recesses, was arising for resistance, and that Stalin in the national peril was endeavouring, by appointing himself field-marshal and never appearing out of uniform, to seem not so much the mandatory of the régime as the leader of everlasting Russia.

The map of the vast battle was spread out on the walls of our offices. There the gigantic effort of the Germans could be seen developing. Their three groups of armies—von Loeb, von Bock and von Rundstedt—had in four months penetrated to the heart of the Russian lands, taken several hundred thousand prisoners, and seized an enormous booty. But in December, round about Moscow, the vigorous activity of Zhukov, powerfully aided by a harsh and premature winter, checked the invader, then made him draw back. Leningrad had not fallen, Sebastopol was still holding out. It seemed that Hitler had not succeeded in imposing on the German High Command the only strategy that could have been decisive, that is, the grouping of all its mechanised forces solely in the direction of the Soviet capital, so as to strike straight at the enemy's heart. In spite of the model victories of the campaigns in Poland, France and the Balkans, the Führer had this time had to offer up sacrifices to the time-honoured errors, distribute the shock resources between his three marshals, deploy a front instead of launching a battering-ram. Surprise once past, the Russians, over immense expanses, would make him pay dearly for it.

Meanwhile we tried to furnish a direct contribution, however modest, to the Eastern front. Our corvettes and our cargo boats took part in the allied convoys which were carrying war material to Murmansk through the Arctic Ocean under the hardest conditions. As I could not succeed, at first, in getting the British to agree that the two light divisions formed in the Levant by Larminat should be engaged in Libya, I gave General Catroux in February the order to prepare the transfer of one of them to Iran and the Caucasus,—which enchanted the Russians and worried the English. Later, when Larminat's troops were after all detailed for the battle against Rommel, I sent to Russia the " Normandie " fighter group (later the " Normandie-Niémen " air squadron), which was to do magnificent service there and was the only Western force fighting on the Eastern front. Inversely, we saw arrive in

London, under the leadership of Captain Billotte, a detachment of about fifteen officers and two hundred men who, having escaped from German prison-camps, had managed to reach Russia, only to be interned there. Released shortly after the beginning of the Germano-Soviet war, they reached us via Spitzbergen, on board a convoy returning from Archangel.

On 20th January, 1942, in a broadcast, I paid tribute to Russia's military recovery and affirmed the alliance we had made with her for the present and for the future. In February Roger Garreau, who till then had been Minister Plenipotentiary at Bangkok and now had joined Free France, was sent to Moscow as delegate of the National Committee. For three years Garreau was to represent France in Russia effectively and intelligently, make all the contacts allowed by the régime and keep us well informed. As soon as he reached his post he saw MM. Molotov and Vichinsky, respectively Commissar and Vice-Commissar for Foreign Affairs, and also M. Lozovsky, Vice-Minister. All three expressed to him with insistence their Government's intention of creating the closest possible relations with Fighting France.

In May M. Molotov came to London. On the 24th I had a very thorough conversation with him. He was accompanied by Bogomolov and I by Dejean. That day, as afterwards, I found in M. Molotov a man who seemed both physically and mentally—lock, stock and barrel—made to fill the office which had been delegated to him. His tone serious, his gestures rare, his politeness thoughtful but stiff, his gaze directed within himself, the Soviet Minister for Foreign Affairs said what he had to say evenly and listened with attention. But he let nothing escape him that appeared spontaneous. Nothing would move him, make him laugh, or irritate him. Whatever problem was raised, one felt that he knew the file about it, that he was registering faultlessly the new elements added to it by the conversation, that he was formulating his official position exactly, but that he would not depart from what had been prepared and decided elsewhere. He had certainly, in the past, brought to concluding the Germano-Soviet agreement with Ribbentrop the same assurance that he brought to negotiating, now, the Western pacts. In M. Molotov, who was and wanted to be merely a perfectly adjusted cog in an implacable machine, I thought I had identified a complete success of the totalitarian system. I paid tribute to its greatness. But however much of what was at the bottom might remain hidden from me, I could feel the melancholy of it.

In the course of our conversation in London, the Soviet Minister for Foreign Affairs reached agreement with me on what his Government and the National Committee should do for each other in the immediate future. Free France would urge the American and British allies to open a second front in Europe as soon as possible. At the same time she would help, by her diplomatic and public attitude, in doing away with the isolation to which Soviet Russia had long been relegated. The latter, on her side, would support us in Washington and London in our effort to re-establish the unity of the Empire and national unity by fighting. This would apply to the administration of our territories,—for instance, Madagascar,— to the so-called parallel, but in reality separatist, enterprises which the Anglo-Saxons were encouraging, and finally to the resistance movements in France, about which Moscow recognised that no foreign Government—even that of the Soviets— had the right to turn any of them away from obedience to General de Gaulle. As for the future, it was agreed that France and Russia should work together over the shaping of the peace. " My Government," M. Molotov told me, " is the ally of those in London and Washington. It is essential for the war that we should collaborate closely with them. But with France Russia desires to have an independent alliance."

The effort of Free France to widen its relations in the directions of Washington and Moscow did not prevent its centre from still functioning in London, or its own affairs— military activity, liaison with Metropolitan France, propaganda, information, finance, economic life of the overseas territories—from being, by the force of things, dovetailed in, as it were, with those of the British. The consequence, for us, was the obligation to maintain closer relations with them than ever. But their encroachments were more painful to us as we grew bigger. And yet the entry of Russia and America into the war, which involved for England, in her turn, the heavy servitudes of an alliance with giants, might well have led her to bring her policy closer to ours and to practise a frank solidarity with us, covering action in Europe, the Middle East, Africa and the Pacific. We would have lent ourselves willingly to such a change, and we sometimes had the impression that certain British leaders were also ready for it.

Anthony Eden, for instance. This British minister, though as British and as ministerial as could be, showed an openness of mind and a sensitiveness that were European rather than insular, human rather than administrative. This favoured child of British traditions—Eton, Oxford, Conservative Party, House of Commons, Foreign Office—was nonetheless accessible to what seemed to be spontaneous and to break new ground. This diplomat entirely devoted to his country's interests did not despise those of others, and remained careful of international morality in the midst of the cynical brutalities of his time. I often had to deal with Mr. Eden. Many questions that we had to discuss were frankly disagreeable. On most of these occasions I admired not only his brilliant intelligence, his knowledge of affairs and the charm of his manners, but also the art he had of creating and maintaining around the negotiation a sympathetic atmosphere which favoured agreement when that was possible and avoided wounds when it was not. Above all, I am convinced that Anthony Eden felt a special affection for France. From her he had derived a large part of his culture. To his political brain she seemed clearly indispensable to the balance of a world assailed by every sort of barbarism. Lastly, this man with a heart did not fail to be sensitive to the plight of a great nation.

However, Mr. Eden's good intentions were not able to make the alliance a rose without thorns. I recognise that he was often thwarted in his efforts by the spiked and touchy qualities he met with in us. But it was chiefly from the British side that the difficulties arose: the suspiciousness of the Foreign Office, ambitions of the colonials, prejudices of the military, intrigues of "Intelligence." At the same time, political society in London, though on the whole favourable to Free France, was subject to influences that were not always so. Certain Conservative circles eyed frowningly these Cross of Lorraine Frenchmen who talked of revolution. Various Labour people wondered, on the contrary, whether de Gaulle and his companions had not a tendency towards fascism. I can still see Mr. Attlee coming softly into my office, asking for the assurances needed to relieve his conscience as a democrat, and then, after he had heard me, withdrawing with a smile on his face.

In the last resort everything depended on the Prime Minister. He, deep down, could not bring himself to admit the independence of Free France. What was more, Mr. Churchill, each time we came into collision on account of the interests for which we were respectively responsible, treated our disagreement as a personal thing. He was hurt by it and grieved in proportion to the friendship which bound us to each other. This attitude of mind and sentiment, added to the devices of his political tactics, plunged him into fits of anger which gave our relationship some rude shocks.

Other reasons, besides, converged to make this great man irascible at that time. The English, while pouring forth meritorious and glorious exertions throughout that period, notably in the submarine struggle, sometimes suffered reverses that were all the more galling because the enemy who inflicted them had not always the material superiority. On 10th December, 1941, at sea off Malaya, the magnificent battleship *Prince of Wales* and the battle cruiser *Repulse* were sunk by Japanese aircraft before being able to fire a shot. On 15th February, 1942, 73,000 British soldiers capitulated at Singapore after a brief resistance. In June, in spite of the considerable resources accumulated in the Middle East by the English, Rommel broke the Eighth Army front and drove it back to the gates of Alexandria, while the 33,000 men who were supposed to hold Tobruk gave themselves up to the Germans with a haste difficult to justify. Mr. Churchill measured, better than anyone, the consequences of these reverses as regards the conduct of the war. But above all, he suffered as an Englishman and as a soldier.

It must be added that some people in governing circles did not hesitate to impute to him, discreetly, part of the blame for the British failures. Although England as a whole cherished Winston Churchill as the apple of her eye, the papers printed, Parliament heard, the committees muttered and the clubs spread judgments about him that were sometimes hostile. The result of all this was that Mr. Churchill was not, during the first months of 1942, in the mood to soften or be at ease, especially towards me.

Finally, and perhaps chiefly, the Prime Minister had made for himself a rule to do nothing important except in agreement with Roosevelt. Though he felt, more than any other Englishman, the awkwardness of Washington's methods, though he found it hard to bear the condition of subordination in which United States aid placed the British Empire, and though he bitterly resented the tone of supremacy which the President adopted towards him, Mr. Churchill had decided, once for all, to bow to the imperious necessity of the American alliance. He therefore did not mean to adopt towards Free France an attitude that would conflict with that of the White House. Since Roosevelt showed himself distrustful towards General de Gaulle, Churchill would be reserved.

At the time of my arrival in London in September, 1941, his ill-humour was great. The Prime Minister had difficulty in accepting what had happened in Syria and the Lebanon between us and England. On September 2nd he went so far as to write to me that, in view of my attitude, he did not think there was any point in his meeting me at present. In the Commons, on September 9th, he made a disquieting statement. True, he recognised that " among all the nations of Europe the position of France in Syria is one of special privilege." But he took it upon himself to add that " there is no question of France maintaining the same position in Syria which she exercised before the war . . ." and that " there must be no question, even in war-time, of a mere substitution of Free French interests for Vichy interests." As usual, Mr.

Churchill's displeasure was accompanied by a systematic tension in Franco-British relations. The London Government affected, for several days, to have no business to discuss with us and to close its doors to us,—which led me, on my side, to suspend all participation by the Free French in broadcasting from London. However, in accordance with the usual swing of the pendulum, a resumption of relations soon followed these vexations. On September 15th I had a conversation with Mr. Churchill which ended well after a bad beginning. He assured me, in conclusion, that his Government's policy relative to the Levant remained as it had been defined in our Cairo agreements.

Wishing to clear the matter up, I saw Mr. Eden several times in October and November. We reached an agreement which laid down the essential points. England recognised that the French mandate was still in existence and was exercised by General de Gaulle, until it should be replaced by treaties duly ratified in accordance with the legislation of the French Republic,—that is to say, in fact, after the war. She admitted that the proclamation of the independence of Syria and the Lebanon by Free France did not modify this position in law. It was also established that the Lyttleton-de Gaulle agreements remained the charter of Franco-British relations in the Middle East.

In fact, when General Catroux instituted on September 27th the independence and sovereignty of the Syrian Republic under the presidency of Sheik Tageddine, and, on November 26th, of the Lebanese Republic under the presidency of M. Alfred Naccache, England, although she had disputed these decisions in advance, accepted them as soon as they had been taken, and recognised the two Republics together with the two Heads of State resulting from them. At the same time I notified respectively the Secretariat-General of the League of Nations on November 28th and, on November 29th, the American Government and all the other allied States, together with Turkey, of the arrangements which had just been made in my name in Syria and the Lebanon. "These arrangements," the notes stated, "do not affect the juridical situation which results from the Mandate Act and must continue to exist until the conclusion of new international acts." The British Government made no objection to these communications. What is more, it had itself suggested them.

It might, therefore, have been thought that the question was settled, at least until the peace. Circumspect though I was, I even wrote, myself, to our delegation in the Middle East that, in my opinion, "in face of the difficulties that England was encountering in the Arab countries, she was like us, anxious to see the mean rivalries of the past succeeded by a feeling of solidarity between the two greatest Moslem Powers." The directive I gave to our delegation was "to avoid everything that might increase the difficulties of our allies and to neglect nothing to facilitate their task by a genuine collaboration, while at the same time maintaining intact the position and rights of France." I was counting, unfortunately, on something that did not exist. In reality British policy, without contesting the legal position in theory, would still snap its fingers at it in practice.

In fact, repeated incidents were destined to keep the Franco-British quarrel alive in the Middle East. There was the recruitment—illegal—of Druze cavalry by the English. There was their claim—rejected of course—to proclaim on their own account the state of siege—that is to say, to take power—in the Jezireh, where disorders had broken out in consequence of the revolt in Iraq. There was their unwarranted interference in the operations of the Grain Office set up by us in the Levant, in which they demanded to be represented with the aim of meddling in the local administration. There was the threat—vain indeed—made by General Wilson to have certain French officials, who were not amenable to him, expelled. There was the attitude of Spears, who used hostile and threatening language and constantly intervened in the relations between our Délégation Générale and the Governments at Damascus and Beirut.

General Catroux steered his ship between the reefs. Although he was inclined to compromise and conceded more to the English than I would have wished, he found himself at every moment faced by fresh intrusions. Whence ceaseless unrest in the Levant, and in London some snarling negotiations.

In May, 1942, British pressure busied itself with trying to have elections take place in Syria and the Lebanon without delay. Our National Committee was naturally not opposed to a consultation of the people, from which fully representative governments would issue. Those we had set up were there only for the transition. This was particularly the case at Damascus, and I for my part was sorry that President Hachem Bey had not resumed his functions. But we considered that, to make the Syrians and Lebanese vote, it would be best to wait for the end of the war,—that is to say, for a moment when the two States would be once more under normal conditions, when our responsibilities as mandatory Power and as defenders would be lightened, and when the English would no longer be there to influence the voting. However, General Catroux, under energetic pressure from Mr. Casey, who had replaced Mr. Lyttleton in Cairo as British Minister of State, made him a promise of elections in the near future,—which the newspapers immediately made public. I had to acquiesce in this arrangement, though I ordered its date to be postponed. But it was easy to foresee that it would form, thenceforward, a copious source of Franco-British friction.

There were to be others. Over Jibuti our allies were playing a double game. While allowing our small force—Commandant Bouillon's battalion and the camel corps—to continue the blockade by land, they themselves had stopped the blockade by sea. From Aden in Arab small craft, and from Madagascar in submarines or in the sloop *d'Iberville*, the supplies required to nourish the policy of wait-and-see were reaching the colony. But the English, meanwhile, were negotiating with the Negus the treaty which set up their tutelage over Ethiopia. Their activity at Addis Ababa explains their inaction over Jibuti. For if, thanks to their help, Free France had been able rapidly to win French Somaliland over and to possess herself, in consequence, of the port, the railway and a considerable force, she would have been in a position herself to offer Addis Ababa the outlet and the security of which it stood in need. On the contrary, as long as Vichy occupied the place, the British held the fate of the Emperor and of his States in their hands alone.

That is why Gaston Palewski was unable to get the Colony effectively blockaded. He could not succeed, either, in bringing the British and Abyssinians to conclude a tripartite agreement instead of one between the two of them. Nonetheless his activity and that of his assistants—Lieutenant-Colonel Appert, commanding the detachment, and Chancel, a young diplomat accredited to Nairobi—were a useful preparation for what followed. The links established by them with various French elements in Jibuti and with the natives, the propaganda which they carried on by leaflets and broadcasts, and their relations with General Platt, caused the rallying of Somaliland to be a mere formality when the day came. At the same time, they made French representation reappear at Addis Ababa. Our rights over the railway were reserved, our religious and lay charities, at one time closed by the Italian occupation, could resume their activity, and the French Legation re-opened its doors. Though I deplored the delays, I could see the fruit ripening on the shores of the Red Sea.

But suddenly the intervention of the English in another part of the Empire brought my uneasiness and irritation to their peak. On 5th May, 1942, a telephone call from a press agency at three in the morning informed me that a British squadron was landing troops at Diego Suarez. Our allies were occupying a French possession by force without even having consulted us!

Now, ever since Pearl Harbour, I had tried, by many means of approach, to discuss the rallying of Madagascar with the British Government: a conference with General Brooke, Chief of the Imperial General Staff, on December 10th; a letter sent to Mr. Churchill on the 16th; a plan for operations handed on February 11th to the Prime Minister, to General Brooke and to the High Commissioner of the Union of South Africa; a fresh letter to Mr. Churchill on February 19th; and finally, on April 9th, a pressing note to Mr. Eden. In all these documents I proposed swift action by a Free French brigade, which would be landed at Majunga and would make for Tananarive with, if by chance it should be necessary, British air support, while our allies would create a diversion by blockading Diego Suarez from the sea. At the same time I claimed the administration of the island for the National Committee.

Meanwhile, since the Union of South Africa seemed to me directly interested in this affair, I inquired as to the plans, if any, of the Pretoria Government. As early as the end of 1941 I had sent Colonel Pechkoff there as delegate of Free France. Personally, Colonel Pechkoff had won the liking of General Smuts, and I expected that, if the Union meant to come in, its Prime Minister would not conceal this from my skilful and loyal representative. Lastly, in March, Médecin-Général Sicé, the High Commissioner at Brazzaville, visited South Africa. From his conversations with Smuts and the Ministers he gained the impression that the Union would not itself take action over Madagascar. It was therefore in London that I deployed my efforts, in the conviction that there were no scruples to be conciliated.

In point of fact, the entry of Japan into the war was threatening Madagascar. It was to be foreseen that Vichy would, sooner or later, be constrained by the Germans at least to allow Japanese raiders and submarines to use the Madagascar bases and paralyse allied navigation off South Africa.

We were well enough informed on the state of people's minds in the island by volunteers who, from time to time, managed to escape from there, and by the crews of ships that called there. The 1940 armistice had at first been badly received. Governor-General de Coppet would not have had trouble, at the time, in joining Free France if he had followed up his own declarations. But he had failed to make up his mind. Vichy had almost immediately replaced him by Cayla, who, assisted by Air-General Jeaunaud, had applied himself to lulling the spirit of resistance to sleep, before yielding place himself to Governor-General Anet. Pétain would be obeyed if he ordered that the Japanese be allowed to do as they like in Madagascar. He would also be obeyed if he ordered resistance to an allied landing. One day or another the Anglo-Saxons would want to make sure of the island. But in that case, given the traditional impulses of British policy, everything made it imperative for Free France to take part in the operation.

It can therefore be understood into what anxieties the action and proceedings of the English plunged us. All the more so since, on the very day of the Diégo Suarez attack, Washington published a communiqué stating that "the United States and Great Britain are in accord that Madagascar will, of course, be restored to France after the war or at any time that the occupation of Madagascar is no longer essential to the common cause of the United Nations." But did that mean, then, that, meanwhile, Madagascar would be taken away from France? To what power, other than Anglo-Saxon, would she be attached? What would be the participation of the French there in the war? What would be left of the authority of France there in the future?

We had to play a cautious game. I waited on purpose for six days before making the contact with Mr. Eden for which he asked. The British Minister, in the conversation I had with him on May 11th, showed a certain embarrassment. "I give you my guarantee," he said to me, "that we have no designs on Madagascar. We want the French administration to continue to function there." "What French administration?" I asked. From what Mr. Eden said I gathered that the English planned to negotiate with Governor-General Anet to establish a modus vivendi that would leave everything in Madagascar where it was, in exchange for which the Allies would remain at Diégo Suarez and supervise the rest of the island.

I told Mr. Eden that we were opposed to this plan. "Either it will come off," I said to him, "and the result will be the neutralisation of a French territory under allied guarantee,— which we will never accept. Or it will not come off, and in a few weeks' time you will have to undertake alone, in the interior of the island, an expedition which will begin to look like a conquest. It seems to me, indeed, very probable that this second hypothesis is the one that will be realised, for the Germans will be able to force Vichy to fight you." "We are engaged," Mr. Eden recognised, "upon an enterprise which in fact may well lead to many complications. But I am in a position to assure you that my Government desires and expects that it shall be you who finally will establish your authority in Madagascar. We are ready to state this publicly." It was agreed that the London Cabinet should publish a communiqué in this sense,—which it did on May 13th, stating: "It is the intention of His Majesty's Government that the Free French National Committee should play its due part in the administration of the liberated French territory, since the National Committee is co-operating with the United Nations as the representative of Fighting France."

That constituted an important undertaking on the part of England. I took cognizance of it on the radio next day. In exchange, in my broadcast, I expressed confidence that the Allies would keep their word. But I publicly rejected any compromise about Madagascar, declaring that it was the will of France that her Empire should be neither divided nor neutralised. "What France wants," I added, "is that Fighting France should in her name direct and organise the French war effort in all its forms and in every field, represent her rights *vis-à-vis* the Allies in the same way as it defends them against the enemy, and uphold and administer French sovereignty in those of her territories which have been, or will be, set free." On the same day I ordered the commander of the troops in Equatorial Africa to get ready a mixed brigade to proceed to Madagascar.

But the British Government's promises and my own statements as to the future role of the National Committee were assuming as solved a problem which was not. Vichy, in point of fact, was still master of practically the whole island. It was soon learned that the British, confining their effort to the capture of Diégo, were entering into negotiations with Governor-General Anet. At the same time the "Intelligence Service" in East Africa was sending to the spot a group of agents led by Mr. Lush. These measures were opposed to what Free France wanted. The re-entry of Madagascar into the war was being retarded by them, Anet's authority reinforced and the division of the Empire prolonged. In addition I was afraid of the possible activities of the British political team, which we had had a chance of seeing at work in the Middle East, at Jibuti and in Abyssinia. We were provided with a sinister sign straight away. Pechkoff, whom I wished to send to Diégo-Suarez to inform me of what was happening, found himself prevented from leaving.

Thus, towards the beginning of June, 1942, heavy clouds were spreading over Franco-British relations. To all the many alarming or disobliging actions of the English in Syria, Somaliland and Madagascar, there were added other measures that confirmed our grievances. In the Gold Coast a British mission, directed by Mr. Frank, was making mysterious contacts with the populations of the French territories in the loop of the Niger. At the same time General Giffard, Commander-in-Chief in West Africa, warned the Free French missions at Bathurst and Freetown that they must leave. When I myself was making ready to proceed to Libya to inspect our troops there, I received from the British Government a pressing request to postpone my journey,—which meant that the means for it would not be given me. In London the members of the Government, the ministries and the British general staffs enclosed themselves in a thick atmosphere of secrecy, not to say mistrust.

It was evident that the Anglo-Saxons were busy working out the plan for a vast operation in the Western theatre. General Marshall, Chief of Staff of the American Army, and Admiral King, Commander-in-Chief of the Atlantic Fleet, had spent some time in London in May and had avoided seeing me. And yet, in what the Allies were manifestly planning to do, France, by virtue of her possessions, her populations and her forces, would be essentially implicated. But no doubt the idea was to keep out of it, as far as possible, her active element, Free France, to dispose of her lands and substance fragment by fragment, perhaps even to take advantage of this dispersal to allot to themselves, here and there, parcels of her property. It was time to react. The Allies must be shown that Free France was in their camp to embody France there, but not to act there as cover, against the French nation, for the abuses and encroachments they might commit to its detriment. The National Committee, after a moving and careful discussion, was unanimous in thinking so.

On June 6th I charged Mr. Charles Peake, the faultlessly distinguished diplomat whom the Foreign Office had attached to us, with making our position known to Mr. Churchill and Mr. Eden. " If it should happen," I told him, " that in Madagascar, in Syria or elsewhere, France were forced, by the action of her allies, to lose any part whatsoever of what belongs to her, our direct co-operation with Great Britain and, eventually, with the United States, would no longer have any justification. We would have to put an end to it. That would amount, in practice, to concentrating ourselves in the territories that are already rallied or will be, and to pursuing the struggle against the enemy to the limit of our strength but alone and on our own account." That same day I telegraphed to Éboué and Leclerc on the one hand, on the other to Catroux and Larminat, to let them know of this decision and to invite them to prepare. I ordered them also to warn the allied representatives attached to them that such was our determination.

The effect was not long in coming. On June 10th Mr. Churchill asked me to come and see him. We spent a packed hour together. After warm compliments on the French troops who were covering themselves with glory at Bir Hakeim, the Prime Minister launched into the question of Madagascar. He admitted frankly that Fighting France had reason to be offended at the way in which the operation had been undertaken. " But we have," he stated, " no ulterior motive about Madagascar. As for what we mean to do there, we have no idea as yet. The island is very large! We should like to come to some arrangement so as not to get lost in it." " What we want," I said, " is for Madagascar to join Free France and come back into the war. For that, we are ready to-day, as I have proposed to you before, to engage troops there." " You are not my only ally," the Prime Minister answered. He thus gave me to understand that Washington was opposed to our taking part. To tell the truth, I had no doubt of it.

I drew Mr. Churchill's attention insistently to the danger caused to our alliance by a certain way of proceeding with regard to the French Empire and—perhaps in the near future —to France herself. He protested his good intentions. Then, suddenly jumping to his feet, " I am the friend of France! " he cried. " I have always wanted, and I want, a great France with a great army. It is necessary for the peace, order and security of Europe. I have never had any other policy! " " That's true! " I replied. " You even had the merit, after Vichy's armistice, of continuing to play the card of France. That card is called de Gaulle: don't lose it now! It would be all the more absurd since you have reached the moment when your policy is succeeding and when Free France has become the soul and frame of French resistance."

We spoke of Roosevelt and of his attitude towards me. " Don't rush things! " said Churchill. " Look at the way I yield and rise up again, turn and turn about." " You can," I remarked, " because you are seated on a solid State, an assembled nation, a united Empire, large armies. But I! Where are my resources? And yet I, as you know, am responsible for the interests and destiny of France. It is too heavy a burden and I am too poor to be able to bow." Mr. Churchill brought our conversation to an end with a demonstration of emotion and friendship. " We still have some stiff obstacles to get over. But one day we shall be in France; perhaps next year. In any case we shall be there together! " He accompanied me out as far as the street, repeating: " I shan't desert you. You can count on me."

Three days later Mr. Eden in his turn set himself to give me renewed and satisfactory assurances as to British disinterestedness about the French Empire in general and Madagascar in particular. He announced to me that " Brigadier " Lush had been recalled and that Pechkoff would be able to leave. " Believe me," he said warmly, " we desire to go forward hand in hand with you to prepare the Western front."

Provisionally, then, things remained in suspense. However, the warning we had given had been heard. It was from now on unlikely that British arbitrariness about our Empire would go beyond a certain limit. There were chances that there would be some respite in the Syrian affair, that Somaliland would be encouraged to rally, and that one day the Cross of Lorraine would fly over Madagascar. What was more, I felt more clearly than ever that, in the last resort, England would not give up her alliance with us.

Among the most keenly interested spectators of the diplomatic drama in which, through a hundred contrasting acts, Free France was to be seen taking up afresh the place of France, were the refugee Governments in Great Britain. In 1941 their circle was enlarged by the arrival of the Greek King and Ministers, and then of the Yugoslav King and Ministers. For both of them what was happening to France was a major subject of anxiety. Betrayed and vilified at home by the " quislings " who were usurping their place, they were fundamentally hostile to Vichy, whose attitude served the collaborators in their countries as an argument. At the same time, and although their sovereignty was not contested by the allied Great Powers, they were nonetheless suffering the painful lot of the weak given over to the discretion of the strong. Lastly, they had no doubt that the recovery of France was the condition for equilibrium in Europe and for their own future. It was therefore with secret delight that they watched the action carried on by Free France to establish her independence. The audience we found in them left nothing to be desired.

On our side, we did not fail to cultivate relations with these Governments which, though deprived of territories, possessed official representation and an appreciable influence everywhere in the free world. Dejean and his colleagues on the National Committee kept in touch with their ministers and officials. Our staffs and services met theirs. I myself saw the Heads of States and principal members of these Governments.

We derived honour and profit from these visits and conversations, for these were men of worth with whom we had to deal. But underneath the externals of etiquette we could discern the drama caused in their souls by defeat and exile. Certainly these Governments, still deploying the ceremony of authority, made a brave show of serenity. But deep down among the anxieties and sorrows in which they were all plunged, each one in shadow lived through his own heart-rending tragedy.

The truth was that, since the entry of Russia and the United States into the war, the leaders of the Western countries no longer doubted that their respective countries would be liberated. But in what state? That was what was obsessing those with whom I spoke,—Dutch, Belgians, Luxemburgers, Norwegians. The noble Queen Wilhelmina; her Prime Minister, Professor Gerbrandy; her Minister for Foreign Affairs, the enterprising M. van Kleffens; Prince Bernhardt of the Netherlands: all with despair saw the Empire of the Indies disappearing, in spite of the magnificent efforts of Admiral Helfrich's fleet, and the resistance carried on in the bush by General Ter Porten. MM. Pierlot, Gutt and Spaak, who together formed a team of wisdom, ardour and skill in the service of Belgium, were submerged in sadness when they mentioned the question of the King. As for the Grand-Duchess Charlotte, her husband Prince Félix de Bourbon-Parma and their happily perpetual Minister, M. Bech, they never ceased imagining the material and moral consequences that Nazi domination might well have in Luxemburg. Lastly, King Haakon VII, exemplary in his confidence and firmness, and M. Trygve Lie, who exerted an indefatigable activity in all fields, grieved as they watched their merchant ships disappearing: " It is our national capital that is sinking," the Norwegians kept saying.

Far more tragic still was the situation of Greece, of Yugoslavia, of Czechoslovakia and of Poland. For, while Moscow's entry into the war guaranteed them the defeat of Germany, it involved other threats for them. Their Heads of States and Ministers spoke of these openly. King George II of Greece and M. Tsouderos, the head of the Government, described to me the appalling misery into which the invasion was plunging the Hellenic people, the resistance it was putting up, in spite of everything, against the enemy, but also the saturation of the starving and of the fighters by the Communist party. At the same time, around the young King Peter II of Yugoslavia and inside the Cabinet presided over, successively, by General Simović, M. Yovanović and M. Trifunović, I could perceive the shocks produced by the events that were dislocating their country: the erection of Croatia into a separate kingdom of which the Duke of Spoleto was proclaimed king; the annexation by Italy of the Slovene province of Ljubljana, and also of Dalmatia, and the competition and, soon, hostility of Tito towards General Mikhailović, who nonetheless was pursuing, in Serbia, the struggle against the invader.

It is true that President Beneš and his Ministers, Monsignor Šramek, M. Masaryk, M. Ripka and General Ingr, gave, on the contrary, the impression that they were confident about the future behaviour of the Soviets. Through the intermediary of M. Bogomolov they entertained apparently good relations with the Kremlin. Their representative at Moscow, M. Fierlinger, seemed to be in favour there. A Czechoslovak corps, recruited from among the Czechs taken prisoner by the Russians in the ranks of the Wehrmacht, was placed on a war footing by the Soviet High Command. It could be seen that, whatever might be his aversion from the Soviet régime, it was mainly on Russia that President Beneš was counting for his own return to Prague and the restoration of the Czechoslovak State.

Conversations with Beneš consisted of lofty lessons in history and politics, which he taught at length without either the listener or the master ever tiring of them. I can still hear him evoking, in our conversations, the fortune of the State over whose destinies he had presided for twenty years. " This State," he would say, " cannot continue to exist without the direct support of Moscow, since it is essential to incorporate in

249

it the Sudeten region with its German population, Slovakia over whose loss Hungary is inconsolable, and Têšín which is coveted by the Poles. France is too uncertain for us to be able to trust ourselves again to her goodwill." " In the future," concluded the President, " we might be able to avoid the hazards of an exclusive alliance with the Kremlin, but only on condition that France resumes in Europe the rank and rôle which ought to be hers. Meanwhile, what choice have I? " So M. Beneš reasoned,—not without my being aware of the anxiety that was always there, deep down in him.

As for the Poles, they had no doubt. In their eyes the Russian was an adversary, even when he found himself forced to fight the common enemy. In the view of the President of the Republic, M. Rackiewicz, of General Sikorski, head of the Government and of the Army, and of the Ministers, M. Zaleski, M. Raczynski and General Kukiel, Soviet expansion would inevitably follow the German defeat. On the question how to dam the ambitions of Moscow back when Berlin had been vanquished, the Poles were divided between two tendencies. Sometimes they were dominated by a sort of pessimist philosophy, from which their despair derived intoxicating illusions, as the music of Chopin draws dreams from grief. At others they cherished the hope of a solution that would extend Poland to the West, concede part of the Galician and Lithuanian territories to Russia and obtain her agreement to refrain from ruling in Warsaw by imposing a Communist Government there. But when they did contemplate an agreement, their psychology was so passion-ridden that it produced rivalry among themselves, uncertainty among the Allies and irritation in the Soviets.

Nevertheless, risky though conciliation might be, General Sikorski was resolved to try it. This man of great character was the right person for his country's destiny. For, having been in the past opposed to Marshal Pilsudski's policy and then to the cocksureness of Beck and Rydz-Smigly, he had found himself, since the disaster, invested with all the authority a State in exile can possess.

As soon as the German armies had entered Russia, Sikorski

had not hesitated to re-establish diplomatic relations with the Soviets, in spite of the passions accumulated in Polish hearts. As early as July, 1941, he signed an agreement with the Soviets declaring null and void the partition of Poland effected by Russia and Germany in 1939. In December he had gone, himself, to Moscow to negotiate the liberation of the prisoners and their transfer to the Caucasus whence, under the command of General Anders, they would be able to reach the Mediterranean. Sikorski had had long discussions with Stalin. On his return, in a description of their conversations, he depicted to me the master of the Kremlin as plunged in the abysses of anguish, but with his lucidity, ruthlessness and cunning in no way impaired. " Stalin," Sikorski told me, " has stated that in principle he favours an *entente*. But what he will put into it and force us to put into it will depend solely on the forces confronting one another,—in other words, on the support we shall, or shall not, find in the West. When the moment comes, who will help Poland? It will be France, or no one."

And so the anxious chorus of the refugee Governments made a muted accompaniment to the progress of Free France. All of them had, like the English, recognised the National Committee in terms full of reserve. But they all considered General de Gaulle as the Frenchman qualified to speak in the name of France. They showed it, for example, by signing with me a common declaration about war crimes,—which was done on 12th January, 1942, in the course of a conference of Heads of Governments. In all, our relations with the refugee States and the reputation they helped to create for us aided us on the diplomatic plane and gained for us the assistance of many imponderable factors in public opinion.

During the world tragedy, to be sure, the great men carried Anglo-Saxon public opinion along with them; but public opinion, in its turn, and in spite of war-time censorships, guided the Governments. We therefore tried to bring it into play on our side. I myself endeavoured to do so by taking advantage of the sympathy and curiosity which our enterprise aroused. I regularly addressed the British and American public.

Following the classic procedure, I chose, from among the associations that invited me to make myself heard, some gathering that suited the moment and the subject. As guest of honour at the luncheon or dinner organised for the occasion, I could see, at the end of the meal, many professionals in the information world or privileged persons who came for the speech joining the guests and discreetly filling up the room. Then, having been complimented by the " chairman " in accordance with British custom, I would say what I had to say.

Not, alas, knowing English well enough, I generally spoke in French. But afterwards Soustelle would come into action. My speech, translated in advance, was circulated as soon as I had made it. The press and radio of Great Britain and the United States made it their business to publish its main points. As regards objectivity, I venture to say that that of the American papers seemed to me relative, for they would stress certain phrases taken out of their context. These phrases, at any rate, " got across." The English papers, though often unrestrained in their criticism, hardly ever distorted the text. It should be added that the Latin-American press, out of friendship for France, esteem for " Gaullism " and, perhaps, desire to make up for the attitude of the United States, did not fail to give prominence to my own statements. In short, except during a few crises when " military necessities " were invoked to stifle my voice, I always found the allied democracies respectful of freedom of expression.

Before going to the Levant in the spring of 1941, I had made speeches to several British audiences, in particular to the Foyles Literary Luncheon Club and to the Anglo-French Parliamentary Group. After my return to London in September and up to the month of June following, I was successively heard by the allied Press representatives, the workers and then the directors and staff of the English Electric tank factory at Stafford, the Royal African Society, the Foreign Press Association, the Oxford University French Club, the English-speaking Union, the City Livery Club, the National Defence Public Interest Committee, the Municipality and principal citizens of Edinburgh, and a meeting organised in the Parliament building for members of the House of Commons. In May, 1942, I held a press conference for the first time. On July 14th, 1941, when I was at Brazzaville, the National Broadcasting Corporation in America had relayed over all its stations an appeal which I addressed by radio to the United States. On 8th July, 1942, the Columbia Broadcasting System carried throughout America, from a special mass meeting in Central Park called by Mayor La Guardia, of New York, a speech in English by " our friend and ally, General de Gaulle." On the 14th, for the French national festival, a fresh message to the Americans. To these main occasions there were added others on which, though obliged to speak without preparation, I still met with a worth-while response: for example, at receptions given for me by the towns of Birmingham, Leeds, Liverpool, Glasgow, Hull and Oxford, by Edinburgh University, by the Admiralty at Portsmouth, by the Brigham and Cowan naval shipbuilding yards, the Talbot works, the Harmelin factories, *The Times* newspaper and, lastly, many clubs, all of them kind and well disposed.

But, while I varied the tone, it was always the same ideas and feelings that I cast to the mercy of foreign echoes. I gave, as explanation for the defeat suffered by France at the start, the outworn military system prevalent in all the democracies at the beginning of the war, of which my country had been the victim because she had no oceans to protect her and because she had been left alone to act as advance guard. I affirmed that the French nation was still, underneath oppression, living on with a deep-seated and sturdy life, and would reappear, resolved upon exertion and recovery. I gave as proof of this the Resistance, which was growing within and without. But I depicted the French people as all the more sensitive to the way in which its allies behaved towards it because it was plunged in misfortune and humiliation, because Hitler's propaganda kept waving before its eyes prospects of recovery if only it would cross over into the totalitarian camp, and because Vichy was wrong only—was I not obliged to use every argument?—in so far as the democracies respected the rights of France.

So it was that on 1st April, 1942, I made a speech that dotted the " i "s in this respect and led to keen controversy. " Let it not be supposed," I declared, " that the kind of miracle, which Fighting France is, is a thing given once for all. . . . The basis of the whole matter is this: that Fighting France means to stand by her allies on condition that her allies stand by her. . . ." Referring directly to relations which the United States were still entertaining with Vichy and to the dark dealings they were carrying on with its pro-consuls, I added: " For the democracies to lean towards men who have destroyed all freedom in France and who seek to model their régime on fascism or a caricature of it, would be to introduce into politics the principles of the poor simpleton who threw himself into the sea for fear of getting wet in the rain. . . ." To set the thunder rumbling I added: " There is here a grave failure to recognise a fact which dominates the whole French question and is known as revolution. For it is a revolution, the greatest in her history, that France, betrayed by her ruling and privileged classes, has begun to accomplish." And I uttered this cry: " It would not be tolerable if the self-styled realism that, from one Munich to another, has led liberty to the very edge of the abyss, were to continue to impose upon ardour and to betray sacrifice. . . ."

The position had been taken up. Free France had succeeded in winning recognition both in the feelings of the public and in the assent of the chanceries, not only as the sword-bearer of France but also as the unshakable trustee of her interests. This result was attained in the nick of time. For at the beginning of the summer of 1942 conditions had combined to enable the war to take a decisive turn. Russia had remained standing and was now passing to the offensive. England, while sending numerous reinforcements to the Middle East, had considerable forces available on her territory. The United States were ready to bring to the West their entirely fresh units and immense war material. Lastly, France, crushed and enslaved though she was in the home country and passive throughout a large part of her overseas territories, was still in a position to engage in the final struggle important military forces, her Empire and her resistence. Just as one unfurls the banner at the edge of the field of battle, I had, in the spring of 1942, given the name " Fighting France " to what, till then, was " Free France," and had notified the Allies of this new title.

For the destiny of France would be at stake in the coming collision. Territory of hers,—North Africa or the home country,—would serve as a theatre of operations. What she did, or failed to do, in face of the enemy, would determine her share in the victory. But it would be on the behaviour of the Allies that her rank in the world, her national unity and her imperial integrity would depend. I could have no doubt that some, and not the least important, meant to see to it that on this supreme occasion the guiding French body should be as dependent and fluid as possible and that Fighting France should be absorbed, if not set aside. But the situation she had acquired in the world was now solid enough for it to be impossible to break her from outside.

On condition that she herself held firm, and that she had the support of the nation in proportion as this emerged in its reality. While carrying on our fight, I thought of nothing else. Would Fighting France, in the coming test, have enough keenness, courage and vigour not to split within? Would the French people, exhausted, misled and torn as it was, be willing to listen to me and follow me? Could I unite France?

VIII. FIGHTING FRANCE

WHILE, between the summer of 1941 and that of 1942, Fighting France was extending her diplomatic campaign, she was herself ceaselessly growing. Although the present account sets forth the development of these two efforts successively, they were nonetheless simultaneous and connected. But the fact that the field of action was continuously enlarging made it necessary for me to place an adequate organism at the head of the enterprise. De Gaulle could no longer direct everything single-handed. The number and dimensions of the problems made it essential to bring points of view and persons of competence face to face before decisions were taken. Steps for putting them into action had to be decentralised. Lastly, since in all States power took the cabinet form, we should be helping to get ourselves recognised diplomatically by adopting it for ourselves. By Ordinance on 24th September, 1941, I instituted the National Committee.

As a matter of fact, I had been thinking of this constantly from the beginning. But the fact that, in the space of one year, I had had to spend eight months in Africa and the Middle East, and, above all, the shortage of so-called " representative " men, had constrained me to postpone it. On my arrival in London after the Syrian affair I could, on the contrary, look forward to a long phase of organisation. Also, while most of the individuals who had joined me early on were not, at the start, very well known, some had become so. I could therefore give the Committee a membership that

General de Gaulle addressing Free French sailors, 1942

*General de Gaulle shaking hands with a member of the
Home Guard at a tank factory in London*

would count. For Fighting France, the National Committee would be the directing organ gathered around me. In it the " Commissioners " would debate all our affairs collectively. Each of them would be required to direct one of the " departments " in which our activity was exercised. All would bear responsibility for the decisions taken. In short, the Committee would be the Government. It would have the prerogatives and structure of one. It would not, though, have the title: I was keeping that in reserve for the day, however far off it might still inevitably be, when an authority with the dimensions of French unity could be formed. It was with the same prospect in view that my Ordinance provided for the formation, later, of a Consultative Assembly, " with the task of furnishing the Committee with as wide as possible an expression of national opinion." A good deal of time, however, was to go by before this assembly saw the light of day.

As was to be expected, my decision caused eddies within the small French groups which, on the pretext of being political, were more or less astir in Great Britain and in the United States. They were willing that de Gaulle should act as a soldier and provide the Allies with the reinforcement of a contingent. But they would not admit that the leader of the Free French should take upon him governmental responsibilities. Not having rallied to me, they rejected my authority and preferred to entrust to foreigners—that is, in fact, to Roosevelt, Churchill and Stalin—the future of France.

I agree that there was a genuine antinomy between the ideas of these circles and my own. For me, in the national tragedy, policy had to be action in the service of a powerful and simple idea. But they, pursuing the same chimeras they had always cherished, would not consent that it should be anything but a choreography of attitudes and groupings, executed by a company of professional mimes, from which nothing would ever emerge but newspaper articles, speeches, platform performances and allocations of office. Although this régime had been swept away by events, although it had cost France a disaster from which it was possible to doubt that she would ever rise again, although these intoxicated people were now deprived of the usual means for their agitation—parliament, congresses, ministerial offices and editorial desks,—they were continuing their game in New York or in London, striving to involve in it, for lack of others, the Anglo-Saxon ministers, members of parliament and journalists. The origin of the troubles caused for Free France by her own allies and of the campaigns carried on against her by their Press and radio lay, often, in the influence of certain French émigrés. They could not fail to disapprove of the sort of political promotion which the institution of the National Committee meant for Fighting France, and they would certainly attempt to counteract the operation.

Admiral Muselier was the man who served them as instrument. The Admiral had a kind of double personality. As a sailor he gave proof of capacities which deserved high consideration and to which the organisation of our small naval forces was largely due. But he was periodically possessed by a sort of fidgets, which impelled him to intrigue. As soon as he knew of my intention to form the Committee, he wrote to me posing as champion of understanding with the Allies and of democracy which, according to him, my policy might well endanger. That these might both thenceforth be safeguarded, he proposed that I should place myself in an honorary position and leave the reality of the powers to him. As for the means he employed in the attempt to force my consent, this was nothing less than the threat of secession by the Navy which, he told me on the telephone, " is becoming independent and continuing the war."

My reaction was clear and the discussion was short. The Admiral yielded, alleging a misunderstanding. For reasons of sentiment and expediency, I made a show of letting myself be convinced, took cognizance of his undertakings and appointed him Commissioner for the Navy and Merchant Marine in the National Committee.

It included: in charge of Economy, Finance and Colonies, Pleven; of Justice and Public Education, Cassin; Foreign Affairs, Dejean; War, Legentilhomme; Air, Valin; action in Metropolitan France, Labour and Information, Diethelm, who had just arrived from France. Catroux and d'Argenlieu, at that time posted abroad, became members of the Committee without portfolio. I allotted to Pleven the burden of ensuring the administrative co-ordination of the civil departments: rank, salaries, distribution of staff, accommodation, and so on. I had wanted from the start, and later tried several times, to widen the membership of the Committee by bringing into it some of the eminent Frenchmen who were in America. In pursuance of this I asked MM. Maritain and Alexis Léger for their help. The replies were courteous, but negative.

The National Committee was working satisfactorily when Muselier brought on a fresh crisis. Back in London after the Saint Pierre expedition, for which he had received our unanimous congratulations, he declared, at a sitting of the Committee on March 3rd, that things were not going to his liking in Free France, tendered his resignation as national commissioner and wrote to me to confirm it. I accepted this resignation, put the Admiral on the reserve of officers and replaced him by Auboyneau, who was recalled from the Pacific. But Muselier then declared that, while ceasing to be a member of the National Committee, he was keeping the supreme command of the naval forces for himself, as though what was in question was a fief of which he was the owner. This could not be allowed, and the matter was settled in advance when, suddenly, the intervention of the British Government began.

This intervention had been prepared for a long time, the instigators being a few hotheads among our émigrés and certain elements in the Commons and in the British Navy. The conspirators had found a helper in Mr. Alexander, First Lord of the Admiralty. They represented to him, as Minister, that if Muselier went the Free French Navy would dissolve, so depriving the Royal Navy of a by no means negligible auxiliary. They persuaded him, as a Labour man, that de Gaulle and his Committee had tendencies towards fascism and that the Free French Naval Forces must be separated from their policy. The British Cabinet, for reasons that had to do with its internal balance and also, probably, with the intention of making de Gaulle easier to deal with by weakening him, adopted Alexander's thesis. It decided to require of me the maintenance of Muselier in his post as Commander-in-Chief of the Free French Naval Forces.

On March 5th and 6th Mr. Eden, flanked by Mr. Alexander notified me of this demand. For me, from that moment, the case was judged. At whatever cost, the National Committee's decision must be carried out just as it was, and England must give up meddling in this French matter. On March 8th I wrote to Eden that I myself and the National Committee had decided that Muselier was no longer Commander-in-Chief of the Navy and that we were not accepting the interference of the British Government on this subject. I added: " The Free French consider that what they are doing at the side of the British and for the same cause implies that they must be regarded and treated as allies and that the support of the British must not be given to them on conditions incompatible with their own *raison d'être*. . . . If this were not the case, General de Gaulle and the National Committee would cease to slave at a task which had become impossible. They hold it, in fact, essential, as regards the future of France as well as the present, to remain faithful to the aim which they have set themselves. This aim consists in raising France up once more and reconstituting national unity in war at the side of the Allies, but without in any degree sacrificing French independence, sovereignty and institutions."

I received no reply for the moment. No doubt, before going any further, the English were waiting to see what would happen inside our Navy. There was no movement of dissidence on any ship, in any training depot or any of our establishments. On the contrary, all the elements of the Free French Naval Forces drew closer to de Gaulle with an ardour proportionate to the difficulties that had been created for him. Only a few officers, forming a group about the Admiral, organised an unseemly demonstration at his staff headquarters, where I had gone to speak to them in person. I then ordered

Admiral Muselier to reside for a month in a place that would
keep him away from all contact with the Navy. I invited the
British Government, in accordance with the jurisdiction
agreement of 15th January, 1941, to ensure the carrying out of
this measure, since it was taken on British territory. Then, as
the necessary assurances were long in reaching me, I went
away to the country, prepared for anything, expecting anything
and leaving in the hands of Pleven, Diethelm and Coulet a
sort of secret testament which entrusted them with the mission
of informing the French people in case I should be obliged
to give up pursuing what I had undertaken and should
not be in a position to explain the matter myself. Meanwhile I had let our allies know that, to my great regret, I
would not be able to resume my relations with them until
they themselves had applied the agreement which bound
them.

This was done on March 23rd. Mr. Peake came to visit
me. He handed me a note informing me that his Government
was not insisting that Muselier should remain Commander-in-
Chief and would see that, for a month, the Admiral was unable
to make contact with any element in the French naval forces.
The British Government, however, recommended him to my
benevolence for some mission suitable to his services. Thereupon Auboyneau, who had arrived from the Pacific, took in
hand the administration and command of the Navy. In May,
wishing to offer Admiral Muselier a chance of serving still, I
invited him to come and see me to settle with him the terms
of a mission of inspection I proposed to entrust to him. He
did not come. A few days later this admiral, who had done
much for our Navy, notified me that his collaboration with
Free France was finished. I was sorry for his sake.

After this painful incident, nothing further happened to
prevent the regular functioning of this " London Committee,"
which various sources of hostile propaganda—not confined to
those of the enemy and of Vichy—represented sometimes as a
group of greedy politicians, sometimes as a team of fascist
adventurers, sometimes as a rabble of communist fanatics, but
for which, I bear witness, nothing mattered in comparison

with the welfare of the country and of the State. The National Committee met at least once a week, with some ceremony, in a large room at Carlton Gardens, known as the " Clock Room." In conformity with its rules of procedure, it heard the report of each of the Commissioners on the business of his department or on any question that one or other of them thought it his duty to raise. Cognizance was taken of documents and information, things were discussed thoroughly, and the proceedings ended with decisions drawn up at the sitting in the form of minutes, later notified to the forces and departments. No important step was ever taken without the Committee having deliberated on it first.

I always received valuable assistance and loyal support from the National Committee as a collective organ, as also from each of its members. Certainly I was still obliged to go personally into everything that was sufficiently important. But the burden on me was less heavy from the fact that I was aided and surrounded by men of worth. No doubt these ministers, none of whom had embarked on public life before, were to some extent lacking in authority and reputation. These, however, they proved able to acquire. All, in addition, had their own experience and individual qualities. The whole which they formed laid open to Fighting France avenues of influence that otherwise would have remained closed to it. I might often encounter, from these collaborators, not indeed opposition, but objections, even contradictions to my plans and acts. In the difficult moments, when I was usually inclined towards vigorous solutions, several members of the Committee had a leaning towards compromise. But, taken all in all, it was better that way. In the last resort, indeed, after he had given me his views, no National Commissioner disputed my final word.

In fact, while opinions might be divided, my responsibility nonetheless remained entire. In the struggle for liberation the one who answered for everything was still, in the last resort, my poor self. Inside France, especially, those who were beginning to turn in growing numbers towards active resistance looked in the direction of de Gaulle. There was a more and more distinct response there to my appeals. There was also a convergence of feelings there, which seemed to me as necessary as it was moving. For, realising that the propensity of the French to divide and the dispersal imposed on them by oppression tended to brand their rebellion with an extreme diversity, I was dominated by the anxiety to bring about the unity of the resistance. This was in fact the condition for its effectiveness in war, its national value and its weight in the opinion of the world.

From the summer of 1941 onwards, what was happening at home was known to us soon after it happened. Independently of what one could read between the lines of the newspapers or hear underneath the words of the radio of both zones, a most complete harvest of intelligence was constantly brought to us by the evidence from our networks, the reports of certain well-placed men who were already taking up positions, the testimony of the volunteers who were reaching us daily from France, the indications supplied by diplomatic posts, the statements made by the émigrés on their way through Madrid, Lisbon, Tangier and New York, and the letters sent to Free Frenchmen by their families and friends and passed through by dint of a thousand tricks. I therefore had in my mind a picture kept always up to date. How many times I was privileged to realise, as I talked with compatriots who had just left the country but had there been more or less confined within their trade or their locality, that, thanks to innumerable efforts at collecting, transmitting and collating information by an army of devoted people, I was as well aware as anyone of French affairs!

What emerged from all this was the degradation of Vichy. The illusions of the régime were being finally dispelled. In the first place the victory of Germany, which had been proclaimed as certain in order to justify the capitulation, became unlikely as soon as Russia was engaged in the struggle, the United States came in in their turn, and England and Free France held firm. The claim to be " saving the furniture from the burning house " at the cost of servitude was clearly ridiculous, in view of the facts that our 1,500,000 prisoners were not coming back, that the Germans were practically annexing Alsace and Lorraine and keeping the north of the country cut off administratively from the rest, that the levies made by the occupier in money, raw materials and farm and industrial products were exhausting our economy, and that the Reich was forcing a growing number of Frenchmen to work for it. The assertion that the Empire was being defended " against no matter whom " could no longer deceive anyone from the moment when the Army and Navy were forced to fight against allies and " Gaullists " at Dakar, in the Gabon, in Syria and in Madagascar, while the Germans and Italians of the armistice commissions did as they pleased at Algiers, Tunis, Casablanca and Beirut, while the aircraft of the Reich were landing at Aleppo and Damascus, while the Japanese were occupying Tonkin and Cochin-China. In the eyes of all, from now on, it was Fighting France that represented the chance of recovering the overseas territories one day, by making sure, one by one, of Equatorial Africa, the islands of Oceania, Pondichery, the Levant, Saint Pierre, Madagascar and French Somaliland, and extending its unyielding shadow before it over North Africa, West Africa, the Antilles and Indo-China.

As for the " national revolution " by which Vichy was attempting to make up for its own capitulation, the impression it gave was of a waste of reforms, some of which in themselves had their value, but which were compromised and discredited by the fact of being associated in men's minds with disaster and enslavement. Vichy's claim to a moral renovation and to a restoration of authority, and even its indisputable effort at economic and social organisation, resulted, outwardly only, in the processions of the legionaries, the hagiography of the Marshal and the proliferation of committees and, as to substance, in base persecutions, in domination by police and censorship, in privileges and in the black markets.

And so, even within the régime, the signs of disarray began to be manifest. From the end of 1940 to the summer of 1942 there were, in succession: the dismissal of Laval, the foundation in Paris, by Déat, Deloncle, Luchaire, Marquet, Suarez,

Free French troops at the Battle of Bir-Hakeim, June 1942

Général Koenig! Sachez et dites à vos troupes que toute la France vous regarde et que vous êtes son orgueil.

C. de Gaulle.

Facsimile of General de Gaulle's message to General Koenig after the Battle of Bir-Hakeim etc., of the "Rassemblement National Populaire" which, with the direct support of the Germans, abused those in office and carried on a noisy campaign of going one better in favour of collaboration; the incessant alterations of Darlan's prerogatives; resignations of members of the Cabinet—Ybarnegaray, Baudouin, Alibert, Flandin, Peyrouton, Chevalier, Achard, and others—who declared, one after another, that the task was impossible; the strange and sudden cessation of the Riom trial; the retirement of Weygand; Colette's attempt to assassinate Laval; the latter's appointment as head of the Government. The Marshal himself made public his distress. "From several regions of France," he said on the radio in August, 1941, "I can feel an evil wind blowing. Unrest is taking hold of people's minds. Doubt is seizing their souls. The authority of the Government is being called in question. Orders are being carried out badly. A real uneasiness is striking at the French people." In June of the following year, on the second anniversary of his request for an armistice, he stated in a broadcast: "I do not conceal from myself the poorness of the response my appeals have met with."

As the pomp and the works of Vichy declined, nuclei of resistance began to form here and there in Metropolitan France. The activities in question were, of course, most diverse, often ill-defined, but all inspired by the same intentions. In one place a propaganda sheet was being edited, printed and distributed. In another the enemy was being spied on to keep a network informed. A few determined men were setting up action groups for the most diverse purposes: raids; sabotage; receiving and distributing war material, either parachuted or transported; welcoming or sending off agents; passing from one zone to the other; crossing a frontier, and so on. Some were forming embryo movements whose members were bound together by rules or simply by acceptance of one and the same state of mind. In short, underneath the passive and sloweddown appearance displayed by life in Metropolitan France, resistance was starting its ardent, secret life. Fighters at home were now thinking how to strike blows at the enemy through the tight-drawn nets of police and informers.

In September 1941, the series of isolated attacks on German soldiers began. A major coming out of an underground station, the commander of the garrison at Nantes, an officer at Bordeaux and two soldiers in Paris, in the rue Championnet, were the first to be killed. Other executions followed. By way of reprisals, the enemy shot hostages in hundreds, threw thousands of patriots into prison and later deported them, and crushed under the weight of fines and servitudes the towns where his men fell. It was with sombre pride that we heard of these acts of war accomplished individually, at the price of immense risks, against the occupier's army. At the same time the death of the Frenchmen who served as victims to Germanic vengeance threw our soul into mourning but not into despair, for it was equivalent to the sacrifice of the soldiers on the battlefields. Yet for elementary reasons of war tactics we considered that the struggle needed to be directed, and that indeed the moment had not come for starting open fighting at home. The harassing of the enemy, then the engagement of our home forces at chosen points, and finally the national rising, which we hoped to obtain one day, would be powerfully effective on condition that they formed a whole and were co-ordinated with the action of the armies of liberation. But in 1941 resistance was barely beginning, and at the same time we knew that literally years would go by before our allies would be ready for the landing.

On October 23rd, therefore, I declared in a broadcast: "It is absolutely natural and absolutely right that Germans should be killed by Frenchmen. If the Germans did not wish to receive death at our hands, they had only to stay at home. . . . Since they have not succeeded in bringing the world to its knees, they are certain to become, each one of them, a corpse or a prisoner. . . . But there are tactics in war. War must be conducted by those entrusted with the task. . . . For the moment, my orders to those in occupied territory are not to kill Germans there openly. This for one reason only: that it is, at present, too easy for the enemy to retaliate by massacring our fighters, now, for the time being, disarmed. On the other hand, as soon as we are in a position to move to the attack, the orders for which you are waiting will be given."

While trying to limit our losses, which in such circumstances were excessive for far too slender results, it was nevertheless necessary to use the emotion caused by German repression in the interests of national vitality and solidarity. On October 25th, the day after the invader had massacred fifty hostages at Nantes and fifty at Bordeaux, I announced by radio: "By shooting our martyrs, the enemy thought he would frighten France. France is about to show him that she is not afraid of him. . . . I invite all Frenchmen and all Frenchwomen to cease all activity and remain motionless, each wherever he happens to be, on Friday, October 31st, from four to four-five . . . for this gigantic warning, this immense national strike will show the enemy the threat enveloping him and will be a proof of French fraternity." On the evening before the appointed day, I renewed my appeal. In point of fact, the demonstration was impressive in many places, above all in the factories. I was reinforced by it in my determination to prevent the resistance from turning into anarchy, but to make of it, on the contrary, an organised whole,—without, however, breaking the initiative which was its mainspring or the partitioning without which it might well have disappeared altogether, at one blow.

In any case its constituent elements, the movements, were now in existence, very resolute in many respects, but suffering gravely from the lack of military cadres. Where they could and should have found them,—that is to say, in what remained of the Army,—Vichy barred their way. And yet the first acts of resistance had come from soldiers. Some officers belonging to the army and regional staffs, were saving war material from the armistice commissions. The intelligence service continued in shadow to carry out measures of counter-espionage and, at intervals, transmitted information to the English. Under the impulse of Generals Frère, Delestraint, Verneau, Bloch-Dassault and Durrmeyer, and by making use, in particular, of the rankers clubs, mobilisation measures had been prepared. General Cochet inaugurated active propaganda against the spirit of the capitulation. Many of the monitors of the Chantiers de Jeunesse,[1] who included a number of ex-soldiers, were training themselves and the others with a view to taking up arms. In what remained of the established units, nearly all the officers, N.C.O.s and men showed unconcealed hope of returning to the fight.

The public, indeed, thought that a very good thing. A news film from France, which I had shown to me privately in London, gave me a striking example of this. In it Pétain was to be seen, in the course of a visit to Marseille, appearing on the balcony of the Hôtel de Ville in front of troops and a crowd astir with patriotic ardour. Yielding to the immense power of suggestion that rose from this mass of people, he could be heard shouting suddenly: " Don't forget that you are all of you still mobilised! " One witnessed the unchaining of enthusiasm which those words caused in that civilian and military assembly, laughing and crying with emotion.

Thus the Army, in spite of the captivity or death of most— and often the best—of its people, was showing itself spon-taneously disposed to officer the national resistance. But that is what the so-called Government, to which its obedience subjected it, did not want. Vichy, practising first the fiction of neutrality, and then collaboration, prevented it from responding to its own vocation and shut it up in a moral blind alley from which no one could emerge without breaking with a formal discipline. Although many military men had none-theless crossed the barrier, in particular those of them who were members of the networks, those, too, who were to enter the secret Army, and lastly those who later formed the " Organisation de Résistance de l'Armée," it is a fact that, at the start, the movements had to improvise their own cadres.

In the so-called free zone, " Combat " of which Captain Frenay had taken the lead, " Libération " in which Emmanuel d'Astier de la Vigerie was playing the chief part, and " Franc-Tireur," whose directing organ was presided over by Jean-

[1] A youth movement formed by Marshal Pétain in 1940; voluntary at first, but made compulsory in January, 1941. (Translator's note.)

Pierre Lévy, were developing a considerable propaganda activity and recruiting para-military formations. At the same time what was left of the old trade union movement—the " Confédération Générale du Travail " and the " Confédération Française des Travailleurs Chrétiens "—was spreading a state of mind favourable to resistance. It was the same with a few groups that issued from the old political parties, especially the Socialists, the Popular Democrats and the Republican Federation. Since the Germans were not occupying the zone, it was of course to Vichy that opposition was being put up, it was with its police and courts that there was a bone to pick. The leaders, indeed, while preparing forces that could, if need be, be used against the enemy, were thinking of the seizure of power, and saw in the resistance not only an instrument of war but also the means of replacing the régime.

The political character of the movements in the Southern zone certainly helped to render them alive and active, to attract into their ranks people of influence, and to give their propaganda a touch of passion and topicality which struck the public mind. But at the same time good understanding and, later, common action between the directing committees inevitably suffered from it. It must be said that the mass of the members and sympathisers hardly worried about the programme which the resistance might apply later, or about the conditions in which it would one day take power, or about the choice of those who would then be called upon to govern. In the general feeling, the only thing was to fight, or at least to prepare for that. To acquire weapons, find hiding-places, work out and sometimes carry out raids,—that was the business. For that it was necessary for people who knew one another to organise on the spot, find a few resources and keep their activities to themselves. In short, while within the movements the inspiration was relatively centralised, action was divided up, on the contrary, into separate groups, each of which had its own leader and operated on its own, and all competing against one another for the terribly limited resources in weapons and money.

In the occupied zone this rivalry disappeared in face of

the immediate danger, but the physical dispersion of people and efforts was even more necessary there. They were there in direct and overwhelming contact with the enemy. It was with the Gestapo that they had to deal. No means of moving about, corresponding or choosing a place of residence without running the gauntlet of strict controls. Any suspect went to prison until deported. As for active resistance, it exposed the fighters to torture and to execution without mercy. Activity, in these circumstances, was extremely dispersed. On the other hand, the presence of the Germans kept in existence an atmosphere that urged men on to struggle and encouraged connivance. And so the movements in this zone took on a tensely warlike and conspiratorial character. The " Organisation Civile et Militaire " founded by Colonel Touny, " Ceux de la Libération," headed by Ripoche, " Ceux de la Résistance," recruited by Lecompte-Boinet, " Libération-Nord," which Cavaillès had brought into being, and lastly, in the Hainaut, in Flanders, in the mining country, " La Voix du Nord," directed by Houcke, formally rejected any political tendency, thought of nothing but the fight and produced swarms of small clandestine groups, isolated from one another.

At the end of 1941 the Communists came into action in their turn. Up to then their leaders had adopted a conciliatory attitude towards the occupier, making up for it by abuse of Anglo-Saxon capitalism and its lackey, " Gaullism." But their attitude changed suddenly when Hitler invaded Russia and when they themselves had had time to find hiding-places and to set up the liaison arrangements indispensable to the clandestine struggle. They were prepared for this, indeed, by their organisation in cells, the anonymity of their hierarchy and the devotion of their cadres. They were therefore destined to take part with courage and skill in the national war, being certainly sensitive—especially some of modest station—to the appeal of their country, but never, as an army of revolution, losing sight of the objective, which was to establish their dictatorship by making use of the tragic situation of France. Hence they tried ceaselessly to keep their freedom of action.

But also, exploiting the tendencies of the fighters who—their own people included—wanted only one single fight, they obstinately attempted to permeate the whole of the resistance in order to make of it, if possible, the instrument of their ambition.

So it was that, in the occupied zone, they formed the " Front National," a group that was purely patriotic in aspect, and the " Francs-Tireurs et Partisans," a force that seemed intended only for the struggle against the Germans. So it was that into these they attracted many elements that were non-Communist but, from that very fact, might serve as cover for their designs. So it was that they camouflaged some of their own people and pushed them into the directing organs of all the other movements. So it was that they were soon to offer me their assistance, though never ceasing to mutter against the " de Gaulle myth."

And I wanted them to serve. There were no forces that should not be employed to beat the enemy, and I reckoned that theirs had great weight in the kind of war imposed by the occupation. But they would have to do so as part of a whole and, to be quite frank, under my control. Firmly counting on the power of national feeling and on the credit given me by the masses, I had from the first decided to assure them of their place within the French resistance,—even, one day, in its guiding body. But I was quite as decided not to let them ever gain the upper hand, by-pass me or take the lead. The tragedy in which the fate of the country was being played out offered these Frenchmen, who had been separated from the nation by the injustice which roused them and the error which misled them, the historic opportunity of coming back into the national unity, even if only for the duration of the fight. I wanted to do what was needed to prevent this opportunity from being lost for ever. So, once again, " Long live France! " would have been the cry uttered at the moment of dying by all those who had given their life for her, no matter how, no matter where. In the ceaseless movement of the world, all doctrines, all schools, all rebellions have one moment only. Communism will pass. But France will not pass. I am sure that in the end it will count for much in her destiny that, in spite of everything, she will, at the moment of her liberation —a fugitive instant, yet decisive in her history,—have been a single, re-united people.

In October, 1941, I heard of the presence in Lisbon of Jean Moulin, who had arrived from France and was seeking to come to London. I knew who he was. I knew, in particular, that as Prefect of the Eure-et-Loir department at the moment when the Germans entered Chartres, he had shown exemplary firmness and dignity, that the enemy, after maltreating him, wounding him and throwing him into prison, had in the end set him free with apologies and expressions of esteem, and that Vichy, having replaced him in his post, had since been keeping him in the wilderness. I knew he wanted to serve. I therefore asked the British services that this man of calibre should be sent to England. I had to wait two months before being given satisfaction. " Intelligence," in fact, was trying to win Moulin for itself. He, on the contrary, was asking to be sent to me. By dint of a pressing letter to Mr. Eden, I managed to get the loyal traveller to his destination. I was later to have equal trouble in obtaining his return to France.

In the course of December I had long conversations with him. Jean Moulin, before leaving for London, had made numerous contacts with each of the resistance movements and had, at the same time, taken soundings in various political, economic and administrative circles. He knew the ground on which I planned to engage him first. He made clear proposals and formulated precise requests.

This man, still young but with an experience already formed by responsibility, was kneaded from the same dough as the best of my companions. Filled to his soul's brim with a passionate love for France, convinced that " Gaullism " must be not only the instrument of the fight but also the motive power of a complete renovation, and penetrated by the feeling that the State was embodied in Free France, he aspired to great undertakings. But at the same time, being full of judgment and seeing things and people as they were, he would be watching each step as he walked along a road that was undermined by the adversaries' traps and encumbered with obstacles raised by friends. Being a man of faith and calculation, with no doubts but general mistrust, an apostle and at the same time a minister, Moulin was to accomplish, in eighteen months, a major task. He was to bring the resistance in Metropolitan France, which had still merely the outline of a symbolic unity, to practical unity. Later betrayed, made prisoner and tortured appallingly by an enemy who had no honour, Jean Moulin was to die for France, like so many good soldiers who, under the sun or in shadow, sacrificed a long, empty evening the better to " fill their morning."

We had agreed that he should bring his efforts to bear first on the movements in the South Zone, to resolve them to form, under his presidency, a common body, that would be directly tied to the National Committee, would make union a reality, issue watchwords and settle internal disputes. That done, he would tackle the North Zone and would try to set up a Council of all the resistance, attached to Fighting France, for the territory as a whole. But as soon as it was a matter of capping with one organism all participants in the struggle within Metropolitan France, two questions arose: that of the political parties and that of the military forces at home.

Given the representative but by no means directive character which I wished to see the future Council take on—and which it would in fact take on,—I did not expect to be able to exclude the parties. That some should exist was inevitable. To my mind, indeed, our misfortunes had come not from their existence, but from the fact that, under cover of decadent institutions, they had wrongly arrogated to themselves the powers of government. Therefore, while reserving them their place, I did not intend that they should now capture the resistance movement. This, after all, by no means arose from their spirit or from their activity, since all of them, without exception, had given way at the decisive moment. But, struck down yesterday by disaster, they were now beginning to pull themselves together. Some of their members, while joining the resistance movements, were at the same time regrouping within the old frameworks.

273

It is true that, having no longer a following to flatter or coalitions to operate or portfolios to haggle over, they believed and made believe that they were returning to the noble sources from which they had their origins; the will for social justice, the cult of national traditions, the spirit of lay rationalism, the Christian flame. Their respective organisms, now thoroughly purged, had no aim, so it seemed, but to bring an immediate contribution to the struggle by mobilising this or that tendency in public opinion. Public opinion, indeed, was once more becoming in some degree responsive to the cunning of these familiar groups, all the more so since they abjured their errors. Lastly, the allies were naturally attentive to the attitude of the party men. These were facts which I could not underestimate if I wanted to build up French unity. I therefore instructed Moulin to introduce into the Council that was to be formed, when the day came, delegates of the parties side by side with those of the movements.

While I meant in this way to see some degree of unity established in the political action in France, I wished it to be the same with the military action. The first difficulty in regard to this came from the movements themselves, for, having recruited fighting groups, they claimed to keep them as their own. What was more, except in a few mountainous or very well-wooded regions, these groups could not exist except in small bands. This applied especially to the *maquis*, composed as they were chiefly of outlaws who had always to keep to the country. The only kind of warfare to be expected of them, therefore, was guerilla warfare. But this could be very effective indeed if the detailed actions formed part of a concerted whole. The problem then was, while letting the various fractions operate autonomously, to bind them together by a flexible but efficient frame which would be attached directly to me. In this way it would be possible to lay down for them, in the form of plans established in agreement with the Allied High Command, groups of objectives against which they could take action as circumstances developed, and especially when —at last!—the landing of the armies came. I made Moulin responsible for leading the movements to this elementary cohesion among their military people. I had to wait, however, for several months before being able to set up a command for the secret army in the person of General Delestraint.

Jean Moulin was dropped by parachute in the South during the night of January 1st. He carried credentials from me appointing him as my delegate for the non-occupied zone of Metropolitan France and instructing him to ensure unity of action among the elements of the resistance there. This would mean that his authority would not, in principle, be disputed. But he would have to exercise it, and I would have to support him. It was therefore agreed that it was he who would be the centre of our communications in France, first with the South Zone, then, as soon as possible, with the North Zone; that he would have the means of transmission under his authority, that our envoys would be attached to him; that he would be kept posted as to movements of personnel, material and mail effected on our behalf from England to France and vice versa; and finally that he would receive and distribute the funds sent by us to various bodies operating in Metropolitan France. Thus provided with prerogatives, Moulin set to work.

Under his drive, supported by pressure from base, the heads of the movements in the South Zone soon formed between them a sort of Council of which the National Committee's delegate assumed the presidency. In March they published, under the heading, " One single fight, one single leader," a common declaration in which they committed themselves to united action and proclaimed that they were carrying on the struggle under the authority of General de Gaulle. Order began to reign in the various activities. In the para-military field, preparations for fusion were going ahead, At the same time, with help from us, Moulin equipped his delegation with centralised services.

So it was that the service called " Opérations Aériennes et Maritimes " received direct from Colonel Dewavrin the instructions relative to the comings and goings of aircraft and boats. Every month, during the nights when there was a moon, Lysanders or bombers, guided by pilots—such as

Laurent and Livry-Level—who were specialised in these courageous performances, landed on the chosen terrain. Men who were each time staking their lives carried out the signalling, the reception or embarkation of the travellers and material, the protection of everything and everybody. Often " containers," parachuted at designated points, had to be collected, hidden and passed on. The " Service Radio," which Julitte had begun to organise on the spot, likewise worked under the delegate's authority, sending to London and receiving hundreds and later thousands, of telegrams each month, ceaselessly moving its stations which the enemy's detector apparatus tracked down, and replacing as they occurred the heavy losses it suffered. Moulin had also set up the " Bureau d'Information et de Presse," directed by Georges Bidault, which kept us posted as to the state of people's minds, especially among intellectuals, workers on social questions, and politicians. The " Comité Général des Etudes," attached to the Delegate, and with Bastid, Lacoste, de Menthon, Parodi, Teitgen, Courtin and Debré working on it, elaborated plans for the future. Bloch-Laine directed financial operations on the delegation's behalf and banked the funds received from London. In this way Moulin, keeping the essential instruments in his hands, made the action of our Government felt in practice. As early as the first months of 1942, witnesses arriving from France brought us proofs of this.

One of them was Rémy. He returned from Paris one night in February, bringing bundles of documents for our services and, for my wife, a potted azalea he had bought in the Rue Royale. His network—" Confrérie Notre-Dame "—was working at full spate. For example, not a single German surface boat arrived at or left Brest, Lorient, Nantes, Rochefort, La Rochelle or Bordeaux without London being warned by telegram. Not a single military work was built by the enemy on the Channel or Atlantic coast, particularly in the submarine bases, without its situation and plan being at once known to us. Rémy had, in addition, organised contacts methodically, either with other networks, with the movements in the occupied zone, or with the Communists. The latter had got in touch with him shortly before his departure and had charged him with telling me that they were ready to place themselves under my orders and to send a representative to London to hold himself at my disposal there.

In March Pineau, one of the leaders of " Libération-Nord " and a man trusted by the trade unionists, came and worked most usefully with us for three months. In April there arrived Emmanuel d'Astier, fully armed with proposals and also with interested schemes, and whom I thought it well to send, before he went back to France, to the United States with some definite information about the resistance. The next to join us was Brossolette, who was prodigal of ideas, could rise to the highest planes of political thought, could measure the full depth of the abyss in which France lay gasping, and placed his hopes of a recovery in " Gaullism," which he constructed into a doctrine. He was to play a large part in inspiring our movement at home. Then one day, having fallen into the hands of the enemy while doing his duty, he was to hurl himself to death to avoid the risk of weakening. Roques, too, had come, bearing messages from a certain number of parliamentarians. Later he was to be executed by the Gestapo. Paul Simon landed in his turn, sent from the occupied zone by the " Organisation Civile et Militaire " to establish liaison. Simon brought to bear his keen intelligence and cold determination, and was to render signal services. He was to be killed by the enemy on the eve of liberation. Lastly Philip, Charles Vallin, Viénot, Daniel Mayer and yet others asked to be brought to London.

My interviews with these men, for the most young, all of them seething with ardour and tense in their fighting spirit and ambition, helped to show me to what extent the régime under which the French people had been living at the moment of the disaster was discredited in its mind. The resistance was not only the rebound of our self-defence reduced to extremities. It was also arousing the hope of a national revival. Provided it did not disperse after victory, one might hope that it would serve as the lever for a profound change of system and for a vast national effort. As I saw its leaders pass before me, having come in answer to my call, I thought that those of them who survived would perhaps form around me the directing team of a great human and French achievement. But this would be on condition that, once the danger was passed, they would still accept that disciplining of minds and claims without which nothing is worth anything and which had—for once!—united them.

The moment had come, in any case, for me to proclaim, in agreement with the whole of the resistance and in its name, the purpose we wished to attain. This purpose was liberation in the full sense of the word,—that is to say, that of man as well as of the country. I did so in the form of a manifesto adopted in National Committee, after having asked the opinions, in France, of the movements and the delegation. In it I declared our intention to see that the liberty, dignity and security, which we had resolved to assure to France in the world through the crushing of the enemy, should be obtainable by each man and woman in our country in his or her life through a change from the bad régime that had denied them to many. I condemned " that moral, social, political and economic régime which had abdicated in the midst of defeat " at the same time as " the one which emerged from a criminal capitulation." And I affirmed: " While the French people is uniting for victory, it is assembling for a revolution." The manifesto was published on 23rd June, 1942, in all the clandestine papers of both zones, as well as by the radios of Brazzaville, Beirut and London.

These conditions governing action at home were what chiefly made it essential for me, during this period, to keep the seat of the National Committee in London. And yet the idea of establishing it on French territory, for example at Brazzaville, often occurred to me. This was so, in particular, every time a crisis arose in our relations with England. But I was forced then to return myself this answer: " How, from the depths of Africa, am I to communicate with our country, make myself heard by it, influence the resistance? In Great Britain, on the contrary, there are the means required for liaison and information. Again, our diplomatic action upon

278

the allied Governments implies relations and an atmosphere which the English capital offers us and of which, quite obviously, we would be deprived on the banks of the Congo. Lastly, I must keep contact with those of our forces which can only be based in the British Isles."

After my return from the Middle East, therefore, I established my residence in London. I was to remain there for ten months.

I can see again my life at that time. Easy to believe that it was packed. To simplify it, I lived at the Connaught Hotel. In addition I took a country house, first at Ellesmere in Shropshire, and then at Berkhamsted near the capital, where I spent the week-ends with my wife and our daughter, Anne. Later we were to make our home in London, at Hampstead. Philippe, after passing through the *Ecole Navale*, was sailing and fighting in the Atlantic on board the corvette *Roselys*, and later in the Channel as second-in-command of motor torpedo boat 96. Elisabeth was a boarder with the Dames de Sion, preparing to enter Oxford. The ordinary people round about us observed a sympathetic discretion. The attitude of the English when they saw me with my family passing along a street, taking a walk in a park or going into a cinema, was as kindly reserved as the demonstrations were fervent when I appeared in public. So I was able, to my advantage, to verify that, among this great people, each one respects the liberty of the others.

Most often my day was spent at Carlton Gardens. It was there that François Coulet (who had become my *chef de cabinet* since Courcel left to command an armoured car unit in Libya) and Billotte (my chief of staff in succession to Petit, now on the mission to Moscow, and to Ortoli, who was commanding the *Triomphant*), presented me with reports, letters and telegrams. It was there that Soustelle summarised for me the day's intelligence, Passy-Dewavrin brought me the reports from France, and Schumann received my directives for what he was going to say at the microphone. It was there that I settled business with the National Commissioners and heads of services, received visitors or persons sent for, gave orders and instructions and signed decrees. Often luncheon, and sometimes dinner, brought me together with eminent allied persons or else with Frenchmen with whom I desired to talk. As for the great labour involved, for me, by the composition of my speeches, I did it at home, in the evenings or on Sundays. Whatever happened, I tried not to upset the functioning of the departments by a badly arranged time-table. In principle, work was not done at night at Carlton Gardens, except in the cipher office.

I had indeed to pay many visits outside. Apart from conversations with British Ministers, staff conferences, and ceremonies to which I was invited by the British Government or by some other of our allies, I used to go, whenever occasion arose, to one of the centres of French life in London. The " Institut Français," which had rallied to me literally from the first moment in the person of its director, Professor Saurat, supplied our compatriots with valuable educational resources and an active intellectual circle. The " Alliance Française " was continuing its work under the driving force of Thémoin and Mademoiselle Salmon. The " Maison de l'Instut de France," up to the day when it was bombed to pieces together with its administrator, Robert Cru, produced from its library documentation of which our services had need. The " Amis des Volontaires Français," a group directed by Lord Tyrrell, Lord de la Warr and Lord Ivor Churchill and composed chiefly of British, and in Scotland the " Comité de Co-ordination de la France Combattante " under the friendly chairmanship of Lord Inverclyde, poured forth for our fighters an assistance that was as intelligent as it was generous. The French Chamber of Commerce played its part in fostering trade between Great Britain and the territories that had rallied to us. The " Centre d'Accueil de la France Libre " received the people who came from France. The French Hospital looked after a good number of our wounded. In associating myself with these various institutions my aim was to tighten in England, as I was trying to do elsewhere, national solidarity.

The " Association des Français de Grande-Bretagne " helped me actively in this. By it in particular were organised

Howard Coster

General de Gaulle

certain big meetings to which civilians and military flocked, making it possible for me to meet the mass of French people, for those present to demonstrate their feelings and heighten their convictions, and for the people at home to hear us,— thanks to the radio, which retransmitted the speeches and the stirrings of the audience. Already on 1st March, 1941, at the Kingsway Hall, before some thousands of listeners, I had defined our mission and affirmed our hopes. On November 15th, in the midst of an assembly that filled the huge space of the Albert Hall, I solemnly formulated the three articles of our policy.

"Article One," I said, "is to wage war,—that is to say, to give the French effort in the conflict the greatest possible extent and power. . . . But this effort is being made by us only at the call and in the service of France." Then, condemning at the same time the pre-war régime and that of Vichy, I declared: "We hold it to be necessary that a rumbling and cleansing wave should arise from the depths of the nation and sweep pell-mell before it the causes of the disaster together with the whole superstructure built on the capitulation. For this reason Article Two of our policy is to restore to the people the power to make itself heard as soon as events shall permit it freely to make known what it wants and what it will not have." Lastly, under Article Three, I outlined the foundations we wished to give to the renewed institutions of France. "These foundations," I said, "are defined by the three mottoes of the Free French. We say: 'Honour and Country,' meaning thereby that the nation can live again only by victory and continue to exist only through the cult of her own greatness. We say: 'Liberty, Equality, Fraternity,' because our determination is to remain faithful to democratic principles. We say: 'Liberation,' for if our efforts cannot conceivably cease before the defeat of the enemy, it must result, for every Frenchman, in conditions making it possible for him to live and work in dignity and security."

The audience on this occasion, by its visible emotion and hurricane of shouting, gave a demonstration which rang out far beyond the precincts of the Albert Hall.

Such meetings were rare. I went on the other hand frequently, under the outward form of a military inspection, to see our volunteers. Our land, sea and air forces, small and dispersed though they were and although we could only make them of bits and pieces, now formed a coherent whole which was continuously consolidating. The plan of organisation which I had laid down for 1942 for the War, Navy and Air Commissioners, was being carried out as provided for. I saw this for myself as I visted the units based in Great Britain. On these occasions the men, as they saw, close to, the man whom they called " le grand Charles,"[1] offered him, through their gaze, their bearing and their keenness, at the exercises, the homage of loyalty that would never compromise.

For our small army fighting in Africa and in the Middle East, there were on English soil no more than training centres. But these were instructing a large part of the cadres. In camp at Camberley, Colonel Renouard paraded for me the battalion of chasseurs, the artillery group, the armoured squadron, the engineers' detachment and the signals unit, from which there emerged, every six months, N.C.O.s and specialists. I moved on to the Artillery Park which, under Commandant Boutet, was putting into condition the French material that had been brought to Great Britain by the base services of the Norway expedition or by the warships arrived from France since the invasion. Arms, ammunition and vehicles were being sent to equip the new formations, concurrently with the material supplied either by the English under the terms of the agreement of 7th August, 1940, or by the Americans under " Lend-Lease." The negotiations and executive decisions required by this major task fell to the " Service de l'Armement." It acquitted itself of it under the direction of Colonel Morin, until that excellent officer was shot down in the air in the course of a long-distance mission. Commandant Hirsh was his successor. In London itself I sometimes saluted the " Compagnie des Volontaires Françaises," which had as its captain Mademoiselle Terré, following in the footsteps of

---

[1] This nickname, of course, carries the two senses of " great Charles " and " tall Charles." (Translator's note.)

Madame Mathieu, and was training well-deserving young girls to become drivers, nurses and secretaries. From time to time I visited the " Cadets de la France Libre " at Malvern, and later at Ribbersford. I had set up their school in 1940 for the sake of students and college boys who had come over to England. We had soon made of it a nursery garden of cadets. Commandant Baudoin was in charge of the Cadet School. Five batches were to come from it,—in all, 211 section or group leaders. Fifty-two were to be killed in action. Nothing gave so much comfort to the leader of the Free French as the contact with these young people, that jewelled spray of hope added to the darkened glory of France.

While the units of the land forces stationed in Great Britain carried out the training of elements intended for fighting elsewhere, it was from British ports that the majority of our naval forces took part—in the Atlantic, the Channel, the North Sea and the Arctic—in the battle of communications. To do so it was essential for us to take advantage of the allied bases. We had in fact no means of our own of repairing, maintaining and supplying our ships. Still less could we equip them with the new resources—anti-aircraft defence, asdic, radar, and so on—required by the evolution of the struggle. Lastly, over the vast theatre of maritime operations of which England was the centre, technical and tactical unity was necessary.

Therefore, while the ships manned by us belonged entirely to us, whatever their origin, while the only flag they flew was the tricolour, while the officers and crews acknowledged French discipline alone, and while they carried out missions solely on orders from their leaders,—in short, while our Navy remained purely national,—we had conceded that, apart from episodes that might lead us to make direct use of it, it formed part, as regards the use made of it, of the total naval activity carried on by the British. This, after all, placed it within an admirably competent, disciplined and active system, which had an effect on its own value. The English, on their side, were highly appreciative of this help, and leant the Free French naval forces a large material support. Their arsenals and their services set all their wits to the conditioning and equipping of our ships, in spite of the differences of types and armament. The new apparatus used by the British Navy was supplied to ours without delay. New ships—corvettes and motor torpedo boats, and, later on, frigates, destroyers and submarines—were offered to us as soon as built. If our small fleet succeeded in playing a part and in upholding the honour of France upon the seas, this was due to allied aid as well as to the merits of our sailors.

I realised this every time I went to see some fraction of it at Greenock, Portsmouth, Cowes or Dartmouth. Given the character of the struggle, given also the limited numbers available to us, we manned only small ships. But on board those of Free France keenness was pushed to the limit of what is possible.

Naturally we first manned ships that had come from France. In the spring of 1942 there remained, of our first five submarines, the *Rubis*, the *Minerve* and the *Junon*, which were busy in Norwegian, Danish and French waters, attacking ships, laying mines and landing commandos; the *Narval* had disappeared off Malta in December, 1940, and the *Surcouf* had sunk with all hands in February, 1942. The destroyers *Triomphant* and *Léopard* and the torpoedo boats *Melpomène* and *Bouclier* had for months been escorting convoys in the Atlantic and the Channel. Then the *Triomphant* left for the Pacific. The *Léopard* went to South Africa; later she brought Réunion over to us; in the end she was to be wrecked off Tobruk. The *Melpomène* moved to the North Sea. The *Bouclier* became one of our training ships. Of our five sloops, three—the *Savorgnan de Brazza*, the *Commandant Duboc* and the *Commandant Dominé*—were cruising about the coasts of Africa; the *Moqueuse* was helping to protect cargo boats in the Irish Channel; and the *Chevreuil*, in Oceania, was patrolling from Noumea and, on 27th May, 1942, brought the Wallis and Futuna Islands over to Free France. Two minesweepers, the *Congre* and the *Lucienne-Jeanne*, carried out their hard task in the approaches to the harbours of Great Britain. Ten submarine-chasers took part in the cover given to allied cargo boats between Cornwall

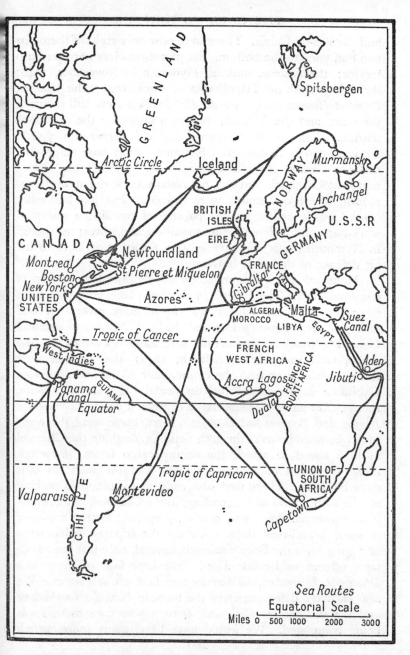

THE BATTLE OF THE ATLANTIC

and the Pas-de-Calais. There were now only eight of them, for two had gone to the bottom. Six patrol-trawlers were put into service; the *Poulmic*, sunk off Plymouth in November, 1940; the *Viking*, sunk off Tripolitania in April, 1942; the *Vaillant*, *Président Honduce* and *Reine des Flots*, which were still scouring the seas; and the *Léonville*, used as a depot for the merchant marine. The auxiliary cruiser *Cap des Palmes* did shuttle service between Sydney and Noumea. Four base ships—the *Ouragan*, *Amiens*, *Arras* and *Diligente*—completed the " naval unit " at Greenock and the *Bir Hakeim* crew depot at Portsmouth, where our sailors were trained. The old battleship *Courbet* was a centre for the passage of recruits, a group of workshops and a depot for ammunition and stores; anchored in Plymouth roads, she gave support with her artillery to the air defence of the great harbour.

Many other ships, supplied by the English, formed part of our small fleet. There were, in the first place, corvettes, built since the beginning of the war for convoy protection and sailing the seas between England, Iceland, Newfoundland and Canada without respite. Nine were handed over to us: the *Alysse*, sunk in action in March, 1942; the *Mimosa*, sunk three months later with the commander of the little division, Capitaine de Frégate Birot, on board; the *Aconit*, *Lobelia*, *Roselys*, *Renoncule*, *Commandant d'Estienne d'Orves*, *Commandant Drogou* and *Commandant Détroyat*. Next, there were the eight motor torpedo boats of the 28th flotilla, ploughing the Channel at high speed to attack the enemy cargo boats that crept along the coast of France by night and the warships that escorted them. There were also eight motor launches making up the 20th flotilla and seconding, in the Channel, our French-built chasseurs. We were, besides, preparing for the manning of some brand-new ships. Among the frigates which were emerging from the British arsenals, several, only just launched, were offered us by our allies. We kept four of these: *La Découverte*, *L'Aventure*, *La Surprise* and *La Croix de Lorraine*. We also earmarked for ourselves the torpedo boat *La Combattante* and the submarines *Curie* and *Doris*, whose construction was being completed. We would have liked many more, which would increase the total of submarines, cargo boats and enemy escorting craft sunk by our ships, and of the aircraft brought down by them. But it was the shortage of man-power, certainly not the lack of ships, that limited our size and our part.

By June, 1942, 700 Free French sailors had already died for France. Our naval forces contained 3,600 sailors in service at sea. There should be added the battalion of Fusiliers, commanded by Amyot d'Inville after the death of Détroyat on the field of honour. There should also be added certain isolated men of the Naval Air Force who, not being enough to form a unit, were serving in the Air Force. Lastly, there should be added the " Commando," now training in Great Britain under the orders of Lieutenant de Vaisseau Kieffer. In May I settled with Admiral Lord Mountbatten, whom the English had put in charge of " combined operations," the conditions in which this very resolute troop would be used. This meant that it would soon take part in the raids on the French coast.

These effectives had been, for the most part, recruited from among the elements of the Navy who were in England in 1940. Some had rallied to us, after having fought us, in the Gabon and the Levant. The same was the case with the crews of the submarine *Ajax*, sunk off Dakar, the submarine *Poncelet*, scuttled off Port-Gentil, and the sloop *Bougainville*, which we had been forced to put out of action in Libreville harbour. A few elements from the active list joined us from time to time from Metropolitan France, North Africa, Alexandria, the Antilles and the Far East. The Navy enlisted all the young Frenchmen it could in England, America, the Levant, Egypt and Saint Pierre. Lastly, the merchant ships gave the naval forces a large part of their man-power.

The most difficult problem for the Naval Commissioner's department was to form the ships' complements of officers. They had to be made up of extremely varied, not to say disparate, elements, by doing violence to the rules of specialisation. We had few officers from the active list. We were therefore training young ones. Under Capitaines de Frégate

Wietzel and Gayral, who successively commanded the
" division des écoles," the Free France Naval School worked
actively on board the *Président Théodore Tissier* and the schooners
Étoile and *Belle Poule*. There came from it, in four batches,
eighty cadets who were to bring to the French Navy a sense
of vocation saturated, from the start, in grief, battle and
aspiration. At the same time the reserve officers, whom we
found on board trading ships or among the Suez Canal personnel, formed a large part of the cadres of our naval forces.
Two hundred cadets recruited in this were to keep watch on
board the frigates, corvettes, chasseurs, vedettes and trawlers
for a total of over a million hours.

In spite of these raids on its man power, the fraction of the
French merchant fleet serving in the camp of the Allies made
an appreciable contribution to their convoys. Out of the
2,700,000 tons—or 660 liners and cargo boats—possessed by
France at the beginning of the conflict, 700,000 tons, or 170
ships, were to carry on with the war effort after the
" armistices." Our Merchant Marine service, directed by
Malglaive and Bingen, and later by Smeyers and Anduze-
Fariz, arranged for the manning of the greatest possible
number of ships by French crews. They also had their say
in the use made of the other ships, of which the British took
charge. In that case, the Union Jack was flown beside the
Tricolour on the poop or at the masthead of these exiled ships.
In spite of everything, 67 merchant ships, totalling 200,000
tons, were manned by us. Twenty had been or were to be
lost; 580 officers and 4,300 sailors were to be concerned in
maintaining this service. By the spring of 1942, over a quarter
had already perished at sea.

The liners were acting as troop-transports. So it was that
the *Ile de France*, the *Félix Roussel* and the *Président Paul Doumer*
brought to the Middle East the British reinforcements from
Australia or from India. The cargo boats, carrying raw
materials, arms and ammunition where they were wanted,
ordinarily sailed in convoys. Sometimes one of them had to
cross the ocean alone. They reached port only to sail again.
Even then, they would be bombed while in harbour. On the

General and Madame de Gaulle

A meeting of the Free French National Committee, 1941. Seated round the table (l. to r.) General Valin, M. Pleven, General de Gaulle (President), M. Dejean, General le Gentilhomme, M. Diethelm

high seas the service was as exhausting as it was dangerous. It meant keeping watch night and day, observing strict rules, perpetually rushing to action stations. Often it meant fighting, firing the ship's gun and manœuvring desperately to avoid the torpedo or the bomb. The ship might sink and a man might find himself struggling in the oily and icy water, with his comrades drowning all around. He might also have the terrible joy of watching the bomber's fall or of staring at the patch of oil beneath which the enemy submarine was going down. One of these ships might even, though a mere cargo boat, be the cause of it, like the *Fort-Binger*, which, in May, 1942, off Newfoundland, sent a German submarine to the bottom.

One day, at Liverpool, Admiral Sir Percy Noble, who from headquarters there directed navigation and fighting over the whole Atlantic expanse, took me to the underground reinforced concrete Operations Room. On the walls, great charts indicated the position, kept up to date hour by hour, of all the Allied convoys, all the warships and all the aircraft that were out, as well as the detected or supposed position of the German submarines, aircraft and raiders. A telephone exchange connected with the outside world, with the radio stations and with the cipher office, and served by calm teams of women—operators, stenographers and messengers—transmitted with barely a murmur the orders, messages and reports sent by the Command to the remote regions of the sea or reaching it from them. Everything was recorded instantly on luminous surfaces. So the immense battle of communications was at every moment outlined and formulated with all its swaying changes.

After having considered the whole, I looked on the maps to see where ours were. I saw them in the good places, that is to say the most honourable. The salute of the leader of the Free French went out, by wireless, to reach them. But then, as I measured how small, numerically,—and for that reason absorbed in a foreign system,—was the share they represented, as I imagined, over there, the ships wasted in inaction at Toulon, Casablanca, Alexandria, Fort-de-France and Dakar, and as I remembered the historic occasion this war was offering to the maritime vocation of France, I felt sadness flooding through me. It was with heavy steps that I climbed the stairs from the subterranean shelter.

A similar sentiment mingled with my pride when I made contact with our airmen at one or other of the British air bases. When I saw their worth and, at the same time, thought what could have been done from North Africa, the Levant or England by the French Air Army if only it had been allowed to fight, I could feel a great chance for the nation being thrown away. But it only made me the more intent on making sure that the efforts of those who had managed to join me should be credited to France. While I of course admitted that everyone in our forces who flew from bases in Great Britain in aircraft supplied by the English must form part of the British air system, I was anxious that our combatants in the air should also constitute a national element.

This was not easy. At the start our Allies were hardly interested in a Free French Air Force. Going straight for what was most practical and most pressing, they welcomed some of our pilots into their units. But all they offered us was to incorporate our air volunteers into the Royal Air Force. I could not agree to that. And so, for nearly a year, the destination of our men remained undetermined. Some, grouped in extemporised French squadrons, had been able to take part in the air battles of Eritrea and Libya. Others, provisionally adopted by British squadrons, took part in the Battle of Britain. But the majority, for lack of machines, organisation and training, were kicking their heels on the edge of the air bases in Great Britain or in Egypt.

The problem, however, was solved in its turn. In the spring of 1941, I managed to settle the questions of principle with Sir Archibald Sinclair, the British Air Minister. An understanding and generous man, he was willing to recognise that the existence of a French Air Force would not be without interest. He agreed, as I asked, that we should form units— actually groups modelled on the squadrons,—the British lending what we lacked in the way of ground staff and carrying out the training of our recruits in their schools. Any pilots we had in excess were to serve in British units. But their position, there, would be that of seconded French officers, subject to French discipline and wearing French uniform. I wrote to Sir Archibald from Cairo on 8th June, 1941, to confirm the agreement negotiated on this basis by Colonel Valin. From that moment he had, in carrying it out, the constant support of Air Marshals Portal in London and Longmore, later Tedder, in the Middle East.

So it was that at the end of 1941 we set up in England the fighter group " Ile de France." Its commander was Scivitaux. When he was brought down over France—whence, indeed, he was to return,—he was succeeded by Dupérier. On the morrow of the Syrian campaign, the fighter group " Alsace " was formed in Egypt: it fought at first in Libya under Pouliguen and then moved to Great Britain, where Mouchotte took command, to be killed in action in the following year. The " Lorraine " bomber group was born in the Levant, under the command of Pijeaud. He, after being shot down behind the enemy lines a few weeks later, managed to regain ours, only to die there. Corniglion-Molinier replaced him. The " Bretagne " mixed group was formed in the Chad, with Saint-Péreuse as its leader, to give support to our Saharan operations. In the spring of 1942 the elements that were to constitute the " Normandie " group—later regiment—in Russia were brought together, partly in London, partly at Rayack. Tulasnes and Littolf were to be successively at its head. After their death it would be Pouyade. Lastly, some of our pilots were, by my orders, placed at the dipossal of the Royal Air Force. Morlaix, Fayolle and Guedj commanded squadrons within it. The two last were killed in action. Glory is costly in the battles of the sky. The Free French Air Force lost, in all, twice as many killed as its effective flying strength.

But while the world character of the war made me determined to see that French forces were engaged in all theatres of operations, I set myself to concentrate the principal effort on the one that interested France most directly,—that is to say, North Africa. Once the Italian Army in Ethiopia was annihilated, access to Syria forbidden to the Germans and Vichy's schemes for action against Free French Africa stifled at birth, Libya was where we had to act.

In November, 1941, the British had taken the offensive there once more. If they succeeded in reaching the Tunisian frontier, it was essential that we should be there with them, having first helped to beat the enemy. If, on the contrary, he managed to drive them back, we ought to do everything to aid them in stopping him before he could overrun Egypt. In any case, it was the moment to deploy the full effort of which we were capable, but by playing our own part in order to win a success that would be truly a French one.

We had two possibilities of action: to push up from the Chad towards the Fezzan the Saharan column which Leclerc had long been preparing, or to engage in Libya, side by side with the English, the mobile forces perfected by Larminat. I decided to do both, but to do so in such a way that the action of our soldiers should directly benefit France.

The conquest of the Fezzan and, after that, the march on Tripoli, would be an operation that could be hazarded only once for all. If, in fact, the business did not succeed, it could not be undertaken again for a long time, given the unheard-of difficulties involved by the formation, equipment and supply of the Chad column. This column should therefore act to the full only if the British, having retaken Cyrenaica, entered Tripolitania. Otherwise it would have to confine itself to harassing the Italians by deep, swift raids.

At the same time I intended that the " Chad front "—if one can go so far as to use this name for a group of inevitably discontinuous actions—should remain a French front. Certainly the start of our Saharan enterprise would have to be co-ordinated with the march of the British Eighth Army. That was a matter of liaison with Cairo. But for the rest Leclerc would continue to be responsible only to me, until the day when, having effected his junction with our allies on the shores of the Mediterranean, it would become logical to place him under their direction. I attached the more importance to this autonomy since the conquest of the Fezzan would place in our hands a guarantee as regards the later settlement of the fate of Libya.

In the course of November and December the British, fighting hard and bravely, penetrated into Cyrenaica. In preparation for their irruption into Tripolitania, Leclerc, with the support of General Serres, at that time over-all commander of the troops in Free French Africa, made his arrangements for launching out at the Fezzan. As for me, my optimism about this was reserved. Knowing that Rommel had managed to disengage himself from the grip of the English and that, Weygand having been recalled from North Africa, the application of the Hitler-Darlan agreement would make it possible for the enemy to supply himself through Tunisia, I was not relying on a rapid progress by the allies towards Tripoli. On the contrary, an enemy counter-attack seemed to me more likely. That is why, while allowing the offensive to be prepared, I kept for myself the right to order its start. As, at the same time, the liaison mission which Leclerc had sent to Cairo had let itself be drawn into accepting his subordination to the British High Command, I made it clear to General Ismay that nothing of the sort was the case, and put the minds of the " Chadians " right as to how things should be in this matter.

In fact our Allies did not enter Tripolitania. For both adversaries the first months of 1942 were a period of stabilisation. Once that was clear, the proper thing for our troops in the Chad was to carry out tip-and-run raids only. Leclerc was burning to do so. On February 4th I gave the authorisation. He acted, rushing through the Fezzan in the course of March with his combat patrols supported by his aircraft, destroying several enemy posts, taking many prisoners and capturing war material. He then returned to his base, having suffered only the smallest losses. To extend this exceptionally valuable leader's zone and resources for action, I gave him command, in April, of all the forces in Free French Africa. Once again I had to overcome protests from his rigorous modesty. From that time he and his troops felt certain that they would capture the oases as soon as events in Libya took a decisive turn for the good. However, they would have to wait ten long months more, under a torrid heat, among the stones and sand, before grasping victory and coming to wash off their dust in the Mediterranean.

But while in the Chad it was necessary for us to postpone the decisive stroke, we were about to find in Cyrenaica, on the contrary, the long awaited opportunity for a brilliant feat of arms. And yet we had had to overcome a great many obstacles before getting the Allies to agree that large French units should be engaged on this ground.

The two light divisions and the armoured regiment formed in Syria under the orders of Larminat had, in fact, not been expected by the British High Command to take part in the offensive started at the end of October. And yet the two large-scale units were solid and well armed. Each of them was motorised and comprised five infantry battalions, an artillery regiment, an anti-tank defence company, an anti-aircraft defence company, a reconnaissance group, an engineers' company and park, a signals company, a transport company, a general staff company, and services. These units, comprising all arms and therefore capable of playing a special tactical part, were real divisions. Although they were certainly "light," I was set on giving them the name they deserved. Larminat, using the arms left behind by Dentz or else gathered from the magazines where the Italian armistice commissions had impounded them, equipped each section with a formidable armament, which our keen and alert volunteers would know how to handle,—none better. So it was that, independently of the divisional artillery, each battalion had six 75-mm. guns of its own. It was also very powerfully provided with mortars and automatic weapons. The troops would have to be lightened for an attack, if the occasion arose. But if holding ground was what was wanted, they had an altogether exceptional fire-power at their disposal.

Having on September 20th approved the composition of the two light divisions, I sent Mr. Churchill, on October 7th, a note to inform him of our desires and our resources. At the same time I wrote to General Auchinleck, Commander-in-

Chief, Middle East, to remind him of how anxious we were that our troops should fight in Libya. I made it clear to Mr. Churchill and to General Auchinleck that, for these operations, I was ready to place the whole of the Larminat Group under the orders of the British High Command and that, at the same time, Leclerc, though acting autonomously, could be launched against the Fezzan at the date they might ask of us. On October 9th I went to see Mr. Margesson, the British Minister for War, and asked him to intervene. Lastly, on October 30th, I indicated to General Catroux the conditions under which it would be right for our forces to be engaged, —that is to say, as large-scale units.

It was not till November 27th that I received the British reply. It was sent to me by General Ismay, the War Cabinet's and Mr. Churchill's chief of staff. His letter amounted to a dismissal of my request as courteous as it was explicit. To explain their refusal our Allies alleged " the dispersal of the French units at various points in Syria," the fact that " they were not trained to act as divisions or brigades," and lastly " the insufficiency of their equipment." They expressed, however, the hope that the future might make it possible to reconsider the question.

Obviously the British Command was counting on achieving the conquest of Libya and overcoming Rommel without the help of the French. It is true that it had on the spot considerable land and air forces and that it believed Admiral Cunningham—who was a magnificent leader and sailor—to be in a position to do more than a miracle and cut the enemy's communications between Italy and Tripolitania.

The disappointment which the English reply caused me can be imagined. I could not tolerate that our troops should remain standing at ease indefinitely, while the fate of the world was being decided in battle. Rather than accept that, I preferred to take the risk of a change of front. I therefore sent for M. Bogomolov and begged him to let his Government know that the National Committee desired that French forces should take part directly in the Allied operations on the Eastern front if the North Africa theatre should be closed to them.

I made, of course, no mystery of my request in London. But, even before Moscow's reply reached me, the British intentions had changed. On December 7th Mr. Churchill wrote me a warm letter to tell me that he had " just heard from General Auchinleck that he is most anxious to use a Free French brigade immediately in the Cyrenaican operations." " I know," the Prime Minister added, " this will be in accordance with your wishes, and how eager your men are to come to grips with the Germans."

I answered Mr. Churchill that I approved of the project and was giving General Catroux the necessary orders. In fact the English, apart from the annoyance that might be caused to them by the possible transfer of the French forces to Russia, were beginning to measure the military advantage that would be involved by our assistance in the battle of Cyrenaica. They realised, indeed, that the enemy there was yielding ground only step by step, that their own troops were suffering heavy losses, and that they would have to reorganise on the spot a command ill adapted to mechanised operations. Giving up the idea of carrying the offensive into Tripolitania, they now expected Rommel to take the initiative again and soon. This prospect made them glad for us to lend them a hand.

In Cairo, then, Catroux settled with Auchinleck the movement of the 1st Light Division towards Libya, and Koenig, instructed to negotiate the details, obtained from our allies a useful complement in anti-tank weapons, anti-aircraft guns and means of transport. In January this division had a few brilliant engagements with some elements of Rommel's who were encircled at Sollum and Bardia and soon gave themselves up. When they saw the processions of German prisoners they had helped to take, our troops felt as though they had had an electric shock. It was most cheerfully that they moved westwards. In the course of February, when the English placed their principal forces at the heart of Cyrenaica, in the so-called " Gazala " position, composed of several zones of resistance, ours were given that of Bir Hakeim, the most southerly. When they were still organising themselves there, they opened an active contest of skirmishes and patrols in the deep no-man's-land that separated them from the bulk of the enemy.

But while the 1st Light Division was thus being given its chance, nothing was being done for the 2nd, which was eating its heart out in the Levant. I meant that it too should take part in the operations. And indeed, on December 10th, M. Bogomolov had come to tell me that my project for sending French troops to Russia met with warm agreement from his Government, and that it was ready to supply our forces on the spot with all the necessary material. I therefore contemplated sending to the East not only the " Normandie " air group, but also the 2nd Light Division. Starting from Syria and passing through Baghdad, it would cross Persia in lorries and then, from Tabriz, be transported by rail to the Caucasus. This was the route taken from the Iranian ports by the convoys of war material which the Allies were sending to Russia. On December 29th I wrote to General Ismay to warn him of my intentions and gave General Catroux the required instructions. The 2nd Division would leave on March 15th for the Caucasus if it had not, before that, been allowed into Libya.

The British High Command raised all the possible objections to the transfer of this unit to Russia. But at Moscow, on the contrary, the Soviets gave it great importance. Molotov, speaking to Garreau, and General Panfilov to Petit, pressed us to carry it out. Mr. Eden, being informed, joined in and wrote to me to support the view of the British military. I could only stick to mine, and it was to mine that the Allied Command consented to come round, at the end of February. Ismay let me know. Auchinleck asked Catroux to put the 2nd Division at his disposal. Leaving Syria, it arrived in Libya in the last days of March.

Larminat, from now on, had his group where it could act: Koenig, in the line at Bir Hakeim with the 1st Division; Cazaud in reserve with the 2nd. The armoured regiment commanded by Colonel Rémy was in the rear, being given new material. A company of parachutists, which I had sent from England, was now training at Ismailia, ready to carry out the raids for which it would receive orders. In all, twelve thousand fighting men, or about a fifth of the total strength which the Allies were putting into action simultaneously. The "Alsace" fighter group and the "Lorraine" bomber group had been fighting in the skies of Cyrenaica since October. Several of our sloops and trawlers were helping to escort the convoys along the coast. Thus an important French force had been gathered in time in the principal theatre. In his justice, the God of Battles was about to offer the soldiers of Free France a great fight and great glory. On May 27th Rommel took the offensive. Bir Hakeim was attacked.

In enterprises in which one risks everything, there usually comes a moment when the person responsible feels that fate is being determined. By a strange convergence the thousand trials in the midst of which he is struggling seem suddenly to blossom into a decisive episode. If it turns out well, fortune will be in his hands. But if it works to the leader's confusion, the whole is lost. While the drama of Bir Hakeim was being enacted round about the polygon of sixteen square kilometres held by Koenig and his men, I in London, reading the telegrams, listening to the commentaries and seeing now shadow, now light in people's expressions, could measure what consequences depended on what was happening out there. If those 5,500 fighting men, who carried each one with him his grief and his hope, who had come of their own free will from France, Africa, the Levant and the Pacific, and who had been gathered where they were at the cost of so many difficulties, were to undergo a sad reverse, our cause would be indeed compromised. On the contrary, if, at this moment, on that ground, they achieved some striking feat of arms, then the future was ours!

The first engagements left nothing to be desired. On May 27th I learned that, while the enemy's main body was passing south of Bir Hakeim to turn the Allied position, the Italian mechanised division "Ariete" had launched some hundred of its tanks against the French position and had lost forty of them, leaving their wrecks on the approaches. On the 28th and 29th our detachments, making sweeps in all directions, destroyed fifteen machines more and took 200 prisoners. On the 30th General Rommel, having failed to settle with the British mechanised formations at the first blow, decided to retire in order to prepare a new manœuvre. Two days later a French column commanded by Lieutenant-Colonel Broche made a dash for Rotunda Signali, over thirty miles to the west, and captured the position. On June 1st Larminat inspected our troops in the field. His report was full of optimism. In the world at large an attitude was forming. Some people, in fact, felt it in their bones that this action might well go far beyond military tactics. Praise for the French troops and their leaders began to appear guardedly in conversation, in veiled phrases on the radio, with a certain caution in the newspapers.

Next day, Rommel seized the initiative. This time he pushed straight at the centre of the position held by General Ritchie, to whom Auchinleck had entrusted the command of the fighting front. The Germans overwhelmed a British brigade at Got-el-Skarab, crossed at this point the big minefield with which the Allies were covering themselves from Gazala to Bir Hakeim and, to widen the breech, sent a division of the Africa Korps against our troops. For the first time since June, 1940, full-scale contact was made between French and Germans. This at first took the form merely of skirmishes, in which we took a hundred and fifty prisoners. But very quickly the front was established for a battle. To the two enemy spokesmen who asked if we were willing to surrender, Koenig sent word that he had not come for that.

The following days saw the adversary tighten his hold. Batteries of heavy calibres, including 155s and 220s, opened an intensifying fire on our men. Three, four, five times a day the Stukas and Junkers attacked them in squadrons of a hundred machines. Supplies were coming up in small quantities only. At Bir Hakeim stocks of ammunition were visibly getting lower, food rations diminishing, water rations being cut. Under the burning sun, in the midst of the sandstorms, the defenders were perpetually on the alert, living with their wounded, burying their dead close by them. On June 3rd

General Rommel summoned them, in his own handwriting, to lay down their arms " on pain of being annihilated like the British brigades at Got-el-Skarab." On June 5th one of his officers came and renewed this ultimatum. It was our artillery that replied. But at the same time, in many countries, public attention was awakening. The French of Bir Hakeim were capturing the attention of the spoken or printed news bulletins more and more. Opinion was getting ready to judge. The question was whether glory could still smile on our soldiers.

On June 7th the investment of Bir Hakeim was complete. The 90th German Division and the Italian " Trieste " Division, supported by about twenty batteries and by some hundreds of tanks, were ready to start the assault. " Hold out for six days longer," the Allied Command had ordered Koenig on the evening of June 1st. The six days had passed. " Hold out for another forty-eight hours," General Ritchie asked. The fact had to be faced that the losses and confusion inflicted on the Eighth Army by the blows of the enemy were such that any operation for relief or aid was thenceforward impossible. As for Rommel, he was in a hurry to rush on towards Egypt, taking advantage of the disarray he detected among the British, and was impatient at this resistance at his rear, dragging on and upsetting his communications. Bir Hakeim had become his chief anxiety and his main objective. He had already come several times to look at the field. He was to come again to urge the assailants on.

Powerful attacks started on the 8th. Several times the enemy infantry, with great artillery and tank reinforcements, attempted, bravely but in vain, to over-run this or that sector of our lines. The day was a very hard one for our men. So was the night, spent in putting the wrecked positions in order again. On the 9th the assaults resumed. The enemy artillery had been still further reinforced with heavy calibres, against which the 75s of Colonel Laurent-Champrosay could not hold their own. Our men were being given no more than just two litres of water every twenty-four hours, which is cruelly insufficient in such a climate. Yet it was essential to hold on still, for with the disorder that was gradually gaining the various elements of the British Army Koenig's resistance now took on a capital importance. " Heroic defence by the French! " " Magnificent feat of arms! " " The Germans beaten in front of Bir Hakeim! " all the trumpets of the news in London, New York, Montreal, Cairo, Rio and Buenos Aires announced at full blast. We were drawing near the aim we had had in mind in obtaining for the Free French troops— limited though their numerical strength might be—a great rôle on a great occasion. To the whole world the guns of Bir Hakeim announced the beginning of the recovery of France.

But what now obsessed me was the safety of the defenders. I knew they would not for long be able to smash attacks supported by such crushing resources. True, I was certain that in any case the division would not surrender, that the adversary would be deprived of the satisfaction of seeing a long column of French prisoners pass before Rommel and that, if our troops remained where they were, he would have, if he wanted to finish with them, to destroy them group by group. But the thing was to rescue them, not to resign oneself to their glorious extermination. I had great need, for what was to come, of these hundreds of excellent officers and N.C.O.s and these thousands of very good soldiers. Their exploit being established, they must now accomplish another, blaze themselves a way through the assailants and minefields, rejoin the bulk of the Allied forces.

Although I was careful not to intervene directly in the conduct of the battle, I could not help letting the British Imperial General Staff know, on June 8th and 9th, in the most pressing manner, how important it was that Koenig should receive, before it was too late, the order to attempt to break out. I repeated this on June 10th to Mr. Churchill, with whom I was discussing the question of Madagascar. In any case the dénouement was approaching, and I telegraphed to the Commander of the 1st Light Division: " General Koenig, know, and tell your troops, that the whole of France is looking at you and you are her pride! " At the end of that same day General Sir Alan Brooke, the Chief of the Imperial

General Staff, informed me that since dawn the enemy had raged against Bir Hakeim without ceasing, but that Ritchie had ordered Koenig to move to a new position if he found this possible. The operation was planned for that night.

Next morning—June 11th—the broadcast and Press commentaries were dithyrambic and funereal. Not knowing that the French were trying to disengage, everyone evidently expected their resistance to be overwhelmed from one moment to another. But behold, that evening, Brooke sent me word: "General Koenig and a large part of his troops have reached El Gobi, out of reach of the enemy." I thanked the messenger, told him he could go, shut the door. I was alone. O heart throbbing with emotion, sobs of pride, tears of joy!

Of the 5,500 men, roughly, comprised in the 1st Light Division before Bir Hakeim, Koenig, after fourteen days of fighting, was bringing back nearly 4,000 uninjured. It had been possible to transport to the rear a certain number of wounded as well as the units. Our troops left on the field 1,109 officers and men, killed, wounded or missing. Among the killed, three senior officers: Lieutenant-Colonel Broche, Commandants Savey and Bricogne. Among the wounded left behind: Commandants Puchois and Babonneau. Some war material, first carefully destroyed, had had to be abandoned. But we had inflicted on the enemy three times the losses we had suffered.

On June 12th the Germans announced that they had "taken Bir Hakeim by storm" the day before. Then the Berlin radio published a communiqué declaring: "The white and coloured Frenchmen made prisoner at Bir Hakeim, since they do not belong to a regular army, will be subject to the laws of war and will be executed." An hour later I had the following note put out in all languages by the B.B.C.: "If the German Army were so far to dishonour itself as to kill French soldiers taken prisoner when fighting for their country, General de Gaulle announces that to his profound regret he would find himself obliged to inflict the same fate on the German prisoners who have fallen into the hands of his troops." The day was not over before the Berlin radio proclaimed:

" On the subject of the members of the French forces who have just been captured in the fighting at Bir Hakeim, no misunderstanding is possible. General de Gaulle's soldiers will be treated as soldiers." And so indeed they were.

While the 1st Light Division was regrouping at Sidi Barrani and Catroux was busy bringing it immediately up to strength again, our " Alsace " air group continued to take part in the redoubled activity of the British fighters, and our " Lorraine " group, together with the Royal Air Force bombers, made a great many attacks on enemy communications. At the same time our parachutists carried out several brilliant raids. So it was that, in the night of June 12th to 13th, their teams destroyed twelve aircraft on the enemy aerodromes in Libya and that Captain Bergé, who was dropped in Crete with a few men, set fire to twenty-one bombers, fifteen lorries and a petrol dump at the Candia airfield before being captured.

Meanwhile the Eighth Army, overcome by sudden moral fatigue, abandoned Cyrenaica, leaving behind a considerable amount of war material. General Auchinleck hoped at least to keep Tobruk, a position that was solidly organised and supplied by sea. But on June 24th the garrison, numbering 33,000 men, surrendered to the Germans. It was with great difficulty that the British managed to recover when they reached El Alamein. One sector of the position was held by General Cazaud and his 2nd Light Division, placed at last in the line in their turn. Among the reserves there figured Colonel Rémy's Armoured Group, hastily provided with material. The situation was grave. The whole Middle East, shaken by disquieting tremors, was expecting to see the Germans and Italians enter Cairo and Alexandria.

This depression on the part of our Allies was to be no more than temporary. A day would come when, thanks to the mastery of the sea, to fresh reinforcements, to great air superiority and, lastly, to the qualities of General Montgomery, they would in the end win the upper hand. Rommel indeed, with his supplies strained, was suspending his advance. Nonetheless, events as a whole made the importance of our action

stand out. General Auchinleck recognised this nobly. On
June 12th he published a magnificent communiqué in honour
of the 1st Light Division: " The United Nations," he declared,
" owe it to themselves to be full of admiration and gratitude
towards these French troops and their valiant general."

In London, six days later, ten thousand French people,
military and civilian, met to celebrate the second anniversary
of the appeal of June 18th. The four tiers of the Albert Hall
were as packed as the safety regulations allowed. A great
tricolour screen with the Cross of Lorraine superimposed was
stretched behind the rostrum and drew the gaze of all. The
Marseillaise and the Marche Lorraine rang out; all hearts
echoed them. As I took my place, surrounded by the members
of the National Committee and the volunteers most recently
arrived from France, I heard every mouth in that enthusiastic
crowd crying out faith to me. But on that day, besides, I could
feel the soaring of joy. I spoke. It was necessary. Action
employs men's fervour. But words arouse it.

Quoting Chamfort's saying: " Men of reason have endured.
Men of passion have lived," I recalled the two years which
Free France had just gone through. " We have lived much, for
we are men of passion. But we have also endured. Ah! what
men of reason we are! . . . What we said, from the first day,—
that France has never left the war, that the authority established
under the shelter of abdication is no legitimate authority, that
our alliances continue—we are proving by deeds, which are
the battles. . . . To be sure, we had to trust that Great Britain
would hold out, that Russia and America would be brought
into the war, that the French people would not accept defeat.
Well, we were not wrong. . . ." Then I paid homage to our
fighters all over the world and our resistance movements in
France. I paid homage also to the Empire, the loyal Empire,
basis of the country's recovery. Certainly its structure would
have to be transformed after the war. But France unanimously
intended to maintain its unity and integrity. " Even the heart-
rending courage displayed in the defence of one part or another
of the Empire against Fighting France and against her Allies
by troops still misled by the lies of Vichy is proof, distorted

yet unquestionable, of this determination on the part of the French. . . ." I drew the conclusion that, in spite of everything, Fighting France was rising from the ocean. " When a ray of her reborn glory touched the bloodstained brows of her soldiers at Bir Hakeim, the world recognised France. . . ."

The tempest of cheers, then the National Anthem sung with indescribable fervour, were the response that came from those present. It would be heard also by those who, at home, behind closed doors, shutters and curtains, were listening-in to the wavelengths that would bring it to them.

The acclamations fall silent. The meeting is over. Each person returns to his task. There I am, alone, face to face with myself. For that confrontation it will not do to take up an attitude or to cherish illusions. I draw up the balance-sheet of the past. It is favourable, but cruel. " Man by man, bit by bit," Fighting France has assuredly grown solid and coherent. But how many losses, sorrows, agonies have been required to pay for this result! We are starting on the new phase with appreciable resources: 70,000 men under arms, leaders of high quality, territories working at full stretch, growing resistance at home, a Government that commands obedience, an authority known, if not recognised, in the world at large. And without question the course of events is bound to raise up more sources of strength. Yet I am not deluding myself as to the obstacles in the path: the power of the enemy; ill-will from the Allied States; and among the French, hostility from the officials and the privileged, intrigues from some people, inertia in a great many and, finally, danger of general subversion. And I, poor man, shall I have the clearsightedness, firmness and skill to master these trials right to the end? Even if, indeed, I contrive to lead to victory a people at last united, what will be its future then? How many ruins will in the meantime have been added to its ruins, and divisions to its divisions? At that moment, with the danger passed and the illuminations extinguished, what waves of mud will break over France?

A truce to doubts! Poring over the gulf into which the country has fallen, I am her son, calling her, holding the light for her, showing her the way of rescue. Many have joined me already. Others will come, I am sure! I can hear France now, answering me. In the depths of the abyss she is rising up again, she is on the march, she is climbing the slope. Ah! Mother, such as we are, we are here to serve you.

INDEX

INDEX

313